Foundations of
Service Level
Management

D1367482

SAMS

Foundations of Service Level Management

Rick Sturm,
Wayne Morris,
and Mary Jander

SAMS

201 West 103rd Street, Indianapolis, Indiana 46290

Foundations of Service Level Management

Rick Sturm, Wayne Morris, and Mary Jander

International Standard Book Number: 0672317435

Library of Congress Catalog Card Number: 99-63620

Printed in the United States of America

First Printing: April, 2000

02   01   4   3   2

Trademarks

Warning and Disclaimer

Associate Publisher
Michael Stephens

Executive Editor
Tim Ryan

Acquisitions Editor
Steve Anglin

Development Editor
Songlin Qiu

Managing Editor
Lisa Wilson

Project Editor
Elizabeth Roberts

Copy Editor
Rhonda Tinch-Mize

Indexer
Kevin Kent

Proofreader
Katherin Bidwell

Professional Reviewers
Ben Bolles
Eric Goldfarb

Interior Designer
Dan Armstrong

Cover Designer
Alan Clements

Copywriter
Eric Borgert

Production
Darin Crone

About the Authors

Rick Sturm has over 25 years experience in the computer industry. He is president of Enterprise Management Associates, a leading industry analyst firm that provides strategic and tactical advice on the issues of managing computing and communications environments and the delivery of those services. He was co-chair of the IETF Working Group that developed the SNMP MIB for managing applications and was a founder of the OpenView Forum. He also is a columnist for *Internet Week*, has published numerous articles in other leading trade publications, and is a frequent speaker at industry events.

Wayne Morris has over 20 years experience in the computer industry. He is the vice president of corporate marketing and a company officer of BMC Software, the leading supplier of application service assurance solutions. He has held a variety of technical, support, sales, marketing, and executive management positions in several companies in Australia and the United States. His articles on systems and service level management have been published in the United States, Europe, and Australia, and he speaks regularly at industry conferences.

Mary Jander has spent 15 years tracking information technology. She is a senior analyst with Enterprise Management Associates (Boulder, CO). Prior to that, she was with *Data Communications* magazine, where she covered network and systems management for an international readership of network architects and information systems managers. She has also worked at *Computer Decisions* magazine and as a freelance writer and copy editor.

Dedication

To Marilyn and David—thanks again for your understanding, encouragement, and forbearance through the entire process of creating this book.

Rick Sturm

To my family on two continents whose understanding, support, and love carry me.

Wayne Morris

To Rusty, with love and gratitude for all your support.

Mary Jander

Acknowledgments

This book generated significant interest and excitement as we put it together. Service level management is a growing management discipline, and there are a number of professionals who are contributing to the growth in understanding and acceptance of proactive service management. This includes industry analysts, members of the press, and courageous individuals within IT departments who have taken a leadership role in implementing service level management, and who have subsequently shared their best practices in industry forums and conferences.

Many of our colleagues and friends contributed their insights and support for this book. To mention them all here is not possible, but we'd like to call out some individuals who made our jobs much easier.

Thanks to Jeanne Moreno, Linda Harvey, and Alex Shootman of BMC Software who have been instrumental in implementing service level management and in educating many others in the methodology and procedures for assuring that service levels can be met. David Spuler, David Johnson, Sharon Dearman, and Shannon Whiting of BMC Software contributed research that helped in many chapters. Amy DeCarlo, Mike Howell, Elizabeth North, and Colleen Prinster with Enterprise Management Associates contributed research and editorial assistance that helped in many chapters and Appendix F. Finally, our thanks go to Sara Nupen with Enterprise Management Associates. She assisted with the creation of several of the illustrations for the book.

Many vendors contributed information to the descriptions of current service level management products. Although it is not practical to list all those companies, our special thanks go to BMC Software, Cabletron, Candle Corporation, FirstSense, Hewlett-Packard, IBM/Tivoli, Landmark, Luminate, and Mercury Interactive for their contributions.

Our thanks go to Rosemarie Waiand and Jan Watson for setting up the Web site, http://www.nextslm.org, which will be used as a repository for templates and also for discussion forums around service level management.

There are many others who had a direct role in developing this book and bringing it to market including Songlin Qiu, Tim Ryan, and Steve Anglin of Sams Publishing and the book reviewer, Ben Bolles.

To all these individuals and others who helped us, we give our thanks and sincere appreciation.

Contents at a Glance

Table of Contents

Tell Us What You Think!

As the reader of this book, *you* are our most important critic and commentator. We value your opinion and want to know what we're doing right, what we could do better, what areas you'd like to see us publish in, and any other words of wisdom you're willing to pass our way.

As an Associate Publisher for Sams, I welcome your comments. You can fax, email, or write me directly to let me know what you did or didn't like about this book—as well as what we can do to make our books stronger.

Please note that I cannot help you with technical problems related to the topic of this book, and that due to the high volume of mail I receive, I might not be able to reply to every message.

When you write, please be sure to include this book's title and author as well as your name and phone or fax number. I will carefully review your comments and share them with the author and editors who worked on the book.

Fax: 317-581-4770

Email: feedback@samspublishing.com

Mail: Michael Stephens
            Associate Publisher
            Sams
            201 West 103rd Street
            Indianapolis, IN 46290 USA

Introduction

Information Technology (IT) departments are receiving pressure in both large and small businesses to operate more like a business and become more efficient. Customers are demanding assurances of service levels from their IT departments, telcos, ASPs, ISPs, and other service providers. New categories of service providers are emerging, such as application service providers (ASP). Increasingly, businesses are turning to out-sourcing of IT functions as a way to control costs and to achieve consistent levels of service. Businesses are increasingly dependent upon service providers, including their own internal IT department and external service providers. No longer can service providers, such as an IT department, just focus on keeping each of the pieces (network, systems, databases, and so on) running. Today's environment demands a comprehensive, customer-focused, holistic approach to management. In some cases, IT itself is becoming the focal point for new business, as evidenced in the growing trend toward managed e-commerce, e-business, application services, and virtual private networks. To fulfill these new roles, IT managers must remain focused on important customers, while still providing affordable service to other clients.

The Need for a Book About Service Level Management

In a way, service level management is similar to the weather. Like the weather, there is much talk about service level management, but little action. Executives recognize the importance of service level management, and Service Level Agreements, even more so. However, a recent study found that a majority of IT organizations have not yet implemented Service Level Agreements with their clients. Why? The answer is quite simple—they do not know how to go about establishing a program for service level management or how to write Service Level Agreements.

This book resolves that uncertainty by showing how to go about establishing a program of effective service level management and how to write Service Level Agreements that will be meaningful.

Who Will Benefit from This Book?

This book is written for those professionals whose organizations are service providers or the client of a service provider. Service providers include IT organizations, telcos, application service providers, out-sourcing companies, and so on. The book has been designed to serve as a practical guide to service level management for the IT managers and other professionals who are responsible for providing services to their clients.

Features of This Book

There has been a lack of readily available documented knowledge about service level management procedures and implementation. This book addresses the theory and methodology behind service level management, and provides an assessment of current technologies and products that can be used to implement proactive service management. The book also provides specific recommendations for developing a service level management discipline within your organization. It includes practical tips, cautions, and notes of interest to help you take advantage of the experiences of the authors and others who have implemented service level management. Templates for building Service Level Agreements, along with sample business justifications supporting service level management investments, should allow the reader to more quickly implement a disciplined approach to service level management.

This book can save the manager of an IT organization or other service provider time and allow the manager to avoid the frustration of attempting to "reinvent the wheel" for SLM. Similarly, this book will help the clients of the service providers to understand what they can reasonably expect from their service provider in terms of service level guarantees. If this book's guidelines are followed, even the process of negotiating a Service Level Agreement can be shortened and made more efficient.

Another valuable resource that this book offers is a comprehensive list of products that can be used to facilitate service level reporting. This list was compiled with many hours of research and can be used to quickly identify products that will be useful in specific situations.

How This Book Is Organized

Over the past five years, service level management has become a hotbed of activity, hype, hoopla, and misinformation. Therefore this book begins by laying out a clear blueprint of what service level management is and what it is not. It then continues with a review of the principles that underlie the effective management of service levels in a service provider's environment, IT environment, or any other service environment.

- Part I: Theory and Principles—presents a detailed guide to creating Service Level Agreements—the heart of any SLM program. It provides a guide to how to go about creating your own Service Level Agreements.
- Part II: Reality—provides practical advice, tips, and guidelines for creating an effective program for service level management. The advice that this book gives can make the difference between creating an SLM program that is

successful and one that is a complete failure—a waste of time, money, and effort. It also looks at the various types of products that are available to help with service level management.

- Part III: Recommendations—provides insights and guidance about the actual contents of a Service Level Agreement. It provides guidance on building a business case for service level management. It provides guidelines for choosing the appropriate metrics for Service Level Agreements. A third key component of this section is guidelines for implementing service level management program in any organization.

- Appendixes—provide detailed information that will be helpful for implementing service level management. The appendices include templates for reports, Service Level Agreements, and follow up assessments. There is also an appendix that contains a comprehensive list of vendors and their products to assist with service level management.

- Glossary—In light of the confusion surrounding service level management terminology, a set of clear, concise definitions is vital to understanding this subject. This glossary contains definitions of over 60 terms important to understanding service level management.

From the Authors

We believe this comprehensive approach to service level management will provide sufficient understanding to enable you to successfully adopt this management approach. This will help you to operate the IT department more like a business and to stay focused on your most important customers.

We expect continued evolution of SLM techniques, technology, and vendor solutions in the industry. We encourage you to commence a dialog and share best practices with ourselves and other colleagues in the industry. To that end, we invite you to visit our Web site, http://www.nextslm.org, where electronic copies of the templates are available together with chat facilities. You can communicate to any of the authors via this Web site or send email directly to the following addresses:

Rick Sturm: sturm@enterprisemanagement.com

Wayne Morris: wayne_morris@bmc.com

Mary Jander: jander@enterprisemanagement.com

Conventions Used in This Book

Note

A Note presents interesting pieces of information related to the surrounding discussion.

Tip

A Tip offers advice or teaches an easier way to do something.

Caution

A Caution advises you about potential problems and helps you steer clear of disaster.

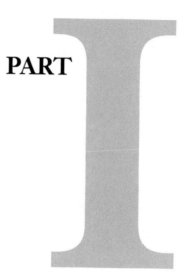

PART I

Theory and Principles

Chapter

CHAPTER 1

The Challenge

Like the peasants in an old monster film, armed with torches and pitchforks, ready to storm the castle—today IT clients are fed up with the service that they have been receiving. They are storming IT castles demanding change. They want improved service and they want it now. This book looks at the problem and how IT can respond to the demands of the user community.

> **Note**
>
> In this book, the terms *users* and *clients* are used interchangeably to identify those people and groups within a company who are the consumer of services provided by IT. The term *customer* is reserved for those groups and individuals who buy the company's goods and services.

The world of business has always been one of change and innovation. The objective of those changes has always been to maximize profits. Owners and managers have constantly sought new ways to achieve this objective. Historically, change has been slow and often subtle—measured in generations or even centuries. However, that has changed. In this century, and particularly since 1940, changes in business practices have accelerated, thanks to the introduction of technologies that stream-line processes and enable new approaches to traditional methods.

Mission Impossible

Information technology (IT) plays a double role in today's global business environment. IT's role in facilitating change is well-known and well-documented. However, it is also subject to forces of change from outside the IT department and even from outside the corporation.

Among the forces affecting IT is the accounting department. Over the past two decades, companies have sought to become even more competitive. In some cases, this has been driven by a desire for increased profits, and in other instances, it is a matter of survival, as competitors force prices downward. This has translated into pressure on IT to reduce costs. IT is being asked to live with smaller budgets—both for capital expenditures and for ongoing expenses. The result is that it is difficult to acquire additional equipment to accommodate the growth in usage most companies are experiencing (increased number of users, transaction volume, number of appli-cations, and so on). Acquisition of more modern, faster, and more reliable equip-ment is made difficult.

Reductions in expense budgets usually translate into reductions in the size of the IT staff because payroll is normally the greatest single expense in an IT budget. Other casualties of budget cuts are salary increases and training for the IT staff. In a competitive job market, the results of these latter items can be higher staff turnover and employees who are less experienced and not as well trained as would be desirable. Ultimately, this limits IT's ability to improve or maintain the levels of service delivered to the end users.

While pressures to reduce costs have been mounting, IT clients, the end users, have become less ignorant and increasingly sophisticated and technically savvy in the ways of computing. They have computers at home. They have computers on their desks in their offices and many have purchased servers for their departments. They are no longer as accepting of excuses or explanations from IT as they once were. The users know what they want and believe they know what is possible. They have aggressive timetables for the delivery of new systems and high expectations in terms of the availability and performance of those systems.

Just as users' technical awareness has risen, so has their reliance on computer sys-tems. The number of mission-critical systems—systems essential to the operation of the business and, ultimately, its very survival—continues to grow daily. Thus, IT's level of responsibility within the corporation has risen significantly. IT has gone from a facilitator of the business process to becoming part of the process and from supporting staff functions to becoming a key element of the business.

Today, some businesses are built solely on electronic commerce. In these cases, the company has no existence except through its computers. Companies like Amazon.com, eBay, e*trade, and the like cease to exist without the functions provided by IT.

However, the criticality of systems is not limited to cyberspace. For industries such as the airlines, financial services, and telecommunications, continuous availability of mission-critical applications is essential. The spread of enterprise resource planning (ERP) applications (for example, SAP R/3, PeopleSoft, Oracle, and so on) has produced another form of mission-critical application. The need for highly available applications with high performance levels has become nearly ubiquitous.

IT has found itself in an unenviable position. CIOs around the world are being told to reduce their budget and improve service levels for an ever-increasing number of applications. In other words, they are faced with the impossible situation of having to deliver "more" with "less."

Divergent Views

IT managers have not been ignoring the needs of their users or the business impacts of the services provided by their organizations. In fact, from the very beginning, IT managers have attempted to measure and assess the performance of the services provided by their organizations. However, they have been limited by perspective and technology.

Historically, IT managers have measured the effectiveness of their organizations by looking at the individual hardware and software components. In the beginning, this made perfect sense—there was only one computer, and it could only run a single program at a time. However, that condition did not last long. Today, analyzing individual components provides information that is relevant and important for managing a specific device or component, but it does not provide a perspective on the overall service being provided to the end user.

Consider the example of Acme Manufacturing. The order entry department has negotiated a Service Level Agreement (SLA) with IT. That agreement calls for the order entry system to be available 99.9% of the time, and no component is to have more than 10 minutes of total downtime in a month. This SLA is incorporated into the objectives for each of the IT department managers. Table 1.1 shows the results for one month. At the end of the month, almost everyone is pleased with the results. All but one of the components have met or exceeded the objectives for availability and for total downtime in the month.

Table 1.1   **Acme Order Entry System Performance for One Month**

Component	Minutes of Downtime	Availability
Building Hub	0	100.00%
Customer Database	4.32	99.99%
Inventory Database	0	100.00%
LAN	6.00	99.99%
Local Server	8.64	99.98%
Order Entry Application	7.54	99.98%
Remote Host	69.72	99.84%
WAN	9.88	99.98%

Obviously, the Remote Host had some problems during the month, but this was because of the failure of a circuit board. Operations had to wait for a service technician to arrive on site and install the new board. Considering this, even the operations group is reasonably satisfied with the performance that IT delivered.

The management of the order entry department takes a much different view of the performance for the month. The end users see a month in which there was a total of 106.1 minutes in which they could not process orders. As shown in Table 1.2, the availability that they experienced was 99.75%—well below the target of 99.9%. (Availability of 99.9% would allow a total unavailable time of 43.2 minutes in a 30-day month.) It is possible that there was some overlap in outages; however, that is statistically unlikely. Also, this example has been constructed using the assumption that outages impacting more than one component would be charged to the root cause. For example, if the remote host fails, it will necessarily result in an outage for the order entry application, the customer database, and the inventory database. However, the outage would only be charged against the remote host because that is the cause of the other components being unavailable.

Table 1.2   **Users' Perspective—Acme Order Entry System Performance**

Component	Minutes of Downtime	Availability
Building Hub	0	100.00%
Customer Database	4.32	99.99%
Inventory Database	0	100.00%
LAN	6.00	99.99%
Local Server	8.64	99.98%
Order Entry Application	7.54	99.98%
Remote Host	69.72	99.84%
WAN	9.88	99.98%
Composite	106.1	99.75%

At this point, IT managers are congratulating each other for the high level of service that they have delivered to the order entry department. Meanwhile, the order entry department managers are hopping mad. The users see IT as being unresponsive and unable (or unwilling) to meet their needs. As they look at the situation, outsourcing the IT function starts to sound like an appealing alternative.

Studies by Enterprise Management Associates have found another problem. Too often, IT fails to provide service level statistics that are meaningful to the end user. Even worse than the component-centric view taken in the previous example, some IT managers substitute techno-babble for meaningful information. For example, it is not uncommon to find IT groups giving reports to their clients that contain such things as packets dropped, page faults, and so on. This type of data might be meaningful to the engineers working with the specific component (for example, the wide area network), but it is little more than gibberish to their clients.

The two communities, the IT organization and their clients, have vastly different perspectives on IT services. IT feels that the client community needs to have more realistic expectations, basing them on what is possible, practical, and affordable. Faced with constraints of immature technology, tight budgets, limited headcount, and scarcity of skilled personnel, IT feels that they should be given credit for being able to accomplish so much. In other words, they feel that they deserve an "A" for effort. On the other hand, the clients' very survival often depends on the delivery of adequate levels of service by IT. They feel that they are paying for the services and should have the right to define what will be delivered.

Technical Challenge

It is true that IT still maintains far too much of a component-centric view of the services that it delivers. Although IT organizations must share in the blame for this continued limited perspective, much of it can be explained by the limitations of the technology available for management reporting. Consider the problem that is reflected in Figure 1.1. This is a simplified illustration of a distributed computing environment. Each type of component has a unique management system attached. Those unique management systems (element management systems) can provide a great deal of information about any single device. The problem presented by these systems is that they also produce a fragmented view of the service. Element management systems are not designed to assess each device in the overall context of the service that it is helping to deliver.

Element management systems are providing information about each component in isolation. It is as if a doctor carefully examines a single part of your body. From that examination, it will be possible to describe the state of that body part. In the case of certain critical body parts (such as the heart, liver, and so on), it might be possible to state how the part is impacting your general health or life expectancy. However, more often it is necessary to consider the part within the context of the total body. It is this perspective that is moving the medical community toward a holistic approach to treatment and diagnosis. There is a similar need within the IT community.

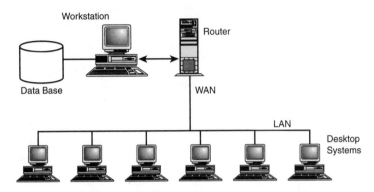

Figure 1.1 *A simple distributed environment.*

In Figure 1.1, there is only a single router, and if the router fails, there is no question that the service is interrupted. However, in a more complex environment—with many routers (see Figure 1.2), alternate paths for data, and so on—the impact of the failure of a single router is not as obvious.

What is needed is the ability to assess the impact of any aberration in the service delivery environment on the service and the end users. Herein lies the challenge—assessing the overall impact when the data is only available on a piecemeal basis. Many companies simply rely on the subjective judgment of the operations personnel. Unfortunately, this is an unreliable approach that cannot produce accurate measurements of the overall level of the service being delivered. Fortunately, new software products are emerging that aim to provide such measurements. We will look at these tools in Chapter 7, "Service Level Management Products."

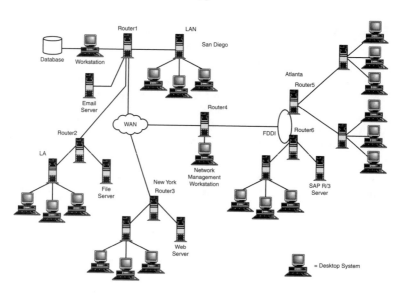

Figure 1.2   *A complex distributed environment.*

What Is SLM?

Service level management (SLM) is the disciplined, proactive methodology and procedures used to ensure that adequate levels of service are delivered to all IT users in accordance with business priorities and at acceptable cost. Effective SLM requires the IT organization to thoroughly understand each service it provides, including the relative priority and business importance of each.

Service levels typically are defined in terms of the availability, responsiveness, integrity, and security delivered to the users of the service. These criteria must be viewed in light of the specific goals of the application being provided. For example, a human resources application might require communications such as email among individuals. An order-entry application might involve multiple cooperating applications such as supply chain management. In all cases, the service should be treated as a closed-loop system with all service levels related directly to the end-user experience.

The instrument for enforcing SLM is the Service Level Agreement (SLA): a contract between IT and its clients that specifies the parameters of system capacity, network performance, and overall response time required to meet business objectives. The SLA also specifies a process for measuring and reporting the quality of service provided by IT, and it describes compensation due the client if IT misses the mark.

Pros and Cons

Some IT managers have a negative perception of service level management (SLM) and Service Level Agreements (SLAs). To begin with, there is a tendency to view SLM as just another fad sweeping across the IT landscape. Certainly in recent years there have been many such fads. Implementing SLM requires time and effort. When IT is already working with limited resources, it is difficult to rationalize allocating some of those resources to work on SLM (especially if it is just a passing fad). Another reason for a negative perception is that in some organizations, the SLM process and the associated SLAs have been abused by the clients of IT. Specifically, the users have succeeded in negotiating unreasonable or unattainable service level commitments and used them as a "club" against the IT organization. Some IT managers believe their organizations expect nothing less than 100% uptime, and they think that signing an SLA merely gives clients a means of documenting the perceived failures of the IT group.

Although these concerns and reservations are understandable and valid, IT management should not allow them to prevent development of service level management, which can be vitally important to the company and the IT organization.

The importance of SLM is demonstrated by its rising popularity. The research firm Cahners In-Stat Group (Newton, MA) reports that the use of SLAs rose 25% among Fortune 1000 companies during 1999, and the market for service level management products is expected to reach $280 million in worldwide revenue by the end of 2000.

Organizations that implement SLM testify to its value in a variety of ways. A comprehensive SLA served as the basis for a lucrative contract between systems integrator 2020 Group Ltd. (Middlesex, United Kingdom) and IMS U.K. and Ireland (Pinner, United Kingdom), a healthcare consultancy. The 2020 Group was enlisted by IMS to help them plan and launch a multisite network requiring 100% reliability. The integrator met this objective by using a "tailored and detailed" SLA, which also helped the team manage the transition to the new network and ensured that 2020's work for IMS was showcased to the best advantage. As a result, the integrator won a lucrative contract to outsource IMS's facilities management on a full-time basis.

At Stanford University (Stanford, CA), the UNIX Systems Support group within the university's Information Technology Systems and Services organization uses SLAs to offer various levels of fee-paid services to staff and students. This approach increases IT's efficiency and allows clients to plan maintenance costs as a regular budget item instead of as an unexpected expense.

There are plenty other SLM success stories. At the National Institutes of Health (NIH, Bethesda, MD), SLAs have been implemented by IT not only to furnish dependable support and timely response to problems, but also to "lower costs through standardized configurations." As an additional benefit, NIH sees SLAs as a means of modeling IT efficiency for other government agencies, thereby taking leadership.

SLM's benefits are so compelling that its use isn't relegated only to IT environments. Seminole Electric Cooperative Inc. (Tampa, FL) also uses SLAs as a key element in its multilevel service offerings. Customers receive cycles of electrical power instead of packets or system capacity.

Other Service Providers

This book has been written mainly from the perspective of IT as a provider of technology services to its clients. However, it is important to note this was done as a matter of convenience for the authors and the readers. In reading this book, it should always be remembered that IT is also a consumer of services. And in this area, IT interest in establishing SLAs with service providers is on the rise. The research firm International Data Corp. (Framingham, MA) announced in September 1999 that 90% of an annual survey of 500 executives said they require SLAs from all service providers. This figure is up from 30% for the same survey in 1998.

As a client or customer of a service provider, all the principles set forth in this book with regard to IT's clients apply equally well to IT in its role as a user of services. Some of the external service providers with whom IT might interface include companies such as Internet Service Providers (ISPs), various forms of communications service providers (telcos), out-sourcing companies, and application service providers (ASPs). Similarly, there might be other service providers within the same company as the IT organization. (Whether a service provider is within the same company as the IT department or external will change the form of the Service Level Agreement, but not the need for the agreement and service level guarantees.) If those organizations providing services to IT do not deliver a consistent, acceptable level of service, IT will not be able to meet its service commitments. It is only reasonable for IT to insist on service level guarantees from its service providers.

This book is also relevant to the non-IT service providers. Companies such as the telcos, ISPs, ASPs, and so on can equally draw on the principles and guidelines in this book, as we will explore in depth in Chapter 11, "Service Level Management as Service Enabler."

The Importance of SLM

All this makes it easy to answer the question, "Is service level management really important to IT?" with an unequivocal "Yes!" For IT, effective service level management is a matter of survival. To understand this, it might be helpful to think of an IT organization as a company. That company's *products* are the services that it delivers to its clients. It is rare to find a successful company that sells its products on the basis of "take it or leave it,"—caveat emptor. Instead, companies go to considerable effort and expense to clearly define both the capabilities and limitations of the product they are selling. Often these are defined in a contract with the buyer. Similarly, a company cannot hope to be successful if it does not implement production controls to ensure that what is shipped is within specifications.

Consider a company that produces sugar (powdered and granulated) and sells it in two-pound bags. First, the specifications ("granulated sugar" and "net weight: 2 lb.") appear clearly on the bag. For reasons of customer satisfaction and cost control, in addition to governmental regulations, the product must meet those specifications.

Note

An IT department without a service level management program is like a sugar producer that puts a "reasonable" amount of product in unlabeled bags. Clearly, this is not a formula for success.

There are six basic reasons for an IT organization to implement service level management. These reasons are as follows:

- Client satisfaction
- Managing expectations
- Resource regulation
- Internal marketing of IT services
- Cost control
- Defensive strategy

Client Satisfaction

The leading reason for implementing service level management is client satisfaction. To begin with, SLM necessitates a dialog between IT managers and their clients. This is necessary in order for IT to be able to understand the client's service requirements. It also forces clients to clearly state (perhaps for the first time) their requirements or expectations. When IT and the client agree on what is an acceptable level of service, they are establishing a benchmark against which IT performance can be measured. IT is able to shift toward a defined objective—the client's requirements. The dialog that is initially established continues through the process with regular reports. Even a process of service level management cannot produce happy clients when service level commitments are not met. However, it will significantly raise overall client satisfaction when commitments are met. It can also help to improve the situation when targets are missed.

Managing Expectations

An ancillary benefit of implementing service level management is that it makes it possible to avoid so-called expectation creep—that is, the ever rising levels of users' undocumented expectations. It is common for people to want improvements over the status quo. If users' requirements are not documented, their expectations are not established at a particular level. Instead, undocumented requirements are free to rise steadily, always staying ahead of the level of service that is being delivered. When Service Level Agreements are negotiated, requirements are documented. Although users might continue to want higher levels of service, the agreement serves as a braking mechanism. IT is able to point to the commitments in the SLA that were previously identified as being acceptable. Any changes require a renegotiation of the agreement and, potentially, additional funding for IT in order to provide the higher level of service.

Resource Regulation

SLM provides a form of governance over IT resources. In some organizations, a powerful user group will sometimes demand support for an application that unfairly ties up resources. With an SLA in place, it is more difficult for a strong minority to outweigh the interests of the majority. SLAs also help IT avoid capacity problems that result when too many applications crowd the network, server, mainframe, or desktop. And because SLAs specify levels of service, they can be used as indicators for ongoing system capacity and network bandwidth requirements. Specific resources will be needed to keep abreast of SLA parameters. And the monitoring and measurement deployed by IT to keep up with SLAs ensures early warning for any new capacity that might be required.

Internal Marketing of IT Services

When used correctly, SLM not only helps IT departments to deploy resources fairly, but also it can be a great marketing tool. By ensuring ongoing, consistent levels of response time and availability, SLAs provide a powerful way for IT to let internal clients know what a terrific job they are doing. Before the advent of SLAs, the only contact many organizations had with their IT departments occurred when something went wrong. This state of affairs tended to place IT in a negative light, causing clients to view IT as a necessary evil and the object of blame for system failures. In changing this perception, SLM takes IT out of the category of a liability and puts it among the company's assets. With the right approach, SLM puts IT in the limelight with other departments—such as finance and accounting—that are charged with sustaining and growing the business.

Cost Control

In the context of cost control, service level management is a double-edged sword. First, it helps IT to better determine the appropriate level of service to provide. Without service level objectives arrived at in dialog with their clients, IT management is forced to guess. Too often, this guesswork leads to excess. That is, it can lead to over-staffing, configuring networks with excess capacity, buying larger, faster computers, and so on.

In the absence of dialog with IT, the users' requirements are established by what is desirable rather than what is affordable. The requirements and expectations are not tempered by the reality of feasibility or affordability. Service level management can also impact costs through moderating user demands for higher levels of service. This can happen in two ways. As discussed in the previous section, service level management can limit the escalation of user demands. Also, as part of the dialog with IT, the financial impact of higher levels of service can also be explained. In some instances, the business case will justify the additional cost of providing higher levels of service. In other cases, there will not be a financial justification and, hopefully, the unnecessary cost will be avoided.

Defensive Strategy

Ultimately everyone is motivated by self-interest. IT managers are no different. It can clearly be in the interest of IT managers to implement a service level management process. With SLM in place, IT has a tool to use in defending itself from user attacks. Clear objectives are set and documented. There is no room for doubt about whether the objectives have been met. In a well-written Service Level Agreement, even the metrics for measuring service levels are defined and agreed to by both the users and IT.

Ultimately, service level management is something that can benefit the user, the IT organization, and the corporation in which they both work. The process of service level management can temper users' demands for higher levels of service. Conversely, service level management can hold IT accountable for delivering agreed upon levels of service, while providing them with clear objectives for service. Outsourcing continues to be very popular. SLM can be the best defensive strategy that IT can have against user dissatisfaction that can lead to outsourcing.

Why Now?

If the case for service level management is so compelling, why is it just now receiving widespread attention? Several reasons help explain the sudden attention that service level management is receiving. First, there has been a dramatic increase in the number of applications (that is, the number of services being provided) and in the relative importance of those applications. Companies are more dependent upon the services that IT provides.

The next factor driving the increased interest in service level agreements is increasing user sophistication and their growing dissatisfaction with the level of service they are receiving. This change in the user community is discussed at the beginning of this chapter.

Probably more important than all the other factors fueling interest in service level management is the fact that technology has matured, making possible end-to-end measurement and reporting available at a reasonable cost. Dozens of vendors, ranging from the very largest to minuscule start-ups, have focused their attention and the considerable talents of their technical wizards on the challenges of service level management. A 1996 Enterprise Management Associates survey of IT managers found only twelve products that were being used for service level management. However, possibly only one of those products (Microsoft Excel) added any value to the process, albeit minimal. Eighteen months later, in May 1998, the number of companies that identified themselves as offering products specifically for service level management had risen to 62. By March of 1999, the number had climbed to 89 (see Figure 1.3).

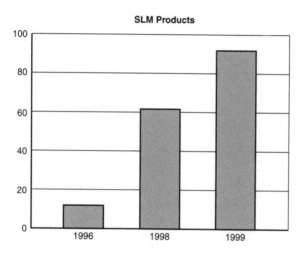

Figure 1.3 *Growth in SLM Products.*

If a company wants to implement SLM, it is a much simpler process than it was even 4 years ago. In the past, collecting the data (if available) and generating the SLM reports was slow and labor-intensive. Sometimes it required custom programs to be written, or expensive data collection products to be purchased. Even then, the results were usually marginal. The situation has improved significantly. The introduction of new products has facilitated the data collection process as well as the merging or correlating of data from diverse sources. Although there are more advances to come, SLM reporting has become dramatically easier.

Summary

In today's global business environment, IT professionals find themselves undergoing pressure to reduce costs and deliver higher-than-ever levels of service to increasingly savvy users. To achieve this, they are deploying service level management (SLM), a methodology for ensuring consistent levels of capacity and performance in IT environments. SLM includes a contract between IT and its clients (whether in house or external to the organization), that specifies the client's expectations, IT's responsibilities, and compensation that IT will provide if goals are not met. Despite some initial misgivings, the value and importance of SLM have been established. Its successful use is well documented in numerous case studies, and its popularity is increasing not only within IT organizations, but also among service providers. A range of new products geared to supporting SLM further testifies to its deployment as an unquestioned requirement in IT organizations worldwide.

CHAPTER 2

The Perception and Management of Service Levels

Service level management (SLM) is the continuous process of measuring, reporting, and improving the quality of service provided by the IT organization to the business. This requires that the IT organization understands each service it provides, including relative priorities, business importance, and which lines of business and individual users consume which service.

There are a number of important aspects that relate to the perception and management of service levels. The first consideration is to ensure that service levels to be managed are measured and evaluated from a perspective that matches the business goals of the IT organization. The IT department supports business productivity by ensuring that the applications used by internal personnel are available to them when required and that they are responsive enough to allow these users to be optimally productive. It is almost certain that failures and errors will lead to a service outage. The IT department must restore the service as quickly as possible with the least amount of disruption to other services.

The IT department must also ensure that automated business processes complete in a timely fashion to meet required deadlines and to enhance effectiveness and profitability. Additionally, if customers directly use or interact with IT services, IT must ensure that their experience is pleasurable—leading to customer loyalty and repeat business.

Service levels are measured and managed to improve a number of quantifiable aspects of the perceived quality of the services delivered. These are described in the remainder of the chapter.

Availability

Availability is the percentage of the time that a service is available for use. This can be a controversial measure of service quality because of the number of different measurement mechanisms. The variability of measurements is a result of differing perspectives of service goals, which vary primarily by the job function of the individual doing the measuring. For example, the network manager typically sees the service as the network connectivity; the system manager views the service as the server being operational; the database administrator sees the service as available access to data held in the database. Hence, quoted availability measurements typically relate to individual components (for example, server availability or network availability) and do not match the IT user's perception of availability. The end user or line of business wants to know that he can access the applications and data required for him to perform productive work.

Note

Unless availability measurement relates directly to the user experience, it will have little positive value and might, in fact, damage the credibility of the IT organization quoting such measurements.

True availability must be measured end-to-end from the end user through all the technology layers and components to the desired business application and data, and back to the end user. Such an aggregate value can be difficult to measure directly and might have to be derived by combining the availability of all the components traversed. Figure 2.1 shows the concept of end-to-end service level management. The reality of a business-oriented IT service might, in fact, be more complex, involving multiple applications, extranets, and Internet connections.

The first step in measuring and managing service levels is to define each service and map out the service from end-to-end. Each of the end users and their locations should be identified together with the path they take to access the business application providing the core part of the service. The data used by the application should be determined along with where it resides and how it is accessed. If the core application needs to interact with other applications, these should also be identified and mapped. In this manner the overall flow of a service or business transaction can be determined, recorded, and used to define transaction types, component dependencies, and appropriate service measurement points.

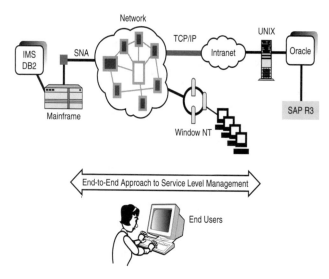

Figure 2.1 *End-to-end service level management.*

Note

This end-to-end definition of service using the user's perspective is required for all measures relating to service quality.

Availability of a service is the capability to successfully complete an entire service or business transaction as defined previously. *Component availability* describes when an individual component the service depends on is operational.

The availability of each service is defined within standard hours of operation for that service. Most IT organizations need to remove applications from service at periodic intervals (called a *maintenance window*) in order to undertake routine maintenance of the application, supporting databases, and underlying infrastructure. Hence availability objectives will also specify planned outages by service, together with the schedule for those outages. The standard hours of operation will vary depending on the nature and criticality of each service. As more services become Internet based, the length of the maintenance window shrinks and might not be acceptable at all.

Availability is the most important factor that influences the users' perception of the quality of IT services. It is also the most critical factor affecting user productivity, particularly if the user depends entirely on a particular business application to perform her job function.

Performance

As with availability, performance must be measured from the end users' perspective and must also relate to the business goals of IT. The performance of a service is measured by the responsiveness of the application to interactive users and the time required to complete each batch job to be processed (also called *job turnaround*). The responsiveness of the application and batch job processing times will be affected directly by the amount of work to be processed (also called *workload levels*). This concept is discussed in the next section.

Interactive Responsiveness

Interactive responsiveness relates to the time taken to complete a request on behalf of a user. The quicker the requests are completed, the more responsive the service. The request could be processing a service transaction or retrieving some information. It is important that any measure of responsiveness match the user experience, hence response time measures must be end-to-end, from the end user's desktop through the business application (including any database access and interaction with other applications) and back to the end user.

The responsiveness of the service is second only to availability as an important factor in the user's perception of the quality of services provided by IT. There is a direct correlation between how fast the application responds to online users and their productivity. An important consideration is the consistency of the interactive response times experienced by the end users. Erratic and unpredictable response times that vary from exceptionally fast to extremely slow will be perceived by the users as unacceptable and far worse than consistent response times that might be merely adequate.

It is important that all applications supported by the IT environment meet their performance goals. If balanced performance is not maintained, one application service might meet its performance objectives at the expense of other application services, which will result in a dissatisfied user community.

Tip

In cases where performance is certain to degrade over time because of increasing workloads, and where responsiveness is significantly better than required initially, some IT departments build in latency that can be removed gradually over time. This ensures that response times can be held constant at acceptable levels, and ensures that unrealistic expectations aren't set.

Batch Job Turnaround

A large amount of processing does not require continuous interaction with either the user or system operator and happens in batch mode or as background tasks. In this case, job streams are scheduled and processed to perform routine operations that produce predetermined outputs such as payroll, financial reporting, inventory manifestos, and so on. Responsiveness of the batch jobs is referred to as *turnaround*. This is the time between submitting the batch or background request and the completion of all processing associated with that request, including delivering output to the required recipients.

In a large IT environment, numerous batch jobs will have to be processed every day, and the volume of jobs typically varies in cycles with peaks at the end of week, month, quarter, and fiscal year.

There is usually a specified "batch window" within which all batch processing has to finish to ensure that the performance, and particularly the responsiveness, of interactive processing is not degraded by the batch processing. Some background tasks are continuous in nature such as print spooling or file system management.

Critical Deadlines

In addition to the normal window for processing all batch jobs, there might be specified times at which certain jobs or tasks must finish to satisfy external vendors or regulation. For example, the payroll run might have to be completed by 2:00 a.m. to ensure that the information is sent to the bank in time for the electronic funds transfer to be completed that night.

Note

Meeting critical deadlines can be very important because there might be monetary damages or penalties for not completing the work by the specified time.

In many cases, the completion of critical deadline jobs will take precedence over completing all jobs within the batch window and might have priority over interactive processing.

User Perception of Performance

Usability studies have identified the relationship between response times and user satisfaction for various user and work profiles. This varies tremendously by the nature of the work involved, the perceived difficulty of the task being performed by the automated process, and the relationship between response time and user "think" time. Similar parameters will affect the user's perception of the adequacy of batch job turnaround. As mentioned previously, consistency of responsiveness is critical to user satisfaction.

Workload Levels

The *workload level* is the volume of processing performed by a particular service. This includes both the rate of processing interactive transactions, as well as the number of completed batch jobs within a given time period.

These service workloads generally relate to specific applications; however, workload processing might span multiple applications and generate work on multiple systems. A service workload uses all the components involved in delivering the service, including using network, system, database, and middleware resources. In order to plan capacity requirements and understand the effect of service workloads, it is very useful to correlate service workloads with individual resource utilization levels across all components that provide the service infrastructure.

Note

The most important measures of service workload volumes are online transaction rates, the number of batch jobs to be processed, and the number of these jobs that will be completed in parallel.

Transaction Rates

Interactive workloads are usually measured as the number of transactions per second; however, it is important to understand the nature of the quoted transactions. Transactions represent a complete unit of useful work. It is important to recognize the difference between a transaction and a system or application interaction. A single interaction is simply one pair of messages in a dialog between the user and the application, such as the user submitting a request for service and receiving an acknowledgment of the request. A single transaction can involve multiple user interactions.

Definition of a Transaction

An *application transaction* performs some business task that results in a change to the data associated with, or the state of, the automated application. A *business transaction* changes the state of a business entity, changes the state of the relationship between business entities, or performs some service on behalf of a business customer.

For example, a business transaction might result in the sale of a number of shares in a publicly traded company. In order to complete this business transaction, a number of different interactions and application transactions might occur. The broker registers the customer's desire to sell the shares using one application transaction. The broker's system checks the stock price from the stock exchange with a different application transaction. Perhaps the broker then lists the volume to be sold and its asking price with a market maker by interfacing to that entity's trading application. A trading house accepts the bid in yet another transaction. Finally, the sale confirmation is sent back to the broker in another transaction, and the broker notifies the customer of the sale. Each of these interactions could be considered a business transaction by itself, but will have little relevance to the customer wanting to sell stock. The customer's perception will be that he completed one business transaction—he sold a volume of stock.

All measures of interactive workloads need to specify whether business transactions or application transactions are being quoted, and if a business transaction, the parties to the business transaction should also be understood, particularly whether one or more of the parties are outside the corporation.

Caution

Measuring business transactions can be complicated unless the application code itself supports such a measure.

Mapping business transactions to application transactions, to underlying interactions, and relating how the supporting technology components were used to process the transaction will be required in order to plan capacity requirements.

Client/Server Interactions

Many applications have been developed using the client/server architecture. In many cases, this is multi-tiered such as an application that is split among the client-side presentation, application server, and database server. This complicates the measurement of the transaction.

Tip

The overriding rule for determining the scope of a business transaction is that it begins with an end user initiating a business action or request and ends when the automated business process fulfills that initial business request.

Using a client/server application architecture increases the need to carefully map the transaction to ensure that all the subordinate interactions are encapsulated by the business transaction definition. This ensures that the measurement of transaction rates and associated response times matches the end user's experience.

Batch Job Concurrency

Another measure of workload levels is the number of batch jobs that are run simultaneously. Most operating systems allow the operator to control the number of background jobs that can be initiated concurrently and the optimal number will vary depending on the power of the system performing the processing and the characteristics of the workloads themselves.

> **Tip**
> Workload balancing is important to ensure that synergistic workloads run concurrently because conflicting jobs (jobs with similar characteristics, such as being CPU intensive or I/O intensive) might lead to thrashing and performance degradation.

It becomes particularly important to carefully control the amount and priority of batch jobs and background processing when these are performed concurrently with interactive processing. There is a very real possibility that these background tasks and jobs will detract from the quality of service provided to interactive users.

Batch Job Dependencies

Batch job stream specifications not only include which jobs to run, but also their sequencing and inter-dependencies. As a simple example, every two weeks a payroll run might include first identifying and flagging new recruits within the employee database, processing all employee records to determine vacation or sick days used by employees, and then processing the payroll to calculate wages and taxes owed. In this case, the first two steps must complete prior to the third step of calculating the payroll numbers.

Complying with job dependencies will place limits on the number of batch jobs that can be run in parallel, hence constraining the overall workload levels. Ensuring that all dependencies are met can also negatively impact the total time required to complete all batch windows. Therefore careful job stream planning, scheduling, and operational management are important aspects of meeting required service levels.

> **Note**
> Where critical deadlines exist, extra coordination is required to ensure that the critical jobs, together with any dependencies, can finish in the required timeframe.

Security

Defining the security of a service includes the definition of who can access the service, the nature of the access, and the mechanisms used to detect, prevent, and report unauthorized access. As applications span multiple platforms and users require access to data across multiple databases, the complexity of the security environment increases tremendously, and multiple security management systems will be employed.

> **Tip**
>
> Coordinating actions and administration across these multiple security systems becomes critical for ensuring consistency of access privileges and reducing the administrative overhead and potential for errors.

Defining Resources

All users and resources—including services, data, applications, systems, and network elements—must be defined to the security systems. To avoid issues with multiple inconsistent definitions, a resource-naming architecture should be defined and adopted. Additionally, a centralized security administration application can be used to automate the coordination and propagation of definitions and updates between multiple distributed security systems.

In more complex environments, it will be very useful to maintain a registry or directory outlining the relationship between the defined resources. For example, as the service is mapped onto the underlying infrastructure (as outlined in the section on Availability), it would be very useful to capture this information and maintain and use it when diagnosing service difficulties and when aggregating component service levels to produce end-to-end service level reports.

Access Controls

When the resources have been defined, access control lists are defined and then used to determine which users have access to which resources, and the nature of the authorized access. Depending on the type of resource to be accessed or used, the nature of the access will vary. For example, a user might be authorized to use a particular service that also requires access rights to certain data objects within a database. The nature or level of the access can range from read, write, update, create, or delete. Depending on her access privileges to the underlying data, the user's ability to invoke the various service options will vary.

> **Note**
>
> Understanding, mapping, and maintaining the resources used by each service is important for understanding which resources a particular user will need to access in order to perform his job function.

The service options available to the user will determine the level of access to each application and resource she requires. Again, the use of a registry or directory service can simplify this aspect of maintaining access control.

Assigning Users to Privilege Classes

To improve the consistency of resource access, users can be allocated to privilege classes that group users together with common profiles. This grouping could be by job function, job level, organization structure, physical location, or some combination of these. In this manner, changes to the access privileges in existing or new resources can be applied to an entire group or class of user simultaneously.

Tip

The use of a registry to hold and maintain this information can simplify the administration of user groups and subsequent granting or revoking of access privileges to resources.

Intrusion Detection

After users, resources, and authorized access privileges have been defined, a continuous process of ensuring only authorized access to resources takes place. The security systems should automatically enforce the security policies as defined by the user group associations and the access control lists for defined resources. Service level management should ensure that the definitions correctly allow access and use of authorized services while refusing unauthorized access.

Another aspect of service management is monitoring the IT environment to detect unauthorized access or attempts to access resources illegally. This includes logging failed access attempts, particularly methodical repeated access attempts; notifying security, system, and service administrators of these attempts in real-time; and exercising escalation procedures to increase the difficulty of obtaining unauthorized access.

Privacy Issues

An important consideration when implementing security systems is to ensure that, where appropriate, the identity of the users is kept private and is not available to unauthorized access. If registries and directory services are used, controlling access to these data stores is an important aspect of ensuring information privacy.

Note

Information privacy becomes more important for those applications that directly touch customers—for example, e-commerce applications—or where applications interface with business partners, such as with supply chain and e-business applications.

The issue of information privacy is a sensitive topic within the Internet community and one that has direct impact on the users' perception of service quality. Standards and regulation can be expected to continue to evolve in this area, and hence service level management must embrace managing information privacy.

Business Ownership of Security

The IT resource definitions, as well as the identity and information associated with users who access those resources, are all business assets, and as such it is important to identify the business owner of IT security. This security business manager must be responsible for defining security requirements, policies, privilege classes, access controls, escalation procedures, and monitoring roles and procedures.

The security aspects of service level management and reporting should be aimed at satisfying the requirements specified by this security business owner.

Accuracy

Service accuracy is a difficult concept to define and measure quantitatively, but the perception of the quality of the service offering will be influenced by a number of aspects relating to the accuracy of the data used for decisions and the accuracy of implementing IT procedures.

Data Integrity

Data integrity is the most significant aspect of ensuring the accuracy of the data used for making decisions. Hardware failures, logic errors, and program architecture issues, as well as operator and user error, can all impact the integrity of data. Ensuring data integrity requires checking the consistency of data and databases structures including views, stored procedures, indices, and so on.

Additionally, defining and implementing appropriate data backup and recovery procedures will improve data integrity by enabling restoration of corrupted data. Recovery of data is addressed in more detail in the section "Recoverability" later in the chapter.

Data Currency

Another important aspect of data accuracy is the currency of data. This is particularly important when data is distributed across multiple data stores such as replicated databases, data warehouses, and data marts. In these cases, the latency, or delay in propagating data changes to the distributed data stores, affects the accuracy of the data. Longer propagation delays result in data that is not consistent across the enterprise, and different users will be working with various versions of the data.

Web servers, e-business, and e-commerce exacerbate this problem because in many cases data is moved from operational databases to data stores outside the firewall—for example, to the external Web site or to the business partner via an extranet.

Caution

Applications using replicated data can result in customers and partners having different and inaccurate data available to them, depending on the frequency of data updates.

Job Control

The accuracy of provided services also depends on ensuring all the required batch jobs are run with the correct sequencing and dependency rules and that critical deadlines are met. This aspect can rely on operator intervention, job scripts, or an automated job scheduler.

Scheduled Maintenance

As mentioned when discussing service availability, most IT environments require maintenance functions to be performed regularly during scheduled downtimes. Service availability is directly affected by the IT department's ability to remain within the scheduled periods. Service quality also depends on the IT department ensuring that all appropriate maintenance—including backups, bulk data moves and loads, database reorganizations, and database schema changes, as well as upgrades to applications, supporting software, and hardware—is completed correctly during the planned downtime. Hence, service management should include precise definition and implementation of scheduled maintenance requirements, frequency, and procedures.

Recoverability

Recovering from unplanned outage conditions as rapidly as possible is necessary to improve the availability of services provided by IT. The ultimate goal of a recoverability strategy is to provide business continuity or as close to this ideal as possible. Hence, the IT organization must be able to recover from multiple types of outages in a minimal time and with minimal disruption to the other services provided by IT.

Types of Outages

Outages can be because of physical failures, logical errors, or a natural disaster. Depending on the nature of the outage, a single service might be disrupted or multiple services might be affected. For example, a physical failure will affect those services using that device or component, whereas a logic error will impact a single service. In either case, the failure might have a cascading effect on other services that use the data or other output from a service initially impacted by the failure. A full disaster will affect all services in that location and all other services that depend on any physical devices in that location.

Note

The vast majority of outages today are because of logic errors rather than either hardware failure or disasters.

Understanding the impact of each outage type and planning for the correct recovery procedure requires knowledge of the relationship between each service and the underlying resources, as well as the inter-relationship between services, particularly in which there is data sharing. The registry or directory of services and associated supporting resources can be invaluable in understanding the effect of an individual resource failure. Similarly, knowledge of the business process, application integration, data model, and the association between data objects and access by application services will allow the impact of one service outage on other services to be assessed.

Levels of Recovery

Recovering from an outage will take place in multiple stages. In the event of a physical failure, the device is repaired or replaced. Then the data must be restored from a back-up copy; the application restarted; and as much lost work as possible, from the time of the last backup to the time of failure, is re-created. Then business processing can be resumed. Each of these processes can be automated to some degree, and the use of additional automation reduces the time required for recovery and can also reduce the possibility of error in the recovery process.

Recovering to a Specified Point in Time

In the event of a program logic error, operator error, or user error, the goal is to recover to the point in time immediately prior to the error that caused the outage. This reduces the time required to resume normal business operations. During normal operation, transactions are captured and logged by applications, middleware, and the database. Following an outage, these logs can be analyzed and used to re-create transactions after the data is recovered from the backup, which provides a snapshot of the data as it existed when the back-up copy was taken.

Those transactions that were completed between the time the back-up copy was made and the point in time immediately prior to the error are re-created. Automated solutions are available that will analyze the logs and generate a script that is replayed to re-create the transactions.

Time to Recover

The time taken for the recovery includes the time required to cease processing, restore a stable environment, recover corrupted data, and re-create lost transactions. The recovery time directly impacts service availability, whereas the ability to recover all data and completed transactions has a direct effect on the accuracy and integrity of the data and the perceived quality of the service.

The time taken to restore a stable environment depends on the extent of any physical damage and availability of additional or substitute hardware resources. The additional recovery time depends on the amount of data to be recovered, the time required to locate and mount the back-up media, the speed of data transfer from the back-up media, the time required to re-create transactions, and the time required to initialize and restart applications and background tasks.

In a disaster situation, or if multiple services are affected by an outage, the time taken to recover an individual service will depend on the procedures used and the priority given to recovering that particular service.

Tip

Recovering the most critical business services and those with the most stringent service-level requirements first helps to increase the satisfaction of users and lines of business.

Affordability

A distinct balance exists between the service levels provided by the IT department and the associated costs of delivering the service. Typically, the higher the availability and performance required, the more costly it is to provide the service. In order to better understand this relationship, and to ensure that lines of business use fully loaded costs when assessing their profit and loss, many organizations charge IT costs directly to the users of IT services.

When allocating costs, a mechanism for calculating IT costs together with a methodology for allocating those costs to the various users and lines of business should be negotiated and agreed to by IT and the user community.

Quantifying Cost

The costs associated with running the IT environment include hardware costs (capital depreciation and expenses), software costs, maintenance costs, personnel costs, telecommunications cost, consultant and professional service costs, and environmental costs. In most cases, the costs associated with operating the IT environment are the largest costs incurred, outweighing the expenses and capital depreciation of hardware and software. This means that effectively managing the environment is very important to keeping these costs under control. Effective service level management can help contain operating costs.

The total IT costs can be calculated relatively easily; however, allocating costs to individual services is complex and can be subject to dispute.

Note

An important decision in the operation of the IT department will be whether to allocate costs at all. If not, IT costs can be considered part of general administration costs.

Tip

Assigning IT costs to lines of business allows IT to be seen as a business partner and service supplier to the business, rather than as a cost center.

This shift in positioning of the IT department as a business partner is subtle but important if IT is willing to take on a more strategic role in helping ensure business success. The goal of IT becomes a combination of improving business efficiency as well as business effectiveness. A further refinement of this is that IT will be measured on return on investment (ROI), rather than simply by total cost of ownership (TCO).

This is a significant step forward in recognizing the business importance of the IT department. As more corporations implement e-business initiatives, the IT department becomes a critical revenue generator for the company, and the strategic role of IT becomes one of helping the company make money.

When assigning costs to lines of business, considerations include what costs to use, what method of allocation to use, and how to demonstrate return on investment and show value for money.

What Costs to Count

Some costs are directly related to the use of IT resources such as CPU, memory, disk space, and application software. Greater utilization of these resources results in increased demand for hardware capacity and software licenses, which can be fulfilled either by reduced service or additional purchases. Environmental costs and IT operations staff can be considered constant overhead within certain limitations. Typically these are stepped functions in which additional staff or perhaps larger floor space become necessary as the IT environment grows past certain size thresholds.

Software development costs vary depending on the demand for custom applications and can normally be related to specific projects or business initiatives.

Software license costs for application software usually increase with the number of users. Assigning application license costs and custom development costs to lines of business is generally straightforward.

Other costs will vary with the size and complexity of the IT environment including additional capacity for contingencies, backups, and hot standby systems, along with utility software and network and system management solutions. These are difficult to assign to individual users or lines of business but are necessary for smooth operation.

Tip

These costs lend themselves more to an agreed-upon allocation as overhead, rather than trying to relate costs to usage by the lines of business.

Assigning Costs to Line of Business

The requirement to assign IT costs to lines of business varies according to each company's accounting practices and desire for profit-and-loss reporting by lines of business. In many companies, IT is seen as a cost center allocated to general administration overhead. However, there is a trend toward viewing IT as a competitive advantage that can increase revenues and enhance market position. In this case, allocating IT costs to lines of business as a cost of sales is very appropriate.

Note

As e-commerce continues to gain momentum, the IT costs might, in fact, become the primary cost of sales for a growing number of companies or specific line of business.

A variety of mechanisms are in use that allocate IT costs to lines of business. In many, usage statistics are gathered including CPU utilization, disk space consumed, output generated, and so on, and a formula is used to calculate a usage cost based on these measurements. Additional costs such as telecommunication, environmental, and labor costs are factored into the formula, such that total IT costs are covered by the sum of the costs allocated to each line of business. This method is popular in traditional mainframe environments where most costs are centered on the centralized processing environment. The relationship between transactions processed and business value is relatively easy to establish because much of the processing is batch oriented, and the interactive processing is very transaction oriented.

The acceptance and growth of distributed computing environments has made collecting usage costs by individual user or group much more complex, and it can be very difficult for lines of business to relate IT resource consumption to the way they conduct their business. Multi-tiered applications mean that more resources across a wider range of desktops, Web servers, application servers, database servers, and corporate mainframes are used to complete single transactions. There is also much greater network complexity resulting in additional equipment, local area network, and telecommunication service costs. These are difficult to allocate based on actual usage.

More simplistic methods have gathered support in distributed environments including allocating costs based on service subscriptions or calculating costs based on volume of business transactions. These are easier to calculate and have analogies that most management can relate to, making them easier to understand and sell to the lines of business.

Service subscription cost allocation is based on the cable television model. Lines of businesses pay for services that are accessed by their personnel, and the cost per user does not vary by the intensity of usage. This is a very simple model, and, provided that the cost per user per service is set appropriately, it is easy to understand and easy to calculate. The price for each service subscription should relate to the cost of providing the service and preferably will also reflect the perceived value of the service.

Caution
The IT department needs to ensure that the sum of all subscriptions sold equals the total costs to be allocated.

Allocating cost by business transaction volumes can be very attractive if business transactions are easily measured. This is an easy allocation mechanism for the lines of business to understand. The IT department and each line of business will have to agree on a suitable cost per transaction. There will be significant work on the part of the IT department to calculate appropriate transaction costs for each transaction type based on resources consumed to perform the transaction, the length of the transaction, and the perceived business value of the transaction.

Caution
Again, the IT department must ensure that the total charges across all lines of business are adequate to cover all IT-related costs.

Relating Value to Cost

The ease of relating IT costs to business value varies depending on the mechanism used to calculate and allocate costs. Typically most lines of business will care little about the actual IT resources consumed, but will understand that they use certain applications and services in order to conduct business and complete business transactions.

Allocating costs based on resource consumption will represent IT as a cost center because it will be difficult for the lines of business to directly associate the cost allocation to business volumes. In this case, the IT services will be viewed more as a commodity, and the lines of business will seek to lower costs either by reducing budget for the IT department or looking for an alternative low-cost provider.

Using service subscriptions can be easy for the user community to understand because there is an analogy to the cable television industry. There is not a direct correlation between cost, usage intensity, and business volumes in this model, and this might cause some confusion when trying to relate business value.

Using business transaction volumes provides a more direct link between cost and business value, and the analogy is bank fees on banking transactions. The difficulty here might be in negotiating a suitable fee per business transaction and differentiating value between the various types of transactions, while still having a simple model that is easy to calculate. This also places the responsibility on the IT department to understand business volumes by transaction type well enough to ensure that total IT costs are recovered.

Summary

As outlined in this chapter, there are many aspects to service level management. The most important concept is to ensure that the definition of the services to be managed relate to the perception of the lines of business and the IT users. The quality of the services delivered to these users will be judged according to the users' ability to safely, effectively, and cost efficiently use the services when required to perform their jobs.

CHAPTER 3

Service Level Reporting

Service level reporting is an important communication vehicle between the IT department, the user community, and the lines of business. It should be viewed as a means for demonstrating the value of IT services and as a way to promote the quality of the services provided by the IT department. Providing the reports in a format that aligns with the goals of the lines of business, and that is easily understood by business managers as well as corporate executives, demonstrates the IT department's understanding and support for key business initiatives.

Effective reporting provides a way to proactively address service difficulties and reduce the negative effect on the reputation of the IT department as a result of a service outage or degradation.

Tip

Proactive reporting of service difficulties can also reduce the load on help desk personnel by decreasing the number of problem reports initiated by users of the affected IT services.

Audience

When determining how best to report on the quality of services provided by the IT department, various audience types should be identified and categorized along with their interest areas and characteristics. Each audience category requires different information that varies in focus, granularity, and frequency. Many common elements can provide the underlying information used in all reports; however, the perspective and presentation format will differ by audience.

Executive Management

Executive management wants to know that the IT department is providing value to the business overall and contributing to business success. As information technology becomes viewed increasingly as a competitive advantage, senior management becomes more attuned to the impact (positive and negative) of the service quality delivered by the IT department. This includes understanding how enhancing the quality of IT services improves business competitiveness and efficiency. Similarly, management understands that outages and degraded service cost the business both in real dollars as well as in related lost opportunity costs. As IT services are provided directly to customers, such as with e-commerce and e-business initiatives, the visibility of service difficulties increases and extends to the press, financial community, and investors who assess the impact of service problems on business viability and performance.

Reports aimed at the executive management team must be highly summarized and outline the quality of service experienced by the company's personnel, customers, and business partners. The report should directly relate the delivery of superior service to associated productivity improvements. Conversely, service outages or degradation should be related to real costs as well as lost opportunity costs in both revenue and staff productivity.

Note

Although reports that include the business impact of service difficulties might be painful and embarrassing, they build credibility and might be very helpful when asking for management's support to fix the problems.

Lines of Business

The lines of business are interested in knowing how the quality of services provided by IT help them to drive more business. This means the reports should relate service levels to business transaction volumes, personnel productivity, and, where possible, customer satisfaction. Reporting the impact of service outages or service degradation in terms directly related to the business is equally important, hence opportunity costs and lost productivity should be determined and reported.

Note

Establishing the relationship between service quality and the ability to optimize business transactions is important.

Increases in business transaction volumes might be related to improved service levels and business expenses might be reduced by improved staff productivity because of better service performance. These types of relationships can be shown with many different types of applications, such as automated manufacturing operations where the bottleneck might lie with computerized control or with customer-facing operations such as reservation systems where computer delays lead to increases in staffing levels and reductions in customer satisfaction. Therefore, it is important that this relationship be explained to the lines of business and utilized in service level reports. The goal is to quantify the business benefits associated with the reported service quality.

Relating customer satisfaction directly to the quality of IT services might be more difficult to capture, and conducting primary research such as customer surveys or providing a feedback mechanism as part of the service transactions might be required. After it is established, the relationship between IT service quality and customer satisfaction can be an important tool for establishing the value of IT and for justifying additional IT resources. If there is an established, credible mechanism for regularly assessing customer satisfaction, tracking the results of service satisfaction against delivered service levels directly shows the relationship and trends.

Internal to IT

IT must be service oriented in order to provide better support for the business. To foster this orientation, the same service level reports provided to the lines of business should be available to and reviewed by all levels of IT management. Many IT departments are organizing first-level support along service lines rather than technology layers. This provides a focus for service level reviews as well as natural interface points for user communities. These service-oriented teams also act as the user advocates within the IT department.

Additional reports showing all underlying technology outages and performance degradation should be produced. Where possible, these reports should be correlated with overall service quality using time as the common variable. These allow IT management and technology-focused second-level support to relate the impact of technology and component failures and degradation to the quality of service levels delivered to the lines of business. Overall service delivery performance should be graded against service level objectives. This ensures all IT personnel know how well the department is performing overall, and how their particular role and the technology they support affects the achievement of these objectives.

Outside Customers

Summarized reports should be available to the customers of IT services who are outside the corporation. These should provide information on the quality of the services delivered to them, and should also outline the steps taken to improve service quality, particularly if customer expectations have not been met.

Tip

Regular customer satisfaction surveys should be conducted to relate the satisfaction of external IT users to the service levels delivered to them.

A powerful business driver can be established if service levels can be related to customer satisfaction and if there is a relationship between customer satisfaction, customer loyalty, and buying behaviors. If these relationships can be demonstrated, the IT department is in a powerful position to show the true value of the services and service quality it provides.

Tip

One aspect of service level reporting that can dramatically improve customer perception and satisfaction is the proactive notification provided by real-time reporting and alerts as outlined in the next section.

Types of Reports

Several different report types are required to provide sufficient detail on all the aspects of service quality and to satisfy the interests and focus of the different audience types. The format and content of each report also varies with the frequency with which it is produced. Reporting frequency is discussed in the next section. This section outlines the components of a service level report; however, not all reports incorporate all components and not all audiences are interested in receiving all components.

Executive Summary

This report provides an overall assessment of achieved service levels including quantitative and qualitative reports against agreed service level objectives. It should provide quick summaries of the quality of the services delivered and, preferably, make effective use of graphs and charts to impart this information. Relating the service levels achieved with any business impact is an important aspect of the executive summary.

The executive summary should be self-contained, particularly for end-of-period reports aimed at senior management and lines of business. If service difficulties have been experienced, they should be highlighted with references to any supporting documentation or detailed reports.

Service Availability Reporting

Service availability should be shown mapped against objectives. This includes distinguishing between normal operating hours, off-hour shifts, and downtime as a result of scheduled maintenance. Availability should be shown by service or application rather than by components, and should represent the experience of users by organization, by location, and by line of business. Roll-up summaries showing percentage availability by service and by line of business will be useful when communicating with the lines of business and senior management.

The only audience who should be interested in the availability of individual components will be the IT department. These reports should be used to evaluate the reliability of technology components and the impact of technology problems on overall service quality. These technology-focused reports can be very useful when reviewing the performance of technology vendors and might also be useful for senior management when justifying the acquisition of additional IT resources.

Performance Reporting

Performance must relate directly to the end-user experience and should be broken out by online transaction responsiveness as well as batch job turnaround. To communicate effectively with lines of business and senior management, responsiveness should be shown by application, user group, location, and line of business.

Tip

It might be beneficial to group transactions based on their characteristics, as well as report responsiveness of those transaction types individually as well as the aggregate performance.

Characteristics that could be used include degree of difficulty, importance to the business, and value based on improved user productivity. This provides a more granular view and helps to associate business value with transaction responsiveness.

To give the IT department a better understanding of the impact of the various technology layers on overall responsiveness, response times and propagation delays by each technology layer (network, operating system, middleware, and database) should be calculated if possible and reported. These should then be graphed against overall end-user response times to show any correlation using time as the common variable. This enables IT management, capacity planners, and performance analysts to focus on the most critical performance issues.

Workload Volumes

The lines of business and senior management want to see workload volumes expressed in terms of business transaction rates. This provides a common basis for discussion of workload levels between the IT department and the lines of business.

Note

Business transaction volume supports a better understanding of the value of the services provided by IT, and provides a foundation for demonstrating the positive (or negative) impact of service levels on business productivity, revenue, and efficiency.

Workload reports external to the IT department should show business transaction volumes by user group, by location, and by line of business.

To increase understanding of workload characteristics within the IT department, business transactions should be correlated with transaction rates and utilization levels for each of the various technology layers. The most interesting measures are traffic volumes and utilization of the network, CPU utilization and transaction rates on the servers, I/O rates on the databases and storage subsystem, and transaction and message rates across the middleware environment. Understanding the relationship between these measures and the business transaction rates is extremely useful when predicting future performance under various business scenarios and supports more accurate business decision based on all costs including required IT resource capacity. Internal IT workload reports should show business transaction volumes as well as technology utilization levels and transaction rates.

Security Intrusion

An important aspect of service quality is maintaining the confidentiality, privacy, and integrity of business data. Thus, reports should be provided on security intrusion attempts, security violations, and compromised or damaged data. Additionally, reports on virus infections and their associated impacts are useful to understanding how viruses are spread and for making decisions on preventive measures. In all cases of data damage or security violations, the report should also include a summary of techniques used to detect the intrusion, the recovery procedures used to restore data integrity, and the processes and mechanisms used to prevent reoccurrence.

These reports should be used when reviewing security procedures with lines of business, and when discussing and recommending additional security measures.

Recoveries

All outages should have an additional report outlining recovery time, technique used to recover, and procedures implemented to prevent or reduce the impact of subsequent occurrences. This report is very useful to ensure that IT operations become more proactive and move away from continuously operating in a reactive mode. The preventive measures might require additional IT resources (human or equipment) and might involve implementing new procedures within the IT department or the lines of business.

Tip

Outlining the real costs, as well as the lost opportunity costs of the downtime caused by each outage together with the incremental expense of preventing future occurrences, allows an informed business decision to be taken.

Cost Allocation

If costs are allocated to the lines of business, either to allow them to be charged back or to provide a pseudo profit and loss statement, an appropriate report will be required. This report should outline the methodology used to calculate IT costs, total costs calculated by this method, the mechanism used to allocate costs to individual lines of business, and the calculated cost for each line of business.

Caution

Using a cost allocation model can lead to unpleasant discussions about the amount of costs involved, unless this report is also accompanied by the associated service level reports showing the value of the IT services in business terms.

Many corporations choose not to allocate IT costs, and treat the IT department as a general administration expense. This overlooks the value of IT as a competitive advantage for the business and overstates the profitability of individual lines of business. In this case, total IT costs are allocated to the lines of business using the formula for allocating general administration costs. This is a simple way of allocating IT costs, but doesn't necessarily provide a true representation of how IT resources are used in reality or the relative utilization and value of IT services to each line of business.

However the allocated costs are calculated, the IT department has to decide whether to produce a single report showing allocated costs for all lines of business, or to produce individual reports for each line of business showing only the costs associated with that organization. This decision depends on the culture of the organization and any associated internal political ramifications.

Report Card Summary

A number of organizations have designed reports that use a school report card format that provides summarized reports that are easily understood by all audiences, rather than highly technical complex reports. Whether using an alphabetic system or a numeric scale, multiple aspects of service are graded and reported. Determining what aspects of service to grade is typically done in conjunction with the user community. Additional underlying information is also provided so that more detail is available if a service level grade is unacceptable.

Figure 3.1 shows a sample service level weekly report card that shows attributes for two services supported by the IT department. In this case, there was a minor outage for the Financials application and a more significant outage for the Help Desk system.

Service Level Report - Week of July 5-7, 1999	
Service	**Oracle Financials**
Measure	*Grade*
Availability for Normal Operations	B+
Proactive Problem Notification	A
Outage Recovery Times	A
Responsiveness for Queries	A
Responsiveness for Update	B
Report Timeliness	A
Security of Data	A
Service	**Vantive Help Desk**
Measure	*Grade*
Availability for Normal Operations	C
Proactive Problem Notification	A
Outage Recovery Times	B
Responsiveness for Queries	A
Responsiveness for Update	B
Report Timeliness	A
Security of Data	A

Figure 3.1   *A sample service level weekly report in report card format.*

Frequency of Reporting

Reports are produced with varying frequencies, depending on the audience and level of detail. The more frequently produced reports contain a very detailed analysis, whereas the summary reports are produced less frequently, are aimed at a higher-level audience, and relate more to the business aspects of service delivery and the resulting business impact of service level quality.

Daily Reports

Reports produced daily are detailed and show the quality of service provided by the IT department during the previous day. All reports and quality grades of the various aspects of service should be provided segmented by application, user group, location, and line of business. The report should also show how the service quality varied by time of day for each of these segments.

Tip

Daily reports are very detailed and are useful for identifying any patterns or trends in workload volumes or service quality that require analysis or improvement.

Detailed, daily reports are primarily for consumption within the IT department and, thus, can be more technology focused. However, the relationship between technology performance and the service quality experienced by end-users should be clearly established.

Figure 3.2 shows a sample daily report for a help desk application. This report clearly shows that the response time experienced by the users in Paris was problematic.

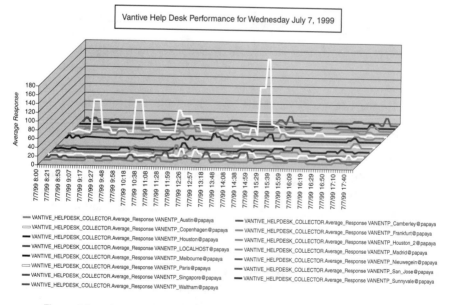

Figure 3.2 *A sample daily service level report showing response times by location for a help desk application service.*

Weekly Summaries

Weekly summaries provide similar information to the daily reports, but are summarized relative to time. The service quality can be summarized by shift or half-shift for each day of the week rather than on an hourly basis. If additional detail is required to explain a pattern or trend, the drill-down detail from a particular day's report should be provided.

The weekly reports should start with a business focus of availability, performance, and workload volumes, provide technology focused reports of these same measures, and highlight any correlation to show the impact of technology issues on overall service delivery. Additional aspects to be covered in the report should be a summary of security violations and attempted intrusion, as well as detailed analysis of outages and recoveries.

Although the primary audience is the IT department, lines of business might also want to review the weekly reports, particularly if the service quality was perceived to be abnormal.

Monthly Overviews

The monthly overview is primarily a reporting mechanism for the lines of business and senior management. It should communicate the quality of services delivered by the IT department succinctly and should relate the quality of IT services to business value.

Tip
The report card format, combined with graphical explanation, enables clear understanding and quick interpretation.

All aspects of service quality should be covered, but allocated costs are not typically shown in monthly reports unless accounting and budget procedures called for monthly reports.

Additional reports internal to the IT department should relate the availability and performance of the various technology layers to the business view of service. This allows the correlation between technology problems and associated business impact to be clearly established so that resources can be focused on the most important issues.

Quarterly Business Summaries

The quarterly summary report showing overall service levels, associated business and productivity leverage, as well as outages and associated costs and lost opportunity costs, can be very useful for a quarterly line of business review conducted by the IT department.

Tip

The quarterly summary report, combined with a line of business customer satisfaction survey, is an excellent vehicle for continuing the communications between IT and its internal and external customers.

These business reports can also be useful for understanding future plans and IT requirements for each business unit and for renegotiating service level agreements as necessary. The quarterly summaries are also where costs would typically be allocated if a chargeback mechanism were implemented. In order to ensure no surprises for the lines of business, additional exception reports might be required more frequently if anticipated costs are exceeded.

Real–Time Reporting

Real-time reporting adds significant value to the users of IT services as an addition to historical service level reporting. Real-time reports increase the satisfaction of the IT user community and also reduce the workload of help desk personnel and overhead on problem reporting systems. Proactive notification of known problems also increases the end-users' willingness to work more flexibly with the IT department to reduce the business impact of outages and service degradation. For example, work shifts might be rescheduled or back-up systems put in operation.

Outage Alerts

Tip

Providing a proactive mechanism that lets users know of problems identified by the IT department significantly increases confidence of the user community in the IT department.

When communicating outage information, it is important to show which users are affected, together with impacted applications, locations, and lines of business. Other important information includes the nature of the problem and its symptoms, as well as the anticipated service resumption time.

This requires a reporting facility using Web or push technology. It significantly reduces the number of calls to the help desk and allows IT personnel to focus their resources and energy on fixing the problem, rather than on responding to user queries.

Planned Downtime

Scheduled maintenance is nearly always disruptive to business operations. This is exaggerated by e-commerce, e-business, and other internal online initiatives that enable business personnel and customers to use IT services at any time of the day or night via Internet access, home PCs, and dial-up networks. When alerting users to planned downtime, information should be provided on the service, location, and user groups affected, as well as the reason for the downtime and any available alternative service offerings.

Tip

It might also improve user relations if the alert is published with sufficient notice to enable the user community to negotiate an alternative schedule for the downtime or to make other business arrangements.

Performance Degradation

Typically, users will experience performance degradation in the form of poor responsiveness before a problem is identified by the IT department, unless technology solutions are implemented to proactively measure the end-user experienced response times. In either case, as soon as the performance degradation is identified, an alert should be sent to all impacted users notifying them of the condition. In many cases, isolating the cause of the performance degradation is complex, and it might be difficult to determine the length of time this will take. However, making users aware of the problem and that the IT department is actively working to improve performance reduces the number of problem reports and calls to the help desk.

Heavy Security Attacks

If the IT department detects security intrusion attempts or a spreading virus, it needs to alert users immediately in order to reduce the potential damage caused by these attacks. The alert should contain the nature of the attack, the immediate steps being taken by IT to contain the attack, and the precautions that users should take to limit their vulnerability. In some cases, the IT department must take certain applications and services offline, and an estimate of the downtime should also be provided. Following the resolution of the security violation or virus, the IT department will need to notify users of how they can recover any lost or corrupted data and the steps to be taken to avoid any repeat occurrences of the attack.

Figure 3.3 demonstrates a sample online reporting system in which one service is currently in warning status and one service is currently in alert status. Drill-down details for each service are available as shown in Figure 3.4.

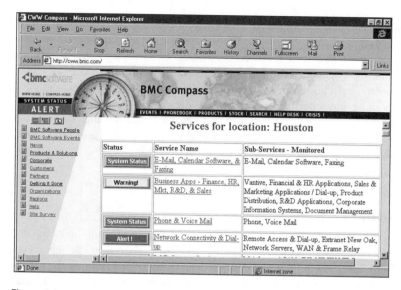

Figure 3.3 *A sample online alert system showing the service status for a specific location.*

Figure 3.4 shows that the first warning is due to a problem with the document management system. This additional information shows the locations affected by the problem together with the organizations, as well as the estimated time for service resumption.

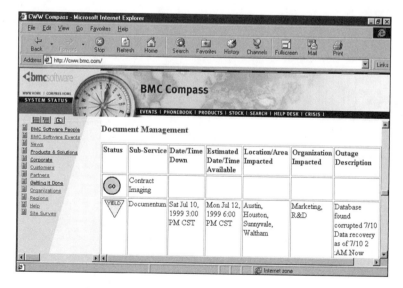

Figure 3.4 *The details of the service disruption alert.*

Service level reporting consists of a variety of report formats, each with different content and production frequency. Each of these reports has a different set of audiences, and the report format and content should be tailored to each specific audience. Effective reporting requires an understanding of the audiences, and service levels should be reported from the audience's perspective. Of particular importance is establishing and reporting the relationship between the delivered service levels and the business impact (both positive and negative). Additionally, real-time alerting and reporting mechanisms are very valuable to the service users, and can significantly enhance the reputation of the IT department as well as reduce the workload on the help desk staff and systems.

Summary

Reporting achieved service levels is an important aspect of communicating between the IT department and the lines of business it services. The reports will vary by audience, frequency, and content detail; however, in all cases, the reports should discuss the quality of services provided in terms the audience understands. If possible, establishing a direct link between service quality and business impact adds credibility to the reports. Additionally, the use of online alerts and proactive notification of service degradation allows the IT department to show greater responsiveness to the IT user community. This improves user relationships while reducing the number of calls to help desk personnel.

CHAPTER 4

Service Level Agreements

Service Level Agreements (SLAs) are central to managing the quality of service delivered by, or received by, an IT organization. More than anything else, SLAs are what people think of when they discuss service level management. Obviously, as discussed in Chapter 3, "Service Level Reporting," Service Level Reports are a key component of service level management. However, without service level agreements, efforts to manage service levels are little more than a collection of good intentions.

The Need for SLAs

Why are Service Level Agreements so important to service level management? The answer is that SLAs set the standard to measure against. It is analogous to having a cooking thermometer that is not calibrated. (There are no gradations on it.) Without calibration, you do not know the range of the thermometer. Therefore, you can use it, but it provides little value. If you stick the thermometer into a turkey and then take it out, it shows that your prospective dinner is hot enough to register halfway up the thermometer. What does this tell you? Is the turkey nearly done, barely thawed, or so overcooked that it soon can be converted to jerky? From the data provided by the uncalibrated thermometer, you simply cannot judge. If you have used this thermometer enough times prior to this, you might be able to interpret its display. However, such interpretation requires considerable experience and is highly subjective.

Take the analogy of a cooking thermometer a bit further. Assume that you are going to cook some steaks for a group of friends. Now these are not just ordinary steaks. They are ostrich steaks. They are quite expensive, and you have never cooked them before. To make matters worse, your friends are quite particular about how their steaks are to be served. Each of your friends tells you how he or she would like their steak prepared. Two of them request rare. One requests medium and one requests medium rare, "but not too rare."

In far too many cases, IT managers are working with uncalibrated thermometers. That is, they are working with data that is difficult to relate to the service levels expected or provided. For example, detailed collections of data (such as packet collisions) might be very useful to network administrators and, indeed, might be related to the level of service being provided. However, that relationship is not immediately apparent.

Because you have never cooked ostrich before, you do not feel that you will be able to visually judge when the steaks are properly cooked. Fortunately, you have a cookbook that tells you the temperature to which an ostrich steak must be cooked for various degrees of completion. Although you have upgraded your thermometer and now have one that has degrees marked on it, you still have a problem. You do not know if the cookbook's standard for medium rare matches your friends' expectations. What should you do? You could proceed to cook the steaks using the standard specified in the cookbook and hope that your friends approve of your decision. You decide that would be too risky. You could tell your friends to cook their steaks themselves, thereby absolving yourself of responsibility. However, you want to impress your friends with your great culinary skills, and telling them to cook their own steaks could hardly be expected to impress them as you are hoping to do. As you ponder your dilemma, you notice that your cookbook contains a short description for each of the labels provided (rare, medium, and so on). You hit upon an idea; you read the descriptions to your friends. A discussion follows in which you learn that your friend who wanted her steak cooked medium rare, but not too rare, in reality would like her steak cooked to what your cookbook describes as medium-well done. The others agree with the cookbook's descriptions. Using your new thermometer, you cook the steaks to perfection and your friends hail you as a great chef.

By now you might be asking, "What do ostrich steaks have to do with Service Level Agreements?". The answer is that the cooking analogy actually represents a very simplistic example of a Service Level Agreement. You and your friends agreed on what would be an acceptable way of cooking their steaks. In essence, you negotiated an agreement about the service (cooking) that you were about to provide and what would be an acceptable level of service (how well done the steaks would be). In doing this, you have settled on a mutual understanding and set a target level for performance.

Functions of SLAs

Like defining how well steaks will be cooked, some basic benefits result from creating a Service Level Agreement. First, an SLA defines what levels of service are considered acceptable by users and are attainable by the service provider. This is particularly beneficial to the service provider. It guards against expectation creep. There is a basic characteristic in human nature to always want more and better—regardless of the subject. If you receive a huge raise, it is likely that, even if the cost of living does not change, you will be hoping for (or even demanding) another raise a year later.

In the case of IT services, if the availability of a key application is increased dramatically—higher than ever requested before—clients will soon become used to that level of availability and begin to demand an even higher level of availability, and they will vilify IT if it is not provided. If the expectations are documented in an SLA, they become a reference point—an anchor—for client expectations. In other words, the SLA provides permanence for the agreements arrived at and documented in it. More specifically, a well-written Service Level Agreement will define not only the expectations (how good is good enough), but it will also define a mutually acceptable and agreed upon set of indicators of the quality of service.

Principles of Expectation Creep

As expectations are met, expectations will rise. People are never satisfied.

People become upset when their expectations are violated.

In the absence of contradictory facts, expectations will be based on what is desirable, rather than what is possible.

Service providers and their clients are like beings from different planets when talking about service levels. They tend to speak very different languages. The result is that it is often quite difficult for them to understand each other. Ultimately, an SLA, through those service level indicators, will provide a common language for communication between the two diverse communities. Documenting the mutual understanding arrived at through the process of negotiating a Service Level Agreement provides clarity.

Note

There are six primary benefits that can be expected from Service Level Agreements. Those benefits are

Provides permanence

Provides clarity

Serves as communications vehicle

Guards against expectation creep

Sets mutual standards for service

Defines how level of service will be measured

Types of SLAs

Broadly, there are three types of SLAs. The one that is most common is an In-House SLA. An In-House SLA is one between a service provider and an in-house client. An example of an In-House SLA would be the agreement between IT and a user department. The second most common SLA is an External SLA. That is, an SLA between a service provider and its client (another company). The third type of SLA is an Internal SLA. The Internal SLA is used by the service provider to measure the performance of groups within the service provider's organization. An example of the Internal SLA would be between the network services group in an IT organization and the overall organization, or perhaps the CIO. The Internal SLA is typically tied to annual reviews of managers and provides a mechanism for holding individuals and groups accountable for their portion of an overall service.

The process for creating an SLA is fundamentally the same for each type of agreement. Likewise, the contents that are found in each different type of agreement are basically the same. The differences come largely in the formality that is attached to the process of creating the agreement, the language that is used, and the consequences that will result if the service level commitments are not met.

In-House SLAs

When the service provider and client work for the same company, familiarity should not be allowed to preclude establishing a detailed, legally binding contract. If the SLA is constructed in a considered, serious way, the results can benefit both parties as well as the company itself. Most large banks and financial institutions, for instance, ensure 100% uptime to external customers by establishing firm in-house SLAs between IT and the various divisions of the organization. The cumulative result of strictly adhering to these agreements is an overall level of reliability that can be used as a selling point to bank customers.

External SLAs

The most rigorous type of agreement is the External SLA. Because it is usually a legally binding contract between two companies, it requires more care in crafting it. Legal review of the External agreement is strongly advised. However, many companies overlook this step and, as a result, end up with an agreement that is of little value. Of course, another error, at least as serious, is to fail to have SLAs with external service providers. The lack of SLAs has proven disastrous for many companies.

Caution

Have External SLAs reviewed by an attorney before signing.

Failing to have an SLA with an external service provider is unconscionable, and yet countless companies do exactly that every year. The problem is not limited to small companies. Some of the world's largest companies have made this mistake. The managers responsible for these contracts are guilty of gross negligence and perhaps a breech of their fiduciary responsibility to their employers. After a contract for service without a service level guarantee has been signed, the client's options are quite limited. To begin, they must hope that the services provided meet their needs. If the services provided do not meet their requirements, for any reason, depending on the specific terms of their contract, they might be faced with tough choices, including enduring, for the remainder of the contract, a level of service that is less than acceptable; terminating the contract prematurely, potentially incurring large penalties for doing so; or attempting to renegotiate the contract. (Of course, the service provider probably has little or no incentive to renegotiate the contract.) Renegotiating the contract might result in higher fees in order to receive the desired level of service. The specific options available will depend on the terms of the contract with the service provider. Any company finding itself in the unenviable position of receiving an unacceptable level of service and no contractual guarantees of the level of service to be provided should seek legal counsel to assist in assessing the available options.

Tip

Always include a Service Level Agreement as part of any service contract with another company.

Internal SLAs

The Internal SLA is a relatively simple matter. It typically is written in an informal manner. In fact, the Internal SLA might not exist as a separate agreement. Instead, its commitments and intent might be embodied in other documents, such as individual or departmental goals and objectives, or even in the criteria for the company's bonus plan. Frequently, the Internal SLA will specify service levels in very technical terms. The use of technical terminology, and even jargon, can be acceptable in this document because all the parties are familiar with the terms and understand them.

SLA Processes

Service level management is a process. While the SLA itself is a document, it is the product of process. Processes are required to create, maintain, and administer the Service Level Agreement.

Creation Process

The process of creating an SLA typically follows a series of predictable steps, which are summarized in the following section. Although this guide is applicable to most SLAs, keep in mind that every situation is different. In many instances, SLAs will need to be tweaked to accommodate special functions and measurements. It is crucial for IT managers to follow their instincts in tailoring each SLA to fit the requirements of particular constituents.

SLA creation begins with a serious commitment to negotiate an agreement. It would be easy to say the groups involved must make that commitment. However, in reality, commitments are not made by groups, but by individuals. In this case, the commitment needs to begin with senior management of the groups involved— that is, the management of the service provider organization and the user or client organization. Ideally, the commitment is made at the very highest levels in the respective organizations.

Assemble a Team

When there is executive commitment to creating an SLA, the next step is to assemble a team of people to actually negotiate the terms of the agreement. It is important that the members of the team be personally committed to the success of the process—that is, committed to creating a fair and reasonable Service Level Agreement.

In order to assemble a team to negotiate an agreement, it is necessary to determine the team size and membership. As with most questions in life, there is not a single, one-size-fits-all answer to this question. In part, the size of the team will be dictated by the culture of the company. However, some guidelines can be offered. The team needs to be large enough that each stakeholder group be represented on the team. (A stakeholder group is any organization that is either engaged in providing the service or is a user of the service.) In most cases, the agreement will have only two stakeholders, the service provider and the user. Although it is possible for the team to consist of just two individuals, that is not very common. The typical size of an SLA negotiating team in a medium to large company is 4–10 people. Every effort should be made to minimize the size of the team, although the realities of corporate politics might dictate otherwise.

Ideally, every team member should have something unique to contribute to the process, such as knowledge about how the service impacts the users, the limitations of the technology being used to deliver the service, and so on. The members need to be, in some respect, subject-matter experts on some aspect of the service delivery or consumption.

Note

In assembling a team to negotiate a service level agreement, there are four points to keep in mind. First, there should be equal representation from the service provider and their client. Second, the leaders of the team should be peers. Third, the members of the team should be stakeholders. That is, they should have a vested interest in the service being provided. Fourth, the team members need to be subject matter experts; for example, knowledgeable about the service and its business impacts.

There should be equal representation on the team from both the user group and the service provider. Too great a disparity in numbers will give an unfair psychological advantage to the larger team.

At a minimum, the leaders from each group need to be peers. It is difficult for effective negotiations to take place if there is a significant disparity in rank among team members. Some companies are more sensitive to this than others. If peer relationships are not considered, this can lead to one group being apt to dictate (possibly unintentionally) the terms of the SLA, rather than negotiating them through a process of exchange between peers. Another requirement for the team leaders is that they have sufficient authority to commit their organization to the SLA.

The negotiating team should have a charter, written by the leaders, that specifies its responsibilities, membership, leadership, structure, and functioning. In terms of functioning, the charter needs to include a schedule for the development of the SLA. It is advisable to make the schedule aggressive. A pitfall of some teams, especially large ones, is that some members almost make a career of the negotiation process. In most cases, depending on availability of the team members, it should be possible to negotiate an agreement in 6–8 weeks.

Tip

Negotiating team meetings should be brief and infrequent. Most of the work will be done outside the meetings.

Negotiate the SLA

Successfully negotiating an SLA (particularly Internal or In-House SLAs) requires that both parties approach the process seeking a Win-Win solution. That is, they should seek to craft a Service Level Agreement that is fair and reasonable to both parties. The result of the negotiation will be a contract. In the case of the In-House and Internal agreements, the contract might not be a legally binding agreement; however, the structure will be the same.

Negotiating an SLA is a process in which information is exchanged in order to seek a reasonable conclusion. The user group needs to be able to communicate their requirements clearly. They also need to be able to explain the business impact of various levels of service.

Similarly, IT (or another type of service provider) needs to be able to assess the potential impacts of delivering proposed levels of services. Those impacts might be financial (additions or upgrades in staff, computers, networks, and so on). Another possible impact of delivering a higher level of service to one group might be that IT would have to reduce the level of service provided to another group. There might be technical limitations on IT's ability to provide the level of service.

Tip

Do your homework before negotiating. You should know the following:

- Cost of delivering a given level of service

- Benefits of the desired level of service

- Service level metrics that are available

Before negotiations begin, it is important that benchmark data be collected. Ideally, both groups will be able to collect data. However, in most cases the service provider will have access to more data. The objective is to know as precisely as possible the level of service currently being provided. It is also important to know what metrics are available regarding the level of service being provided. It might be great to agree to provide an average end-to-end response time of 0.5 seconds. However, if it is not possible to measure end-to-end response time, the effort spent negotiating that item in the SLA has been wasted.

Document The Agreement

As noted previously, the SLA is a contract. When the negotiations have been completed, the next step is to document what was agreed upon. The basic components of a Service Level Agreement are as follows:

Parties to the agreement	Exclusions
Term	Reporting
Scope	Administration
Limitations	Reviews
Service level objectives	Revisions
Service level indicators	Approvals
Non-performance	
Optional services	

Parties to the Agreement

This will normally be the two groups that negotiated the agreement; that is, the service provider and the user group that is the consumer of the service.

Term

Typically, the term of the SLA will be two years. Creating an SLA is too much work to warrant an agreement term of much less than two years. Alternatively, technology and business conditions change too rapidly to be able to confidently expect the agreement to be valid beyond two years.

Scope

This section will define the services covered by the agreement. For example, an agreement might specify that it covers an online order entry system, the facilities where the users will be located, volumes of transactions anticipated, when the service will be available (days of the week and hours of the day). Note that this section does not specify the levels of services to be provided. In the preceding example, nothing is mentioned about the percent availability for the service.

Limitations

This section of the agreement can be thought of as the service provider's Caveat clause. This section basically qualifies the services defined in the Scope section of the agreement. The service provider is saying, "We will provide the services covered by this agreement as long as you don't exceed any of the limitations." Typical limitations are volume (for example, transactions per minute or per hour, number of concurrent users, and so on), topology (location of facilities to which the service is delivered, distribution of users, and so on), and adequate funding for the service provider. These types of limitations are quite reasonable.

In order to enter into the Service Level Agreement, the service provider has to believe that they have adequate resources to meet the commitments of the agreement. Making this commitment without these limitations would be like someone agreeing to feed you and all the members of your household for a lump sum payment of $10,000. This might be a good deal for either party of this agreement. If your immediate family consists of just yourself and your very petite wife, the person agreeing to provide the food has struck a great bargain. However, one month into the term of your agreement, your five children (two of whom are training to become sumo wrestlers) move back into your house. Also, you decide to host a foreign exchange student. The student happens to be 300-pound weight lifter. Suddenly the balance of the equation has shifted. Without limitations in the agreement to provide food for your current household, the other party to the agreement will start losing money after the second month of feeding your enlarged household. In business, equally dramatic changes can occur. Mergers and acquisitions can bring sudden increases in workload, as well as shifts in traffic network patterns. Closing or opening facilities will shift workloads and might require new links for your network. Consolidation of functions into fewer locations might change traffic patterns. Growth of the business is also a source of additional data to be handled.

Service Level Objectives

More than any other factor, the service level objectives are what most people think of when they refer to SLAs. The service level objectives are the agreed upon levels of service that are to be provided. These might include such things as response time, availability, and so on. For each aspect of the service covered by the agreement, there should be a target level defined. In fact, in some cases it can be desirable to define two levels for each factor. The first will be the minimum level of service that will be considered acceptable. The second will be a *stretch objective*. That is, the second number will reflect a higher level of service that is desirable, but not guaranteed. Clearly, the second category is optional, and if it is utilized in an SLA, it will normally have some type of incentive or reward associated with meeting it.

The most popular categories of Service Level Objectives are availability, performance, and accuracy. Availability can be specified in terms of the days and hours that the service will be available or as a percentage of that time. It is generally best to specify the time period when the service is expected to be available and then define the minimum acceptable percentage of availability. Performance can include measurements of speed and/or volume. Volume (also referred to as throughput or workload) might be expressed in terms of transactions/hour, transactions/day, or gigabits of files transferred from one location to another. Speed includes the always-popular response time objective. However, speed is not limited to just response time. It could also include time required to transfer data, retrieve archived files, and so on. The objective for accuracy is basically centered on the question of whether the service is doing what it is supposed to do. For example, are email messages delivered to the intended recipient? Although availability, performance, and accuracy are the most popular categories for objectives, they are by no means the only objectives. Other categories include cost and security.

In any discussion of service level objectives, a question always raised is, "What is the right number of objectives?". Although there is not a specific number that is always the correct number to use, this is a case in which the principle of brevity has merit. Including more objectives does not automatically raise the quality of the SLA. In general terms, 5–10 service level objectives are usually sufficient. This number of objectives is usually sufficient to cover the most important aspects of the service. Including more objectives usually means that less important objectives are being introduced and drawing attention away from the more important ones. If there appears to be a large number of critical service level objectives that need to be included in the agreement, the SLA team should carefully consider the possibility that they are attempting to cover more than one service with the agreement. If that is the case, they should redefine their effort and write separate SLAs for each service.

Tip

Limit the number of service level objectives to 5–10 critical objectives.

Service level objectives cannot be any randomly chosen set of characteristics. These must be able to meet certain criteria in order to qualify for inclusion in a service level agreement. First, a service level objective must be attainable. There are far too many cases in which, for a variety of reasons (none of which are valid), a service level objective is included in an SLA even though it cannot be met.

Consider the example of choosing user response time as one of the service level objectives to be included in an agreement. Assume that for this example it is possible to measure the response time. The parties agree upon an acceptable target for average response time. However, there is a problem. The site covered by this agreement is in a remote area of Indonesia. The server being accessed is located in Terre Haute, Indiana. The connection consists of a T1 link to an earth station, followed by two satellite links to reach an earth station in Jakarta, Indonesia. From the Indonesian earth station, there are a series of microwave links to the user location. In total, the propagation delay alone for this connection is greater than the total response time allowed in the Service Level Agreement. The result is that no matter how hard the IT organization tries, they will never be able to meet the response time commitment in this Service Level Agreement. The example in Figure 4.1 illustrates this connection.

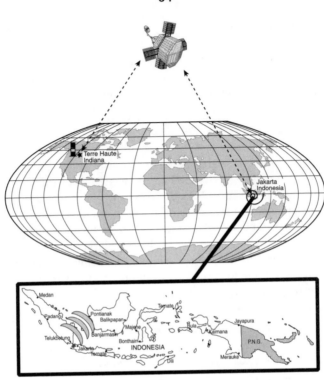

Figure 4.1   *Propagation delay makes service level objectives unattainable.*

You might wonder why an IT organization would ever commit to a service level objective that it cannot meet. There are a variety of reasons for this. The IT representatives on the SLA team might have been poor negotiators. The user team might not have negotiated in good faith, approaching the process from a win-lose perspective. The negotiators might not have been peers with the more senior representatives on the user team. Another possibility is that the IT representatives failed to do their homework. Even if the team members, individually, lacked specific knowledge about the connection in question, they certainly should have been able to research it and make an informed response to the request for this level of service for user response time.

Note

In order for service level agreements to be successful, the criteria that they use to measure the level of service must be

Attainable	Meaningful
Measurable	Controllable
Understandable	Affordable
Mutually acceptable	

A service level objective must be meaningful to all the parties to the agreement. Another way of stating this is to say that it must be relevant. An IT organization might consider an important metric to be CPU utilization for the servers used to deliver the service in question. However, from the users' perspective, the relevance of this to the service they receive is difficult to grasp.

Another requirement for a service level objective is closely related to the need to be meaningful. That is, the service level objective and its associated metrics must be understandable. Interviews of IT managers by Enterprise Management Associates has found that some of them are providing the users with statistics that are intended to reflect service levels. Unfortunately, those statistics tend to be ones that are easily captured, and mean little to anyone other than a network engineer or system administrator. Two of the more popular statistics reported were packet collisions and dropped packets. Although these might impact the level of service being delivered, they are not readily related to what the user is experiencing. In fact, these statistics meant little or nothing to nearly all the users receiving the reports. Thus, those statistics failed the tests for being understandable and for being meaningful.

The next requirement for a service level objective is that it must be measurable. Among users, a very popular service level objective is user (that is, end-to-end) response time. Certainly, this is one of the key factors shaping the users' opinions about the level of service they are receiving. Unfortunately, measuring user response time on an end-to-end basis is still a technical challenge today. At the other end of the feasibility spectrum is the availability of a service. This is relatively straightforward and can be measured with a minimum of effort and difficulty. If it is not possible (and affordable) to measure something to represent a service level objective, that objective is worthless and should not be included in an agreement.

A service level objective belongs in an SLA only if it represents something that is controllable. That is, the service provider must have the ability to exercise control over the factors that determine the level of service delivered. If unlimited resources are available, it is difficult to conceive of a common IT-provided service that is not controllable. However, faced with the limitations of the real world, such conditions become much more plausible. Consider the IT manager in a Third World country. The manager's budget does not permit the purchase of a standby generator to prevent service interruptions during the frequent power failures. Strikes by union workers, poor service by a telco (with no reasonable alternative), and so on are just a few of the factors that can place certain service level objectives beyond the control of the service provider. When assessing whether an objective is controllable, consider providing exclusions (or waivers) for factors that are not controllable and that might impact the level of service provided.

As has been previously mentioned, no organization has unlimited resources. The amount that can be spent on delivering any service is limited. Therefore, in setting service level objectives, it is also necessary to consider whether the desired level of service is affordable. (This might also be thought of as being cost effective.) The first way to look at this is by considering whether the desired level can be delivered within the existing budget of the service provider, without adversely impacting any other services. If it can, there is no question that it is affordable. If it cannot, the question becomes more difficult to answer. It is necessary to consider the business value of the desired level of service compared with the current level. In one case, the client of an IT organization was adamant that for the service in question (order entry system), they absolutely had to have 99.999999% availability. The current availability for that system was 99.999%. Instead of digging in their heels and insisting that the higher availability was impossible, the IT organization did their homework. They researched what changes would be required in order to deliver the requested availability and the cost of those changes. They returned to the user organization and explained that they would be happy to provide the desired level of service if (as was the company policy) the user organization would provide the necessary funds. It was explained that the cost of the necessary changes would be $87 million initially and $8–$10 million per year thereafter. Suddenly the user organization decided that a more modest increase would be acceptable (99.9999%). Another aspect of affordability pertains to the cost of collecting the data for service level reporting. Like so many things, this often becomes a tradeoff between precision and cost.

Finally, the service level objectives that are included in an SLA must be mutually acceptable to all the parties to the agreement. It is not possible for a viable, effective agreement to be arrived at if one of the parties to the agreement simply dictates the terms of the agreement. Creating an SLA is a process of negotiation to arrive at a result that both parties consider acceptable and that they both feel they can live with for the term of the agreement.

Service Level Indicators

As noted previously in this chapter, every service level objective must be measurable. More precisely, something must be able to be measured that is indicative of that service level objective. In a sense, a service is an elusive, intangible thing that cannot be directly measured. Instead, it is necessary to measure something that both parties agree reasonably represents the service level objective.

Consider the service level objective of the availability of a system (such as an order entry system). This might seem very simple and straightforward. However, look at it more carefully. Some IT managers tend to look at the problem too simplistically and feel that it is sufficient to monitor the application software. They think that if the application is running, it is available. However, there could be a variety of problems that prevent the user from accessing and using the application. The problem could originate in the client or the server, each of which has a series of potential trouble spots. Or the problem could be in one of the many network connections linking the client to the server: A router could be down in the network, the communications server at the user site could be down, or the application could be running but not responding because it is waiting for some critical resource. Any of these examples would prevent the users from being able to access the application. From the user's perspective, however, the truth is that the application is unavailable.

Tip

Remember that the user's perspective is the one that counts.

Therefore, it can be seen that careful thought must go into defining what indicators will be used to provide metrics to represent each service objective. In some cases, the service level indicators will be the same as the objective they represent. In other cases, the indicators are an indirect representation of the service level objective.

Consider the case of the availability of an order entry system. Ideally, there will be a single indicator for the service's availability; that is, an indicator which reflects the overall availability of the service to the end user. Unfortunately, in the case of the order entry system, there is not a way to directly measure the availability of the service. However, it might be possible to develop an estimate of the service's availability. Perhaps a special application can be constructed that will reside at the users' location and periodically test the service's availability (perhaps by submitting an inquiry transaction). However, security and other concerns might preclude such an approach.

Continuing with our example, in the event that it is not possible to develop a single measurement that represents the overall availability of the service, it becomes necessary for the SLA to define what will provide an adequate approximation of the service's availability. One approach might be to track the availability of each of the components required for the delivery of the service (for example, application, server, network, application, and so on). Obviously, this is not a perfect solution, but it might be good enough. If more precision is necessary, it is possible to analyze and correlate the data to provide a better view of overall availability. However, greater precision will normally carry with it greater complexity, greater cost, and higher likelihood of error. Remember that perfection is unlikely and compromise is an inherent part of the SLA process.

Whatever is chosen, the SLA needs to document each of the service level indicators that will be used to represent each of the service level objectives. It will be necessary to specify the data source for each of the indicators.

Non-Performance

If the Limitations section of the agreement can be considered the service providers' Caveat section, the Non-Performance section can be considered the Consequences section. That is, this section spells out what will happen in the event that the service provider fails to meet the commitments that are spelled out in the SLA. Typically, if the service provider fails to meet their obligations, the agreement will detail the penalties that might be expected. The most obvious penalty is financial, particularly in the case of an external service provider. With external service providers, you should also include a clause that provides your company with the option of terminating the contract in the event of significant non-performance. Be careful in dealing with external service providers. Some of them will propose a remedy for non-performance that consists of credits to be applied toward future services. However, if they are providing an unacceptable level of service now, why would you want a discount on future services? That is somewhat like going to a restaurant for dinner and having a horrible meal with service to match the quality of the food. At the end of the evening, you complain to the manager. As consolation for the poor meal that you have just had, he offers you a gift certificate so that you can come back another time and have another meal at no cost. However, if the food was truly terrible and the waiter incompetent, would you really want to go back and have another meal that might potentially be equally bad? The same is true of services in the business world. Be sure that the compensation offered is really something that would have value to your company. The purpose of the penalties (other than termination) is not to compensate your company for the poor service. Rather, the purpose is to provide sufficient incentive for the service provider to provide the level of service for which you have contracted. This principle can be illustrated by one company's approach to software acquisitions. The company insists that any vendor contractually promise that if they do not respond to problems in their software on a timely basis, they will pay the company a small amount of money (a percentage of the annual maintenance contract). The maximum amount of money that could ever have to be paid, even in a worst-case scenario, is insignificant to both companies. Many vendors will do almost anything to keep from including such a clause in the contract. Dramatic discounts have resulted from vendors trying to avoid this service level commitment for their software support service. The reason that this particular clause is so objectionable is that it is outside of the vendor's normal processes. If a vendor actually fails to meet the nominal requirements of the contract, he will have to issue a check to the customer. Issuing a check to a customer is not something that a vendor normally does. Although they have processes for taking money from customers, they don't have processes for giving them money because of poor service. Therefore, to comply with this condition requires exception processing. It most likely would require an escalation of the problem within the vendor's organization to obtain the approvals necessary to issue the check to the customer. Although raising the visibility of a problem within their company might not be something that the sales organization or the support organization consider desirable, it is clearly in the customer's best interests. Another interesting aspect to the use of this contract clause is that it has almost never actually been applied. The reason that it has not been applied is twofold. First, and most importantly, the vendors will turn their organizations inside out to make sure that they don't have to make the penalty payment. Second, in all honesty, the terms that the customer specifies are so loose that almost any action on the vendor's part will satisfy the language of the contract. However, in their fear of incurring any penalty, the vendors seem not to recognize this and go far beyond what is required in the contract.

One last point about this example is warranted. The penalty is calculated as a percentage of the annual maintenance fee. The result is a potential penalty that is miniscule. Consider a software product that costs $30,000 and has an annual maintenance fee of $4,500. The contractual penalty for not responding to a complaint from the customer about a problem would be calculated based on the amount of time in excess of that allowed in the contract. Assume that the agreement specifies that the vendor will respond to a serious problem within one business day. If the vendor actually takes three business days to respond, the violation of the agreement would be two days. Even though the violation is in business days, the maintenance agreement is specified in calendar days, and therefore the penalty is calculated using business days. The 2-day violation is divided by 365 calendar days. This result (0.005479) is then multiplied times the annual maintenance fee. Therefore, in this case the penalty would be $24.67! A ridiculously small amount, yet sufficient to make very large companies jump through hoops to avoid it. A simpler alternative to determining the amount of the penalty is to simply specify a dollar amount for a period of time (minutes, hours, days, and so on) of violation of the agreement.

Although in the previous example a token penalty was sufficient, you cannot always rely on a token payment to produce the desired effect. The key to a penalty for non-performance being effective is that it must cause pain or discomfort within the service provider's organization. The objective is to maximize the discomfort so that in the future the service provider will choose to ensure the proper level of service is delivered, rather than to suffer the discomfort that will result from non-performance. The most obvious way to cause pain is through a large financial penalty. However, smart service providers won't agree to terms that can result in very large penalties. Also, although financial penalties are possible with internal service providers, they are more difficult to implement. Another drawback to the financial penalty is that a large penalty can cripple the service provider, making it even more difficult for them to meet their commitments. On the other hand, a small penalty applied to an unscrupulous service provider can become another incidental cost of doing business for them—less expensive than providing the level of service specified in the agreement.

Tip

Penalties for non-performance should be sufficiently large so that they will cause pain within the vendor organization. However, even small penalties can be constructed in such a way as to make them painful.

Creating effective penalties for non-performance calls for creativity. Some of the best penalties do not involve money. For example, an effective requirement might be specified that in a case of non-performance, the head of the service provider's organization must meet with the head of the client organization and provide an explanation. It might be even more effective if it was stipulated that the meeting had to be in person, at the client's office, and within 48 hours of the determination of the non-performance condition. You will be most successful in creating effective penalties if you know as much as possible about the service provider. This way, you can better understand which penalties will have the maximum effect within their organization. The bottom line is that you must be creative to be effective in defining penalties for non-performance. Also, never accept a service provider's claim that they never agree to penalty clauses. First, they probably already have done so with other clients. Second, they will do so if they want your business, particularly if you are creative in defining the penalties.

Tip

Do not accept a service provider's claim that they never agree to penalties for non-performance. This is almost certainly untrue and even if true can be circumvented through persistence and creativity.

It is very important that both parties have a clear understanding of what constitutes non-performance. Consider the example of an agreement that specifies a response time of 2.2 seconds for the order entry application. Is that requirement an absolute threshold that must never be crossed? Or is the response time specification actually referring to an average? Alternatively, there might be some allowance for the threshold to be exceeded under certain circumstances (refer to the section "Limitations") or for a maximum number of transactions in a given time period or for a maximum allowable period in the busiest part of the day. What is most important here is that both of the parties have a clear understanding of what constitutes a violation of the agreement and therefore warrants some consequential action.

Caution

Beware of non-performance remedies that provide the compensation in the form of future services. Bad service is never a bargain.

In constructing the non-performance section of the agreement, creativity and flexibility are important. These are particularly important when dealing with internal service providers. It does not make sense to negotiate a penalty for non-performance that consists of reducing IT's budget. That would effectively reduce their ability to meet the users' requirements. Instead, non-financial penalties should be considered (for example, reductions in individual bonuses, and so on). Also, as an alternative to penalties, internal service providers can be motivated by rewarding them for meeting or exceeding the service level commitments in the SLA.

Optional Services

There might be additional service components that are not normally provided, or that are not provided at this time. However, if there is reason to anticipate that the user might want some of these options within the term of the SLA, it is wise to include a provision for that in this agreement. For example, a company might not currently be open for business on Sunday, allowing IT to perform batch processing and system administration work during the day. However, if it is anticipated that Sunday work will be required during the Christmas holiday season—hence, requiring the availability of the online systems—the possibility should be included in this section of the agreement.

Exclusions

In addition to spelling out the services that are covered by the agreement, the SLA should also specify what is not included in the agreement. Some common sense is warranted here. Obviously, if the agreement covers the online order entry system, it is not necessary to specify that the agreement does not include the payroll system. Instead, the exclusions that are specified in the SLA are those categories that might reasonably be assumed to be covered. For example, it might be appropriate to specify that the service encompassed by the order entry system's SLA does not cover the entry of orders by customers via the company's Web site. Clearly the e-commerce activity, although important to the company and a means by which orders can be received, is not part of the current order entry system. The e-commerce component is too distinct to be covered by the SLA for the online order entry system. It has different users, employs different software, is accessed differently, and so on. What might be appropriate to consider for inclusion in the agreement would be the interface through which e-commerce orders are received by the order entry system.

Reporting

The reports generated for the Service Level Agreement are key components of the SLA process. Without reports, the agreement is left merely as a statement of good intentions. The lack of reports would mean that it would never be possible to contrast actual performance against the stated objectives contained in the agreement.

The reports must be relevant to the service level objectives and reflect the service level indicators. Like the service level objectives, users must readily understand them—even the ones who have no understanding of the underlying technical issues. In many cases, graphs are the best way to represent the information about the service level performance. However, remember that some users will want to look at the data more closely. Therefore, it is advisable to have the supporting data available in tabular form for those who want to review it. Another recommendation is to keep the reports simple and focused. Although it might be easy to distribute copies of a report already being produced that includes the required information (plus a lot of other information), it is unwise to use this report. Instead, it is better to distribute reports that contain only the specific information required by the SLA. Additional information can be confusing or lead to misunderstandings. Reports might contain information about multiple service level indicators, but should not contain extraneous data.

Tip

Remember that graphs can convey more information and be more readily understood than tables. Therefore, whenever possible, use graphs to display information about actual service level performance.

The SLA should contain a list of each of the reports that will need to be produced in support of the agreement. For each report, the SLA should specify the name of the report and when it will be produced (frequency). It should also indicate which service level indicator(s) are reflected in this report. There should be a brief description of the content of the report and possibly even an example of the report itself. A description of the source of the data for the report should be included in this section of the agreement. Although this might seem tedious, it does prevent misunderstandings later. Also, it can serve as a limited guard against unethical manipulation of the reports during the term of the agreement. For each report specify the following:

- Report name
- Frequency
- Service level indicator(s)
- Content
- Data sources
- Responsibility
- Distribution

Who Can You Trust?

A certain degree of caution is appropriate with the SLA reports, particularly if the employees producing the reports stand to gain personally from the results reflected in the reports. A large company learned this lesson painfully. The company had an internally developed trouble ticketing system. The system was not terribly sophisticated, but it was adequate for the needs of that company. One day, an executive got the bright idea that he could motivate the IT department employees to provide better service (higher availability) by linking their quarterly bonuses to the level of service that was being delivered to their clients. On the face of it, this seemed like a reasonable idea. The question then became how to measure the service being delivered. Someone hit upon the idea of using the trouble ticketing system. This seemed reasonable because it did track every outage and, by implication, could then be used to calculate the remaining availability.

Data from the trouble ticketing system was analyzed and it was agreed that this could be used to provide a reasonably accurate indication of service availability. The decision was made to implement the plan.

It should be noted that the trouble ticketing system was not perfect. Its greatest weakness was the fact that it relied on individual IT employees (Help Desk) to manually enter information about service interruptions. The employees were quite good about opening trouble tickets when a problem occurred. However, when they were very busy, or if multiple people were involved in resolving the problem, sometimes a trouble ticket might not be closed at the time that the problem was resolved. This could result in some trouble tickets being open for several days, or even longer. This problem had been discovered a couple of years earlier and the program was modified to allow anomalies like this to be corrected. At the end of each month, any apparent problems of this type were researched and new information was entered to reflect the correct duration of the problem. This facility became the source of a problem of a very different type.

The employees responsible for researching outages and, if appropriate, entering the correct information were part of the same group whose bonuses were tied to service availability. It did not take long for these individuals to figure out the facility used to correct errors in outage durations could also be used to ensure that their group always met or exceeded the objectives that had been established for service availability. Within a couple of months of implementing the idea to link bonuses to service availability, availability had soared. The executive who had conceived the plan was congratulating himself and his team.

Executives from the user departments grumbled that they had not seen any improvement in service. However, this was initially dismissed with the thought that the users would never be satisfied no matter how much service improved. After about eight months and continued complaints from the user departments, supported by their own documentation of problems, the IT department decided to investigate the situation. The investigation did reveal that the employees had been falsifying the records in order to meet availability objectives and thereby maximizing their personal bonuses. As a consequence, the link of availability to bonuses was discontinued and accurate reporting returned. Amazingly, no one was ever disciplined for this scam.

The SLA needs to specify who will be responsible for producing the reports. The responsibility should be specified by position or group rather than by individual. It is also necessary to include specifications about the distribution of each report. As illustrated in the sidebar, care must be taken not to create a situation in which a conflict of interest might arise and lead to the reports being compromised. At a minimum, it should list the groups, or positions, that are to receive the reports. However, it is also desirable to specify whether the report will be produced in hard copy or electronic form. If electronic copies are chosen, the SLA should specify how the report would be distributed (email, Web, and so on).

Administration

This section of an SLA describes the ongoing administration of the SLA and the processes that it specifies. In this section, there needs to be a description of the ongoing processes and a definition of where in the organization responsibility for each process lies.

Reviews

Periodically, the SLA needs to be reviewed to verify that it is still valid and that its processes are working satisfactorily. It is possible for a review to occur at any time, if both parties are agreeable to doing so. However, the SLA needs to specify times when regular, periodic reviews will occur. In a typical agreement, with a term of 24 months, three reviews should be scheduled. The first review should be held six months after the agreement is put in place. The other two reviews should occur in the twelfth month and the eighteenth month.

In a review of an SLA, some fundamental questions need to be addressed. The first question is whether the agreement and its associated processes are functioning as intended. Particularly in the first review, it is important to address the question of whether the agreement and its service levels are still acceptable. The reviews need to consider whether any changes are required. For example, it might be necessary to replace a service level indicator because data is no longer available for it. Or, it might be necessary to redefine responsibilities or report distributions because of an organization restructuring.

SLA reviews can range from very informal to very formal. They can be little more than two department heads (for example, the former negotiating team leaders) discussing the SLA over a cup of coffee. Alternatively, at the other end of the spectrum, the review might consist of reconvening the entire SLA negotiating team. The method chosen will depend in large part on the culture of the company, the warmth or coolness of the relations between the departments involved, and the user department's satisfaction with the service levels being delivered.

Revisions

When an SLA is put into place, it should be expected that revisions to it would be necessary. The agreement is not set in concrete, nor are the organizations that it serves. Revisions are very common and tend to be driven by a variety of factors including: requirements, technology, workload, staffing, staff location, mergers and acquisitions, and so on. When revisions are necessary, a new agreement will need to be written and approved. As with the agreement reviews, the process can be quite informal or require a lengthy negotiation process.

Approvals

After all the details for an SLA have been defined, and all the parties are in agreement, the agreement needs to be signed. In the case of an SLA with an external service provider, this is obviously necessary. With internal service providers, the need to sign the agreement might be less obvious, but it is just as important. In signing the agreement, both parties are formally acknowledging that they are in agreement with its terms and are committed to its success. The person signing the agreement for the service provider should be the person who has authority over all aspects of the services covered by the agreement. Likewise, the user signing the agreement should be the overall department head, that is, the person to whom all the users of the service report. However, regardless of level, the individuals signing the agreement must have authority to sign the agreement and have an interest in its success.

Summary

Service Level Agreements are a key component to any service level management process. To begin with, they provide a basis for effective dialog between the client and the service provider. They can be beneficial to both the service provider and the client because SLAs hold both parties accountable. That is, the client is forced to define the level of service that will be considered acceptable. On the other hand, the service provider is held accountable for delivering the level of service to which they have agreed. To be effective, the SLA must be negotiated fairly and in good faith. When established, the SLA is one of the most effective vehicles available to the service provider for managing client satisfaction.

CHAPTER 5

Standards Efforts

Industry standards for service level management are not very mature at this time, and in general there is a lack of industry-accepted methodologies, practices, and standards in place. Most standards efforts have focused on infrastructure management rather than service management. This is at least partially because of the difficulty of setting standards for defining, measuring, and managing services, which is a more complex issue than standards for monitoring and configuring individual devices and components.

The most notable standards effort to date has been driven by the UK Government's Central Computing and Telecommunications Agency (CCTA). CCTA has delivered a documented methodology for managing service called the IT Infrastructure Library (ITIL). Other efforts include the Service Level Agreement (SLA) Working Group created by the Distributed Management Task Force (DMTF) and the Appl MIB by the Internet Engineering Task Force (IETF). A more focused effort, the Application Response Measurement (ARM) Working Group is supported by several vendors, as well as a special interest group sponsored by the Computer Measurement Group. The rest of this chapter looks at these efforts in more detail.

Tip

Standards efforts continually change over time, with some efforts gaining momentum whereas others lapse, and new initiatives are regularly introduced into the industry. It is worthwhile to check the following Web sites regularly to ensure that you are aware of new developments:

http://www.dmtf.org (Distributed Management Task Force)

http://www.ietf.org (Internet Engineering Task Force)

http://www.cmg.org (Computer Measurement Group)

http://www.exin.nl/itil/itinf/home (IT Infrastructure Library)

IT Infrastructure Library

The IT Infrastructure Library (ITIL) was initially developed for use within UK government IT departments by the Central Computing and Telecommunications Agency (CCTA). This library consists of 24 volumes available to interested parties. The use of the ITIL has spread outside the UK government and, in fact, has a significant amount of support throughout Europe. Awareness and support for ITIL in the United States is very limited, although an organization has been established in the United States to try to increase its acceptance.

The ITIL has a number of service management modules that cover topics including help desk operations, problem management, change management, software control and distribution, service level management, cost management, capacity management, contingency planning, configuration management, and availability management. The volumes provide a methodology for defining, communicating, planning, implementing, and reviewing services to be delivered by the IT department. They include guidelines, process flowcharts, job descriptions, and discussions on benefits, costs, and potential problems.

The specific module on service level management refers to the relationship between service level managers, suppliers, and maintainers of services. ITIL sees service level management as being primarily concerned with the quality of IT services in the face of changing needs and demands. Figure 5.1 shows how IT users, service providers, and suppliers relate via the use of Service Level Agreements.

This module also outlines the responsibilities of the service level manager as

- Creating a service catalog that describes provided services
- Identifying service level requirements relating to each service and user community
- Negotiating Service Level Agreements between service suppliers and IT users
- Reviewing support services with service suppliers

- Setting accounting policies for cost allocation
- Monitoring and reviewing services
- Reporting on achieved service levels

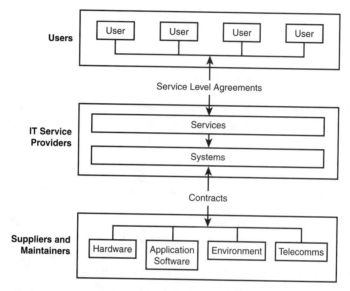

Figure 5.1   *The relationship of users, providers, and maintainers of IT services.*

ITIL specifies many benefits of service level management including achieving a specific, consistent level of service, balancing service levels against the cost of providing them, increasing user productivity, and defining a more objective relationship between IT users and service providers. It also spells out potential problems including resistance to change, the difficulty in formulating service level requirements, the problems associated with establishing costs, and the danger of agreeing to overly-ambitious service level targets before an appropriate baseline is established.

The ITIL endorses the principle that IT services are there to support the business and help staff to do their work well. Two concepts are embodied in all its modules:

- A lifecycle approach to service management
- Customer focus

ITIL advocates that IT service managers have appropriate input to development projects to ensure that operational requirements are taken into account during development, testing strategies are created, capacity requirements to support the new systems are understood, and service expectations are understood from the beginning. ITIL emphasizes the importance of service quality, and states that quality service comes from keeping close to the customer and communicating effectively with the customer.

ITIL views service management as a single discipline with multiple aspects and advocates taking an integrated approach to implementing service management. Hence ITIL recommends the use of a single repository for configuration data that is available to the help desk and used as a base for change management, problem management, and contingency planning as an important implementation consideration. The base ITIL modules don't specify which order to implement all aspects of service management because they can be implemented either consecutively or simultaneously.

Note

ITIL does not cover all aspects of implementation management, and recommends the use of formal project management as well as complete procedure documentation, risk management, audits, and regular reviews.

The ITIL approach gained the support of the British Computer Society, which has validated the training and examinations associated with ITIL's Certificate in IT Infrastructure Management. A number of user groups have formed to support ITIL, including the IT Infrastructure Management Forum and the IT Service Management Forum. These user groups comprise IT departments of government and commercial organizations as well as academic bodies and vendor representatives. EXIN, the Dutch equivalent of CCTA, has become a partner in ITIL and is helping to fund the ongoing updating and re-issuing of the library.

Several thousand professionals in Europe have been trained and certified in the ITIL methodologies, and multiple authorized vendors provide ITIL certification training, almost all of whom are located in Europe. A large number of organizations in Europe are training their IT staff in ITIL methods; however, it is important to recognize that smaller environments should scale down the processes and methods appropriately.

Note

Training in ITIL methods does not mean that you are ready to implement the methodologies immediately as learned in your IT organization. ITIL starts with the presumption that no current service management methodology, products, or processes are in place, and this will not be the case in most organizations. The goal is to adopt and adapt those methodologies that bring an appropriate level of discipline and the most benefit to the organization. These should be implemented in a phased approach to build on and extend existing practices.

It is recommended that service managers become familiar with the concepts and methodologies provided by the ITIL and use this information as a framework to review current service management processes with the IT department. Then, select those areas in which no formal procedures exist and that appear to have the largest potential return on investment in terms of better support for the business and IT user. High priority should be given to those practices that will help improve the quality and consistency of IT service delivery. Use the ITIL methodology as a starting point and alter it to better suit the size and maturity of your organization and the scope of the services to be managed.

Distributed Management Task Force (DMTF) SLA Working Group

The Service Level Agreement (SLA) Working Group is a task force of DMTF members, who are focused on extending the DMTF's Common Information Model (CIM). The CIM's aim is to allow the definition and association of policies, rules, and expressions that enable common industry communications with respect to service management.

The *Common Information Model (CIM)* is an object-oriented information model that describes details required to manage systems, software, users, and networks. A conceptual management framework is provided that establishes object definitions and classes, and uses the following layers:

- Core Model—Applicable to all domains of management (domains include systems, applications, devices, users, and networks).

- Common Models—Common to particular management domains but independent of a particular technology or implementation.

- Extension Models—Technology-specific extensions of the Common Models.

An important aspect of CIM is the ability to define and represent relationships between objects. This is very useful when trying to show the resources used by various applications and the users who implement those applications.

Note

The Common Information Model began as a component of the Web Based Enterprise Management (WBEM) initiative and has gained significant support from hardware, software, and management vendors in the industry.

The SLA Working Group is extending the syntax and metaschema of CIM to embrace the concepts of service management. The concept of a service spans across multiple areas of the CIM schema, such as network support of the service, software used to deliver the service, and end users who consume the service. Core Model extensions are being created, and these will also allow for further subclassing within the Common Models for domain-specific usage. In addition, policies will be supported for representing management goals, desired system states, or the commitments of a Service Level Agreement.

The working group is seeking to address a number of issues including

- Various types of policies and linkages with methods to allow detection and response to policy violations

- Mechanisms for end-to-end management of policies and rules across multiple domains

- Specification of priority and ordering of rules and expressions together, with mechanisms for conflict resolution

- Interfacing with other working groups to allow use of policies and rules for systems, applications, a network's availability, and performance management

At this time the SLA Working Group is in a very early stage, and it is unclear whether significant progress will be made and, if so, whether the work will gain broad acceptance in the industry. As this work is likely to continue to evolve, it is recommended that interested parties monitor the efforts through the DMTF Web site, at http://www.dmtf.org.

Internet Engineering Task Force (IETF)— Application Management MIB

The IETF has issued RFC 2564 Application Management MIB that, although not focused on service level management, does have a number of elements that can assist in measuring and managing service quality. The areas of most interest are the definition and measurement of units of work; response time monitoring; monitoring resource usage by application such as I/O statistics and application layer network resource usage; and facilities for controlling applications such as stopping, suspending, resuming, and reconfiguring applications.

The Appl MIB is complementary to the SysAppl MIB that focuses on system-level managed objects for applications. Both the SysAppl MIB and the Appl MIB have a significant limitation in that they specifically exclude any applications running on multiple systems. This means that client/server applications or applications that use multitiered architectures are not covered by the Appl MIB. A number of tables are associated with the Appl MIB including the following:

- Service-level tables that map services
- The Open Files table that contains information on files currently open for the running application elements
- The Open Files Cross-reference table that accesses information about open files using the names of the open files as an index
- The Open Connections table that provides information on read and write activity by an application element across connections

- Transaction Statistics tables that hold information about transaction streams, including the number of transactions processed and transaction throughput

- The Running Application Element Status table that augments the information contained in the SysAppl MIB table with additional status, open connections, and error information

- The Running Application Element Control table that provides the ability to exercise some control over the running application elements including suspending, reconfiguring, or terminating a running element

Of these, the most interesting with respect to service level management are the Transactions Statistics table and the Running Application Element Control table. The requirement that the application runs on a single system is a limitation that needs to be considered as part of any management solution implemented using the Appl MIB standard.

Note

As the Appl MIB is still a proposal in RFC stage, it will be some time before it is finalized and additional time before there is any significant support and implementation of software products that use this standard to provide management information.

Application Response Measurement Working Group

Hewlett-Packard and Tivoli (a subsidiary of IBM Corporation) cooperated to produce an API specification called Application Response Measurement (ARM). This is designed to measure business transactions from an end-user perspective, as well as measuring the contributing components of response time in distributed applications. Response times are one aspect of understanding the service being delivered to end users. The ARM Working Group has expanded to include representatives of BMC Software, Boeing, Candle, Citicorp, Compuware, Landmark, Novell, Oracle, SAS, SES, Sun, Unify, and Wells Fargo, along with Hewlett-Packard and IBM.

The actual API specification is relatively simple and requires placing API calls within the application code to designate the beginning and end of business transactions. Additional optional API calls can be used to indicate progress in long-running transactions. The ARM API defines six procedure calls:

`arm_init:`	Initializes the ARM environment.
`arm_getid:`	Names each transaction that will be monitored.
`arm_start:`	Denotes the start of a transaction instance.

arm_update:	Updates statistics for a long-running transaction.
arm_stop:	Registers the end of a transaction instance.
arm_end:	Cleans up the ARM environment prior to shutdown.

The ARM Software Developer Kit continues to be refined. Version 2 addressed the issue of client/server transactions that span multiple tiers by supporting the correlation of transactions and sub-transactions. This allows a better understanding of where bottlenecks and delays might be occurring in more complex transactions. Version 2 can also be used to provide information on the size of transactions, such as a count of bytes or transactions processed, which might be useful to show the status of long-running transactions. The new update API can also be useful in providing additional error code information or an indication of transaction progress such as the account record currently being processed.

Caution

The ARM API is intrusive and must be used during the application development or retro-fitted if the application is already in service. Because many of the applications used within an IT department are produced by third-party software vendors, the IT department will not have access to the source code of these applications. Hence retro-fitting the applications for ARM might be impossible unless the vendor agrees to make the modifications. It might be possible to use remote terminal emulation and embed ARM API calls with the scripts; however, there are other mechanisms for simulating transactions and gathering statistics that might be simpler to implement. As ARM does not have widespread acceptance yet, reliance on it as the only way to measure end-user response times might be premature.

Summary

No single industry standard exists for service level management that has broad acceptance. Although a number of initiatives are underway, the best approach is to keep apprised of standard developments and use a best practice approach. The methodology of the ITIL—suitably modified for your particular organization, together with suitable mechanisms for measuring aspects of service quality—can provide a base platform for successful implementation of service level management. As standards continually evolve and new initiatives appear frequently, it is wise to monitor the various standards organizations via their Web sites.

PART II

Reality

Chapter

CHAPTER 6

Service Level Management Practices

This chapter examines the current practices in use today in typical corporations and organizations. Most of the information used to draw conclusions has come from the United States, although anecdotal evidence suggests that common practices in other countries are quite similar. In general the current state of service management, particularly for newer applications and services across distributed enterprises, is somewhat immature. Although a number of organizations proactively manage the services they provide, the definition, understanding, and scope of service management vary tremendously from organization to organization.

Lack of Common Understanding

In late 1998, Enterprise Management Associates surveyed readers of *InternetWeek*, and the report[7] was published in November. It was found that 21% of high-ranking IT executives could not define service management or identify the tools they would use to implement it, and 81% said they needed more information on the subject. Even among organizations that practice service management, the scope and understanding of this discipline varied. Of those who could define service level management, the most common answer (around 35% of those surveyed) associated the term with meeting or improving end-user perception of the service, which might be a specific application or network service[6].

Several industry research firms have concluded that there is significant confusion in the industry and in the marketplace around service level management. For example, META Group titled a May 1999 research note "Service Level Mess," citing hype from vendors as helping to increase this level of confusion. META Group also indicated that the service level management market maturity would begin in 2001.

Many IT organizations look at service level management as simply a reporting function, or perhaps a mechanism for gaining some advantage by documenting Service Level Agreements (SLAs). An April 1999 report by Forrester Research found that most organizations with documented Service Level Agreements reap little more than bureaucracy from those agreements[4]. They related that most SLAs

- Arise from provincial objectives, such as to support chargeback or to defend in-house jobs from outsourcers
- Specify irrelevant metrics, such as component utilization measures
- Lack teeth where no penalties exist for not meeting the agreement
- Don't drive improvement because they don't assess customer satisfaction, and are not revised when there are changes in business or technology best practices

In a research survey published in February 1998, Forrester found the result of management problems to be downtime (38%), poor performance (20%), slow problem resolution (18%), impact on revenues (15%), high IT costs (13%), and user dissatisfaction (13%). Forrester Research believes that corporations need better ways to measure IT department performance and must align the IT department with business goals. Effective service level management can help achieve these goals[5].

Note

A number of industry research firms cover service level management, particularly since interest has grown within their client base. Although we quote from several of these firms, it is very likely that if you use the services of a different research firm, it will also have a practice that covers service level management.

The industry research firm Gartner Group outlines common pitfalls of today's Service Level Agreements as being too complex, with no set baseline, leading to staff overcommitment in trying to meet unrealistic goals. These unrealistic objectives might be set by the IT organization in response to customer demands and, in many cases, the agreements are too one-sided and don't clearly specify the responsibilities of both parties.

Different industry analysts emphasize different aspects of service level management. Hurwitz Group advocates that a service level agreement needs to specify three service level objectives: user response time, application availability, and application recoverability. Hurwitz Group also sees service level management as an iterative process that extends beyond Service Level Agreements and must be managed as outlined in Figure 6.1.

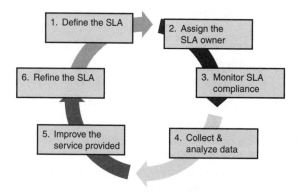

Figure 6.1   *The SLA management process as defined by Hurwitz Group.*

In contrast, Giga Group believes that the three critical areas of Service Level Agreements are response time, application availability, and cost of service delivery. Giga Group recognizes that cost analysis is a complex subject, but highlights the need to consider cost as it relates to achieving a specified set of service levels. Forrester Research sees service level management as consisting of ensuring business application availability, performance planning to enhance the infrastructure to meet response time requirements, and administrative support to provide the day-to-day operations.

META Group advocates an approach it calls Service Value Agreements (SVAs), which is an evolution from a static SLM model to a dynamic one that is oriented around business-focused process management. In META Group's assessment, less than 25% of IT organizations would implement service management from a quality discipline wherein the IT department is aligned with the goals of the lines of business and has appropriate compensation programs to ensure SLA goals are met[1].

The increased attention from industry analysts, as well as more service level management articles appearing in trade publications, will help to educate IT professionals. The general level of understanding and acceptance will also increase as more industry forums evolve to include the opportunity for the sharing of best practices around service management. At this time, there is no common agreement even among the industry analyst community regarding the definition, scope, and process for managing services effectively. As outlined in Chapter 5, "Standards Efforts," few standards have emerged and none have any significant support. We can expect the situation and the maturity of service management to continue to improve, particularly if accepted standards do emerge.

Tip

While waiting for standards to emerge and evolve, including the basics such as common definitions, you might want to become involved in groups such as the Distributed Management Task Force and the IT Service Management Forum. You could also attend selected, focused trade shows and conferences where you can share your experiences and listen to best practices in use at other organizations.

Current Service Level Management Practices

Most IT organizations today don't practice service management as a defined, continuous process of quality improvement. Various research studies show, however, that many organizations have implemented some aspects of service management that typically begin with some form of documented service level agreement and expand to include service level monitoring and reporting. A minority of IT organizations have also included a disciplined approach to continuous improvement for both achieved service levels and customer satisfaction.

A research report published in April 1999 by META Group shows that IT organizations implementing service management quality programs place emphasis on the following five areas[2]:

1. Management by fact using captured performance data. Some IT organizations are also using this information to determine the performance bonus component of IT management compensation.

2. Continuous improvement, which means meeting user expectations that continue to increase while balancing service levels, timeliness, and cost.

3. Customer satisfaction surveys to ensure end-user priorities and perceptions are clearly understood.

4. Design for quality including a focus on change management, standardization, training, and end-user tools.

5. IT leadership in helping lines of business to create competitive advantages using new technology and services.

International Network Services conducts an annual online survey on service level management. The 1999 INS survey showed that, of those respondents who have implemented service level management, 63% were satisfied with their organization's SLM capabilities versus only 17% in the previous year. Although satisfaction was increasing, the same survey indicated that 90% of the respondents felt improving their SLM capabilities was an important goal—the same number as the previous year. This is a good indication that service level management is, in fact, a continuous improvement process, with most IT organizations seeking better capabilities[3].

The 1999 INS survey also found that organizational issues including processes and procedures were the most significant barriers to implementing or improving service level management. A number of other challenges related to the difficulties in defining, negotiating, and measuring Service Level Agreements. Also noted was the problem of justifying the cost/benefits to upper management.

The degree to which the IT department has implemented sophisticated service management varies by the perspective of the IT department. If the IT organization sees itself as a partner with the lines of business and responsible for helping those business units gain market advantage and improve profits, continuous service improvement comes more naturally. The nature of Service Level Agreements and management is also different for services the IT department provides internally and services it contracts for with external suppliers.

Management of Services Provided by the IT Department to the Corporation

Most IT departments evolve their service level management along two vectors:

- The IT department begins by setting internal goals and then extends them by negotiating and formalizing an agreement with the lines of business.
- The metrics used to determine quality of service and the scope of the service management processes increase and improve.

In all organizations, the users of services provided by the IT department have a set of expectations about the quality they want to be delivered by those services. The starting point for managing service quality is, typically, when the users complain, the IT department attempts to fix the problem. When user complaints escalate and the IT department is continually in a fire-fighting mode trying to meet user expectations, the IT management typically seeks to put in place more proactive processes and procedures.

This generally starts with a review of current management practices and an attempt to establish a baseline of the quality of services being delivered by the IT department. To understand service quality, a review is typically undertaken of reported problems, including the trend in the number of problem reports, the time to close problems, the number of backlogged problems, which organizations are most affected, and which IT functions are handling the greatest number of problems. Following the review and the establishment of a baseline, the IT department can then set a number of measurable, internal goals that will lead to service improvement.

Tip

To be most effective, the initial service quality goals should be simple, easy to understand, and clearly measurable. There should also be a link between achievement of the goals and incentives for the IT staff responsible for the service, such as a bonus component of their compensation.

Internal to the IT Department

The IT department typically begins the journey toward more disciplined service level management by examining internal management processes and setting some internal performance goals. In many cases, this starts with the procedure for reporting, documenting, tracking, and resolving problems.

Processes that become more formal include the method used to document and categorize problem priority and severity, how problem status is reported to affected users, and how problems are escalated. Associated goals include how quickly help desk calls are answered, how quickly the assigned support specialist will respond to the user reporting the problem, and how quickly the problem will be fixed (which normally varies according to the assigned priority or severity). Problem hand-off procedures between the various areas within the IT department are also formalized, together with project status reporting and processes for handling crisis situations. Together with these documented procedures and goals, the IT department might identify requirements for supporting infrastructure and tools, such as phone systems, a problem-tracking system, and associated knowledge database.

The IT department might also set other internal goals around the delivery of new services to the organization, such as how quickly the department will respond to requests for new desktop equipment, or to equipment moves, or to additional network connections.

Additionally, the IT department might implement certain system-performance–oriented goals that are based on observed behavior patterns. For example, in many organizations, the IT department attempts to keep utilization levels of distributed servers below 75% because the department has observed increased frequency of user calls complaining of poor performance if system utilization goes beyond that level.

In most cases, these early steps establish a baseline of procedures and internal processes necessary to ensure consistency of approach to service delivery. This approach often helps the IT department understand the current level of service delivery and highlights which areas require most improvement. Although an important first step, real service level management will not begin until the IT department establishes agreements with internal clients and external suppliers.

Note

Even after Service Level Agreements are established outside the IT department, internal agreements will still be required to define interfaces between the various areas within the IT organization, along with expected operating procedures and performance goals.

Agreements with the Lines of Business

There is a natural maturation of the types of agreements the IT department might enter into with the lines of business. Initially, these will be informal agreements with very ad hoc service quality measurement and reporting. This might result from a problem situation with the service delivered to a specific line of business or particular application. In order to factually examine the situation, the IT department must collect information relating to the problem, service availability, service degradation, notification procedures, and the problem resolution process.

Having captured this information, a baseline of service quality can be established and documented and the IT department can work from this baseline to improve service quality and user satisfaction. After this process is followed for one application supporting one line of business, it is a natural process to extend the process to other lines of business and other applications and services. At this stage in the maturation process, a number of Service Level Agreements may be negotiated and documented. However, in many cases, these agreements address the most bothersome lines of business or the most visible applications from the perspective of the IT department.

The next stage in developing more effective service level management practices is to address the prioritization of the lines of business and the applications and services provided by the IT department from a business value perspective.

Caution

Determining business- value–based Service Level Agreements might be a difficult concept for all lines of business to accept. It typically requires senior-management-level and sometimes executive-level sponsorship to ensure complete buy-in by the lines of business.

Only half the participants in the 1999 INS survey had SLAs in place, versus 87% who stated that they had some form of service level management. This indicates that a large number of organizations were still in the ad hoc stage of managing service levels. The survey also indicates that the acceptance and implementation of Service Level Agreements will improve as 60% of the respondents planned to implement either initial or additional SLAs, at which time 65% of respondents will have at least one SLA in place. Interestingly, IT departments recognized the importance of mapping resources to the most critical applications and services, with 42% of respondents making this an objective for Service Level Agreements[3].

The 1999 INS survey also examined the primary objectives for developing Service Level Agreements between the IT department and lines of business. The most prominent themes were setting and managing user expectations and assessing their satisfaction, understanding service priorities and mapping resources accordingly, and measuring the quality of the services provided by the IT department. Figure 6.2 provides additional detail on this aspect of the survey.

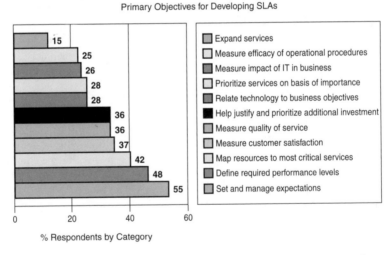

Figure 6.2   *The top objectives for developing SLAs between the IT department and internal organizations—1999 INS service level management survey.*

In addition to negotiating Service Level Agreements, the IT department must measure service levels to understand the quality of services provided to lines of business. Most IT organizations begin by measuring the availability of services they provide, and then add capabilities to measure performance or the responsiveness of the service to end users. Again, there is a maturation process wherein the IT department typically begins by measuring and monitoring the availability of various technology components before it can measure the end-to-end availability of the service from the user's perspective.

This approach is also shown in the 1999 INS survey, where network availability was selected as very important by 90% of respondents. This is a technology view of availability. The secondmost important metric was customer satisfaction, which can be achieved only if the user experience is perceived to be acceptable. The thirdmost important component was network performance, followed by application availability and application response time. This supports the typical view of first addressing availability, and then performance, while at the same time moving from a pure component view to one that centers around the application and the end-user experience.

Management of Services Provided by External Suppliers

The primary external services supplied to the IT department are the networking services provided by telecommunications companies or Internet service providers. External Service Level Agreements with these carriers are becoming important parts of the relationship between the IT department and the service providers. In a joint study conducted in 1999 by McConnell Associates and Renaissance Worldwide, 46% of IT managers said they have established external SLAs with their providers, and 80% of those agreements include penalty clauses for failure to deliver required service quality[6].

When managing the services provided by external suppliers, IT managers have a set of objectives different from the one they have when setting Service Level Agreements with lines of business. The 1999 INS survey shows the top three priorities of external Service Level Agreements to be

- Define required performance levels (58% of respondents)
- Measure quality of service provided by service providers (52%)
- Measure customer satisfaction (34%)

This is demonstrated by the results of the McConnell/Renaissance survey, which showed the most important service level metrics for wide area network providers to be

- Utilization rates (78% of respondents)
- Throughput (72%)
- Error rates (67%)
- Availability (66%)
- Response time (61%)
- Reliability (50%)

These results are consistent with the 1999 INS survey that showed the top three elements included in external network service provider SLAs to be

- Network availability (77% of respondents)
- Network performance (73%)
- Network throughput (64%)

Tip

Telecommunications companies and Internet service providers are becoming much more competitive and aggressive in trying to increase their respective market shares. If you don't have a formal service level agreement with your supplier, you should be able to use the competitive pressures to negotiate one that includes penalty clauses for failure to deliver the required level of service.

For the most part, telecommunications service providers and Internet service providers are offering SLAs that guarantee high levels of network performance. To illustrate this, we will look at a sample of providers offering such agreements; however, note that this is meant to be only representative and not exhaustive.

AT&T offers SLAs for its domestic, international, and managed frame relay environments. AT&T provides SLAs in five areas including provisioning, service restoration time, latency, throughput, and network availability. Each of these areas has agreed-upon service levels and if they are not met, AT&T credits customers for monthly charges and maintenance fees based on the terms outlined in each customer's contract.

GTE Internetworking offers SLAs for its Internet Advantage dedicated access customers. These SLAs include credits for network outages, the inability to reach specific Internet sites, and packet losses. GTE guarantees only its own backbone, but customers can test to identify packet losses or delays within that portion of the network. GTE also keeps performance statistics on a central database, which allows verification of customer claims of poor performance.

MCI WorldCom's networkMCI Enterprise Assurance SLA extends performance guarantees across all its data services. These include guarantees for availability, performance such as transit delays, and network restoration time.

NaviSite Internet Services provides Internet outsourcing solutions and offers the SiteHarbor product family of service guarantees. These guarantees cover the database server, Web server, network infrastructure, and facility infrastructure. NaviSite includes penalties in the form of free service if the guarantees are not met.

Sprint's Frame Relay for LAN service is backed by performance guarantees for network availability and network response time. Sprint also offers performance guarantees for its Frame Relay for SNA service. In both cases, Sprint provides customers with financial credits if performance guarantees are not met.

UUNET Technologies offers SLAs for frame relay, dedicated circuits, and Internet access services. These cover network availability, latency, proactive outage notification, and installation interval guarantees. Again, with each of these there are financial penalties if UUNET fails to meet the performance guarantees.

In summary, offering Service Level Agreements and managing the quality of the services they provide is seen as a competitive necessity by the telecommunications and Internet services providers.

Tip

IT departments should ensure that they have Service Level Agreements in place with external suppliers, and that those agreements are monitored and regularly reviewed. Without appropriate service quality from these suppliers, it is extremely difficult, if not impossible, for the IT department to meet its own Service Level Agreements with the lines of business.

Typical Agreements

Currently, most Service Level Agreements for services provided by the IT department are fairly simple and are more focused on specifying roles, responsibilities, and procedures. The 1999 INS survey found the top elements included in internal SLAs to be:

- Assignment of responsibilities and roles (64% of respondents)
- Goals and objectives (61%)
- Reporting policies and escalation procedures (61%)
- Help desk availability (59%)

Below these were more performance-oriented metrics including network availability, network performance, application availability, and application response time.

The structure of most Service Level Agreements begins with a statement of intent, a description of the service, approval process for changes to the SLA, definition of terms, and identification of the primary users of the service. A number of procedures are described, including the problem-reporting procedures, definition of the change management process, and how requests for new users will be processed. Typically, the schedule of normal service availability and schedule of planned outages is specified.

Following this definition of roles and procedures, any specific performance objectives are specified. In most of today's SLAs, these goals tend to be limited to availability measures and response times and resolution times for reported problems. In some cases, additional measures and objectives are stated for application-response times. Today, very few internal Service Level Agreements either specify the costs of services or provide a cost allocation mechanism. Similarly, very few agreements specify penalties for the IT department if service level objectives are not met.

In general, these Service Level Agreements are early in the maturation cycle, but they establish a dialog between the IT department and the lines of business and catalog the services provided by the IT department. These Service Level Agreements also establish the procedures for the lines of business to interface with the IT department, and begin to set expectations as to the service levels that can be measured and delivered by the IT department.

Service Level Agreements with external suppliers tend to follow the standard offerings of the telecommunication service providers and Internet service providers. Although these are probably adequate for small and medium corporations, larger organizations might be better served by negotiating custom agreements.

Reporting Practices

Just as Service Level Agreements are somewhat immature at this time, so are the service level reporting practices of most IT departments. The majority of service level reports are very detailed, component-level availability and performance statistics that are incomprehensible to most recipients outside the IT department. Some organizations produce useful reports showing the number, severity, and type of problems reported by users of IT services, including response and resolution times. These help the IT department show its responsiveness to the lines of business and can be used to determine whether the problems are systematic, underlying technology or staffing issues requiring attention.

Some organizations do manage to provide service level information by application, by location, and by user; however, unless the IT department has invested in a sophisticated toolset and employed a rigorous methodology, this information has to be generated manually.

Tip

Unless you can provide service level metrics in terms that users can relate to and that represent their experience, it might be best to disseminate the service level reports only within the IT department. Technology-oriented component reporting confuses the lines of business and reduces the credibility of the IT department.

Proactive reports of service difficulties and scheduled outages can be extremely effective in increasing user satisfaction and the credibility of the IT department. Some sophisticated IT departments are deploying technology solutions that allow them to notify users via Web-based applications, synthesized voice units, voice mail, and email.

Types of Products in Use

The Forrester Research 1998 report on Service Level Management included a survey on the use of management tools. The results indicated the following tool usage[5]:

- Systems management tools (70% of respondents)
- Network management tools (60%)
- Applications/database management tools (35%)
- Management frameworks (28%)

The more widespread use of systems and network management tools as compared to the use of application management tools also explains some of the immaturity of service level management. Looking at the network or system in isolation does provide the ability to measure or manage service from the user's perspective. The lines of business use applications that automate a business process or task. Hence, their concern is that the application be available and responsive to the users, who have no visibility to or desire to know the availability and performance of the underlying infrastructure, such as the network and the systems.

The 1999 INS survey examined the effectiveness of service level management tools. Figure 6.3 shows the survey respondents' assessment of tool effectiveness.

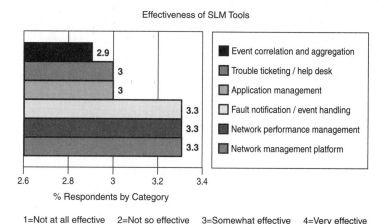

Figure 6.3 *The effectiveness of SLM tools—1999 INS service level management survey.*

The perceived relative ineffectiveness of application management tools versus network management tools also explains part of the difficulty for IT departments to implement more mature service level management. As these products and the application management market mature, there will be a direct benefit to IT departments wishing to manage service levels from the application and end-user perspectives.

A more detailed look at service level management products is provided in Chapter 7, "Service Level Management Products."

Summary

Today's service level management practices in most IT departments are still immature; however, many organizations are improving their abilities significantly. Because service level management is a continuous process, the maturation of the discipline and industry will not occur overnight, but will be a gradual process.

Many organizations are investing in management tools, and are putting service level agreements in place with the lines of business they serve, as well with external providers of services to the IT department. These initiatives support a more sophisticated approach to service level management and improve the quality of services provided by the IT department.

References

1. META Group, *Service Management Strategies Delta*, 10 February 1999, File:754

2. META Group, *Service Management Strategies Delta,* 30 April 1999, File:778

3. Rick Blum, Jeffrey Kaplan/International Network Services, *INS 1999 Survey Results - Service Level Management*, 10 May 1999

4. The Forrester Report, *IT Pacts Beyond SLAs,* April 1999

5. The Forrester Report, *Service Level Management,* Volume 15, Number Four, February 1998

6. Tim Wilson/InternetWeek, "Service Level Management: Build Stronger External Bonds," 10 May 1999

7. Enterprise Management Associates, Service Level Management Market Research Study, 30 November 1998

CHAPTER 7

Service Level Management Products

T he market for management tools displays an interesting phenomenon. Periodically, a new area of interest emerges and becomes the hot topic for several months or, in rare cases, even a few years. When a new hot topic emerges, there is usually a stampede among companies in the vendor community to address the new market opportunity. Some companies race to develop and deliver new products. Others will tweak and refine their existing products. Still others will simply change their marketing materials to slant them toward the new area. This approach is sometimes legitimate. That is, the company's product really does meet a need in this emerging market space. Unfortunately, there are other cases in which even though the product does not really meet any needs related to the hot topic, the vendor still claims it does.

What makes a topic "hot?" Changes in technology are frequently responsible for moving a topic to the front burner. That is because new technologies are exciting, interesting, and usually make possible things that heretofore had been impossible.

New products can generate a "buzz" that leads to an area becoming a hot topic. Also, a shift in user interests will sometimes be the driver for interest in a particular arena. Sometimes press coverage can become a driver independently of any of these factors, or it can be fueled by these factors. Also, vendor publicity can become both a driving force and also lead to increased press coverage.

Today, SLM is one of the latest hot topics. Predictably, there has been a flood of products, from new and established companies, aimed at this market segment. However, with SLM, there is a fundamental problem. There is not a clear definition of terminology. Therefore, vendors are free to create their own definitions— ones that include their products in the domain of service level management. Unfortunately, this plethora of definitions has created confusion within the user community.

In this chapter, we will provide a framework for classifying and assessing SLM products. This will enable managers to better decipher the confusing array of products offered for SLM. And hopefully, it will give managers the means to find SLM solutions that meet their organization's particular requirements.

We will use our own classification system to scope out SLM products. Keep in mind, however, that it's possible for SLM tools to fit into more than one category. And when given the chance, most vendors will insist that their products "do it all." Still, for our purposes, SLM products can be grouped into the following broad functional categories:

- Monitoring
- Reporting
- Analysis
- Administration

Monitoring Tools

When a Service Level Agreement has been negotiated, it is necessary to capture data about the actual quality, or level, of service delivered. To do this, managers need to use tools to monitor the performance of the service. These monitoring tools comprise software or hardware that retrieves data about the state of underlying components driving the service. This data is stored in a database for future reference or interpreted and put into reports. (Reporting tools will be discussed in the next section.)

Basic Strategies

Monitoring tools collect data in two ways: In the first approach, *primary data collectors* capture data directly from the network elements underlying the service (bridges, routers, switches, hubs, and so forth). Some also gather input from software programs that affect overall service availability (applications, databases, middleware, and the like).

Most primary data collectors are not dedicated to SLM. Instead, they are typically management systems that gather data for a range of purposes, one of which is SLM. For example, Hewlett-Packard's OpenView Network Node Manager (NNM) monitors an enterprise network for a range of parameters, including network availability. Although this data can be used for SLM reporting, it also aids troubleshooting by tipping off network operators about degraded performance. HP provides a separate SLM reporting package that works with NNM. That product, called Information Technology Service Management (ITSM) Service Level Manager, also takes input from other HP applications.

Another class of product, *secondary data collectors*, has appeared (see Figure 7.1). These tools do not need to communicate directly with the managed environment (although some of them are able to do so, if necessary). Instead, they extract data from other products that are primary data collectors. Tools such as Luminate's Service Level Analyzer fit this category. Infovista's Vistaviews is another example. This product retrieves data from third-party management applications, including BMC Patrol and Compaq Insight. Also, it comes in versions capable of interacting directly with routers, Ethernet switches, and WAN gear. Secondary data collectors like Service Level Analyzer offer a means of extending management platforms from different vendors for SLM monitoring, while filling in where management systems might be absent. This approach offers a number of advantages. First, it eliminates the need for redundant agents throughout the distributed computing environment. Second, redundant management traffic is eliminated by relying on original sources. Third, this approach eliminates the need for the redundant storage of large quantities of data.

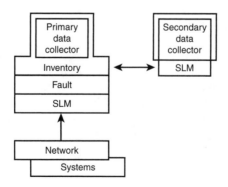

Figure 7.1 *Primary and secondary data collectors.*

Knowing whether a product is a primary or secondary data collector helps determine how an SLM monitoring tool fits a particular environment. To get a better sense of actual requirements, however, it's important to gauge how products fit the manager-agent model.

Both primary and secondary data collectors are designed according to this engineering scheme (see Figure 7.2), in which each device or software program uses an integral mechanism called an agent to collect data about its status. This information is automatically forwarded to a central application called a *manager*, usually in response to a poll signal or request. Many agents in a network can be set up to communicate with one or more managers. For a comprehensive description of the manager-agent model and its implementation in various products, see Appendix F, "Selected Vendors of Service Level Management Products."

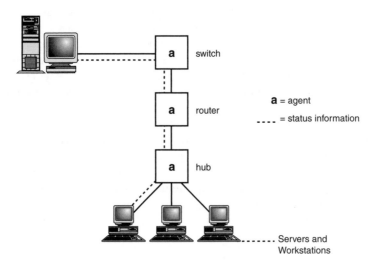

Figure 7.2   *The manager-agent model.*

The manager-agent model can help prospective buyers determine what they need to look for in an SLM monitoring tool. If a company already has an SNMP manager such as HP's OpenView NNM, for instance, all that might be needed is an SLM package capable of using NNM data. That's because most network devices today are shipped with integral SNMP agents, ready to send data to any vendor's standard SNMP manager on request.

In other cases, special agents will be needed to furnish additional information for SLM reports. Suppose that, for example, a catalog retailer needs to track how well its call center has performed in a given month. Data will be required about the functions of the CSU/DSUs, routers, and network connections that bring customer orders into the call center. SNMP agents embedded in those devices, plus standard RMON probes, can furnish this information. And if the retailer has HP OpenView NNM installed, the data can be easily captured.

But the retailer's IT department also needs to know how quickly orders are processed after they're taken over the phone. To obtain this input, software agents will need to be placed on the call center's database server. Because most database servers don't come with SNMP agents installed, the retailer will need to purchase an application that includes special agent software. In this example, another OpenView product, HP's IT/Operations, could be purchased to track the server database via agents bundled with the product. Data from IT/Operations could then be combined with NNM data for use in HP's ITSM Service Level Manager.

Our hypothetical retailer might take a different tack if OpenView NNM wasn't available. If BMC Patrol were installed, for instance, server agents would already be in place. The problem then would be to purchase an SLM monitoring tool to capture data about the underlying network. The retailer could choose secondary SLM data collectors like Quallaby's Proviso to add data about routers and other gear to the system information from Patrol.

In some instances, IT will need to obtain data for SLM from a legacy application, device, or system that does not have its own standard SNMP agent. In this case, IT personnel might have to build agents that can report either directly or indirectly into existing management solutions. This requirement is not as difficult to meet as it might seem. It is relatively easy to construct an SNMP agent using object modeling via Visual Basic or Visual C++. If need be, reporting tools and alerting programs also can be constructed or augmented in a relatively straightforward fashion. Keep in mind that it will be easier to augment SLM tools that support open, well-documented databases and formats.

Data Capture

SLM monitoring tools use a range of methods to capture data. In the implementations previously described, agents are used to check on the devices and software underlying a network service. Other techniques include the use of probes and simulation. Take a look at each of these methods, along with their key benefits and drawbacks.

Agents

Most products classed as primary data collectors—including HP OpenView NNM and IT/Operations, or Tivoli Netview and Tivoli Management Framework—use agents to retrieve information about the hardware and software components that support a particular service. This data can then be forwarded to SLM tools from the platform vendor or third parties.

Several types of agents can be used with SLM tools: Hardware agents comprise software or firmware embedded in network devices that retrieve status information via SNMP or proprietary commands. Nearly all devices in today's corporate environments ship with embedded SNMP agents. All devices from Cisco, for instance, ship with integral agents that use special commands to capture information about device status. This data is converted within the agent to SNMP for transmission to local or remote manager applications from Cisco and other vendors.

Another type of agent important to SLM products is the RMON agent, which consists of code installed at the network interface to analyze traffic and gauge overall network availability. Many RMON agents are packed into standalone boxes called probes (see the next section for more on these). Alternatively, RMON agents are sold as firmware embedded in switches, hubs, and network interface cards. All major hub and switch vendors include RMON agents in their wares.

Because SNMP agents aren't ubiquitously installed on servers or within software packages, many SLM products come with specially designed agents. These agents consist of code that resides on a server and taps log files for information on the performance of databases, network applications, middleware, or the operating system itself. BMC Software offers Patrol agents for a range of distributed databases as well as mainframe environments. These agents report back to BMC's Patrol manager, which in turn is accessible to a range of third-party applications from vendors who've partnered with BMC.

The chief benefits of agent technology are its flexibility and support for mixing and matching of products from different vendors. Software agents also can be used to extract data from a range of sources, as previously noted. Agents also are versatile: Any standard SNMP agent works with any SNMP manager, and vice versa. Even proprietary agents can be integrated with third-party managers—as long as the vendors are willing to cooperate.

On the downside, agent technology can add a processing burden to networks and systems if it is not well planned. Communication between agents and managers is usually based on the client/server model, in which data is exchanged between the two entities over a network. When SNMP is used, this means that packets are transmitted back and forth across a TCP/IP connection. This traffic can tax bandwidth on network links set up to handle mission-critical applications. Congestion can result, especially in large networks, in which many devices are "talking to" a central manager console. One way to avoid congestion is to set up the manager console to poll agents only at specified intervals, or to retrieve only certain types of data from the agents, such as critical alarm information.

Poorly designed SNMP and proprietary agent software also can burden a host computer, causing slowdowns in response time. However, broad experience by IT organizations in many industries over several years, coupled with computer models, both support the conclusion that only in an extreme worst-case situation can the traffic between managers and agents be expected to exceed 1% of the available bandwidth.

The growth of the Internet has prompted many vendors to investigate Web-based techniques, such as Java applets and XML (eXtensive Markup Language), as an alternative to traditional manager-agent communications. Some products, including Trinity from Avesta (a company recently purchased by Visual Networks), e-Specto from Dirigo, and FrontLine e.M from Manage.com put these techniques to work monitoring the availability and health of e-commerce services. Using the Web saves bandwidth and system resources and eliminates the need to set up multiple consoles for management from remote locations. Instead, managers can obtain SLM data from any location via Web browsers. Today, most Web-based management products rely on proprietary protocols and interfaces. But ongoing work by the Distributed Management Task Force (DMTF) is aimed at creating formal standards for Web-based management.

Note

Agent software embedded in hardware devices and network servers is used to gather status and configuration data for transmission to central management consoles. Agent technology has been standardized by the IETF using SNMP, which allows third-party platforms and applications to gather input from multiple sources in the network, regardless of vendor or brand.

Probes, Packet Monitors, and CSU/DSUs

Many SLM products rely on specialized applications or devices to retrieve data on network performance. In this category are probes, packet monitors, and CSU/DSUs equipped with specialized monitoring capabilities. Each of these products passively scrutinizes packets at the network interface and parses them in order to retrieve information on latency and throughput. Probes and packet monitors also analyze flows for insight into the specific applications traversing the net, as well as their overall quality.

Probes consist of standalone hardware devices containing RMON and RMON II agents along with packet parsing and filtering engines similar to those used in protocol analyzers. Apptitude and Netscout Systems are examples of probe vendors. Packet monitors are similar, although often they don't require dedicated hardware but are sold as management applications—the Ecotools product from Compuware and Application Expert from Optimal Networks are examples.

Probes and packet monitors obtain accurate, multi-layer performance data through direct contact with network traffic. On the downside, these products are usually limited in scope and scalability, and their focus is strictly on network traffic; they cannot capture data about the status of devices or specific databases or applications.

Probes are limited in other ways too: A probe designed to monitor leased-line services, for instance, won't track traffic operating above rates of 2.048 megabits per second (Mbps). And the number of links a probe can handle is limited to its physical port capacity: As the number of monitored links increases, more probes need to be purchased.

Note

Probes and packet monitors use agents embedded in packet-filtering devices to track and report the status of network traffic as it moves over LAN or WAN connections. The RMON MIB standardizes this data for compatibility with any SNMP console.

A range of vendors of CSU/DSUs have entered the SLM market by adapting their equipment for use as SLM monitoring tools. ADC Kentrox, Adtran, Digital Link, Eastern Research, Paradyne, Sync Research, Verilink, and Visual Networks all fit this category. Each of these vendors offers a series of CSU/DSUs that keep track of physical-layer performance while divvying up WAN bandwidth to enterprise segments. These products are comparatively inexpensive, and they can be a convenient solution for organizations that want to press existing equipment into the service of SLM monitoring. On the downside, these units only track the performance of WAN links. They don't monitor routed segments. And they might not work on international networks—although most of the CSU/DSU vendors furnish standalone probe versions of their monitors for use overseas.

Note

Some WAN CSU/DSUs come with integral agents that track the physical-layer performance of WAN connections and apply this data to SLM reports.

Simulation

SLM vendors rely on a range of data capture techniques in addition to traditional agents and probes. Some vendors use simulated application flows, for instance, to test the fitness of network connections. FirstSense, Ganymede Software, Jyra Research, Mercury Interactive, and NextPoint Networks take this tack, in which simulated transactions are sent over an IP intranet in order to get consistent readings on response time and availability. In some instances, RMON and SNMP data is added to the mix to fill out the network performance profile.

Besides offering a consistent view of network application performance, simulated transactions offer a way to view end-to-end response time—something that can't be measured by tools that gauge latency alone. On the downside, these tools add traffic to the network; a fact that concerns many network managers. Simulation tools also are restricted to gauging client-server response time. They cannot furnish information about the performance of specific transactions within applications. That type of granular information requires the use of software agents such as those from BMC Software, Candle, Landmark, or Luminate.

> **Note**
>
> Some vendors provide software that is capable of simulating specific types of network traffic or transactions over LAN and WAN links. The simulation tools furnish a way to test multiple connections in a uniform way.

SLM Domains

Effective use of SLM monitoring calls for a skillful application of the basic strategies and data capture techniques previously outlined. But just having the tools isn't enough; a manager needs to apply the tools at the right times in the right places. Like a carpenter equipped with wood and a hammer but no nails, SLM tools won't deliver good information if they're not used in the proper combinations. And the right mix of tools differs with each organization.

One step toward success is to examine the portions of a network that need to be monitored, and then put tools in place to generate the needed SLM data. In general, networks can be described as having the following components or *domains*:

- Network devices and connections
- Servers and desktops
- Applications
- Databases
- Transactions

Taken together, these domains control the quality of network services. An accounting department, for instance, can't run effectively unless all personnel—including debit and credit professionals, tax accountants, the controller and the CFO—are all properly connected over the intranet, which in turn requires switches, hubs, and routers to be in working order. Likewise, the servers and workstations used by the staff need to be configured correctly. But no IT manager needs to be told that response time can slow to a crawl even if the underlying devices and servers are working. Applications can be awkwardly designed, databases clogged with useless entries, and transactions poorly structured.

To get the best SLM information, it is usually, but not always, necessary to install products to monitor each domain. To get the best read on the quality of the accounting services in the previous example requires tools to deliver input on network availability and response time of applications. If multiple sites are involved, a probe might be used to track the quality of WAN links furnished by a carrier. Based on the network design and ongoing performance input, it might be important to adjust the level of monitoring, increase the number and quality of tools in one domain, or consolidate tools across others.

To know how to best coordinate a solution that fits a particular organization's requirements, it's important to know the basic functions of each domain, the tools typically used to monitor those functions, and where and when they're applied. Take a closer look at each of the domains in turn (see Figure 7.3) and examine how the basic strategies and the data capture techniques that we've already covered are applied in each. Examples of currently available products will be furnished for each domain.

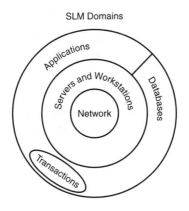

Figure 7.3 *Interdependent SLM Domains.*

Network Devices and Connections

The quality of the underlying network is key to SLM monitoring. After all, no networked service or e-business application can operate without reliable physical connectivity. Monitoring a network requires keeping track of whether each device is operating, and how well all components are working in concert. Getting this data calls for a two-pronged approach that includes tracking the availability of individual devices and monitoring the performance of network connections. Typically, performance data includes information about the throughput, or quantity of delivered packets, and the latency or delay between devices on a particular connection.

Availability and performance data can be obtained by tapping standard SNMP and RMON/RMON II agents located in hubs, switches, routers, and other gear. As previously noted, this can be done via primary data collectors such as HP OpenView or Tivoli Netview, both of which, like other platforms, support their own SLM tools as well as those of third-party vendors. Alternatively, a growing number of management systems dedicated to performance monitoring and reporting also support SLM, including Keystone VPNview from Bridgeway, ProactiveNet Watch from ProactiveNet, and Netvoyant from Redpoint Network Systems. Each of these products can take the place of a primary data collector to feed its own SLM reporting tools. They can be used where no primary data collector is in place, or where there is a primary data collector in a central location that needs to be augmented at remote sites.

Deciding which SLM monitor to use depends in part on the size and design of the network. In large nets, it might be practical and economical to simply extend a platform like OpenView to include SLM monitoring by using tools from the platform vendor. It might also make sense to deploy the platform's scalability options. HP, Tivoli, and other vendors of SNMP management platforms furnish software called a midlevel manager that gathers data at specific segments or sites and sifts it for selective transmission to a central console, reducing the amount of bandwidth and processing required to monitor multiple sites.

Most mission-critical networks these days rely to some extent on carrier connectivity. To keep track of how well the carrier is contributing to service levels, probes may be deployed at specific WAN links (see Figure 7.4). Probes can be polled just like any other SNMP or RMON device. More in-depth data, however, can be obtained by using the application that is sold with the probe. In many instances, this app can be set up with a bit of tweaking to transmit data to OpenView or to a third-party SLM tool.

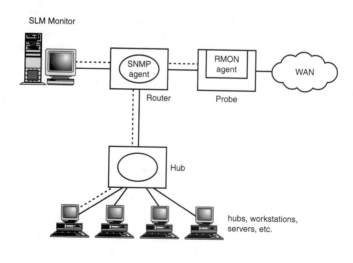

Figure 7.4 *Typical configuration: Network monitoring for SLM data.*

Servers and Desktops

As the user interface to mission-critical applications, servers and desktops are key to SLM success. If response time is poor or there is a failure of server transmission, service has failed, even if network devices are running properly.

But servers and desktops are often missing from the view of SLM monitoring tools. Although specific SNMP MIBs, such as the Host Resoures MIB, have been defined to track some elements of computer systems in a standard way, these aren't typically used to track performance for SLM. Instead, gathering data on the relevant criterion, *response time*, usually requires proprietary agents or simulation tools. Both types of products measure the time it takes applications to traverse the net, either from server to desktop or vice versa, and compare this data to established service levels. Some products also compare response times for different types of applications and indicate how much network latency contributes to the overall measurement.

Most SLM monitoring tools for desktops and servers keep track of response time by issuing simulated transactions from desktop to server, or by using agents placed at either location to gauge server or desktop responses to live application requests. Examples of products in this category include FirstSense Enterprise from FirstSense Software, VitalSuite from Lucent, S3 from NextPoint Networks, and ResponseNet and ResponseWeb from Response Networks.

Products like these show how well service levels are being met from the end-user's perspective. But many are restricted in the range of applications they simulate or monitor: Although most support Internet applications such as POP3, SMTP, Telnet, FTP, and Domain Name Service, not all track Web transactions via HTTP. Also, many are restricted to using SQL queries associated with particular applications like Oracle, PeopleSoft, or SAP R/3. And all of them require some software to be deployed at the desktop, which can make them ungainly to maintain in large networks. Exceptions include NextPoint, which uses Java applets to control simulated transactions, and FirstSense and Response Networks, which allow agents to be distributed over the Internet.

Applications, Databases, and Transactions

Tools that furnish in-depth details on the performance of applications, databases, and transactions are required wherever SLAs depend on software performance. They also can be useful where applications are complex but underlying networks are stable. Because these software elements are all monitored using the same techniques—specifically, specialized agents or packet monitors—it makes sense to group them into a single category when considering product selection.

The agents used for this domain differ significantly from those used to monitor response time for servers and desktops. Although these agents still measure the time it takes a server to respond to a desktop request, they also monitor the health and functionality of the application's inner workings. They do this by residing inside the software itself: monitoring the keystrokes, commands, and transactions deployed by the service. They can identify applications that send too many requests to the server, or highlight those that use transactions that are awkwardly constructed.

Because they're so detailed, these agents are specially designed to keep tabs on specific brands of apps or databases. The Collaborative Service Level Suite from Envive Corp. and Luminate for SAP R/3, for instance, track SAP R/3 databases. ETEWatch from Candle Corp. monitors the response time of Lotus Notes, PeopleSoft, and SAP R/3 applications. Empirical Director from Empirical Software gathers performance data in Oracle databases as well as a range of operating systems. Smartwatch from Landmark Systems can be set up to track the performance of a variety of middleware packages, operating systems, and applications. And BMC Software furnishes a comprehensive framework suite encompassing Patrol, Best/1, and other packages for managing all these elements.

Application agents differ in their monitoring orientation: ETEwatch and Smartwatch, for instance, monitor the performance of applications from the work-station perspective, whereas Envive and Luminate take the response time view from the server. Which view is more valid is generally a matter of opinion. Proponents of the workstation approach claim their wares gauge end-to-end response times, whereas vendors of the server approach say their agents are easier to maintain because they don't have to be placed on desktops throughout the network.

Monitoring specific transactions within applications represents the most sophisti-cated type of application monitoring. It also requires the user to deploy the highest level of expertise. That's because products like Smartwatch call for users to select the transactions they want to monitor. This calls for in-depth knowledge of how applications are structured, as well as a sense of the specific transactions that require most attention. For most organizations, a product like Smartwatch will need to be run by a programmer.

Packet monitors can furnish granular information about software performance by analyzing application traffic. Optimal's Application Expert, for example, depicts specific application threads using color-coded graphs; managers can visually pick out bulky command sequences that might be holding up response time.

A key consideration in choosing a software-monitoring tool is its ability to inte-grate with other vendors' wares, particularly vendors that offer other SLM solu-tions. BMC Software, for example, has integrated its tools with HP OpenView, Tivoli, and a range of other third-party management platforms and applications. And vendors such as Compuware and Envive also have made integration with platforms and frameworks a priority. No SLM shopping expedition is complete without a thorough check of a vendor's partnerships and integrated solutions.

Ultimately, a range of tools is available to support SLM for applications, databases, and transactions. But choosing solutions that fit requires in-depth scrutiny of a particular organization's SLA priorities, available expertise, and need for products that integrate with other parts of the overall SLM monitoring scheme.

Application Response Measurement (ARM): A Rising Phoenix?

It could be the best-kept secret of SLM: Application Response Measurement (ARM), a standard method of instrumenting applications for management. Initially created by Hewlett-Packard and Tivoli four years ago, ARM comprises APIs designed to be built into networked applications, enabling them to be monitored for a range of performance characteristics, including response time. HP and Tivoli provide free ARM software development kits, and BMC and Compuware support ARM in their application-management products.

Despite all this, ARM seemed, until recently, doomed to obscurity. Even the vendors that supported it weren't able to furnish customer testimonials. Some claimed ARM deployment was in the works but had taken a back seat to other projects, particularly Y2K updates. Other vendors said companies considered ARM so strategic that its use was often kept secret. In the meantime, no volunteers stepped forward to testify to successful ARM implementation.

But ARM's fortunes might be changing. This year, The Open Group, itself newly re-launched after suffering several years of second-class industry citizenship, has declared ARM an approved building block in its overall Open Group Architecture for making intranet services as reliable as dial-up voice networks. It remains to be seen whether the ringing endorsement of Open Group members like Compaq, Fujitsu, HP, Hitachi, IBM, NCR, Siemens, and Sun will make a difference in users' readiness to rewrite their applications with ARM. But coming under the Open Group umbrella will give ARM a boost by furnishing certification and testing for ARM implementations and promoting ARM use in large-scale enterprise software integration projects.

The FCAPS Approach

SLM can be approached not only by domain, but also by function. When doing this, the time-tested ISO model of management serves as a useful starting point. This theoretical approach, dubbed *FCAPS* for short, calls for five basic categories of tasks to be included in any comprehensive network management scheme:

- Fault management
- Configuration
- Accounting
- Performance management
- Security management

We will examine how each of these functions might incorporate SLM monitoring and reporting—and how commercial products can be used to fit the specific requirements.

Fault Management

These days, it's rare to find a network that isn't equipped with some form of fault-reporting software or hardware. The SNMP management systems of the early 1990s were focused primarily on reporting broken links and devices, and the descendants of these early OpenView and Netview systems remain in many organizations today.

Also in today's organizations are the techniques of fault reporting that originated ten years ago. The trouble is, yesterday's fault management systems are no longer able to meet the needs of today's burgeoning networks. The reason is sheer numbers: Larger and more complicated networks breed lots of alerts that can cause as many problems as they solve. When a router breaks, for instance, the management system will not only receive alerts from that device, but also from all the hubs, workstations, servers, and other gear that depend on that router for connectivity. Weeding through the resulting avalanche of alarms can delay troubleshooting and repair—resulting in missed service levels.

To cope with this, a new breed of product has emerged that works alongside standard SNMP managers, sifting their alerts and reporting only those the manager needs to see. Included in this category is Netcool/Omnibus from Micromuse, which lets managers gather and filter events from multiple management systems, including those supporting non-SNMP protocols. In effect, Netcool/Omnibus acts as a manager of managers, providing a single console in which selected events and alerts are displayed to streamline troubleshooting. Another group of products takes event filtering a step further, using built-in intelligence to identify the root cause of network problems from telltale patterns of alerts. The Incharge system from System Management Arts, Eye of the Storm from Prosum, and tsc/Eventwatch from Tavve Software fit this category.

Configuration

Ideally, successful SLM includes the ability to control as well as monitor network devices and connections. But this capability is only just starting to emerge, as vendors add traffic-shaping capabilities to their SLA monitoring tools. The Wise IP/Accelerator hardware/software product from Netreality, for example, combines a traffic monitor and shaper with SLA reporting tools. This lets managers assign bandwidth to applications according to priority. Mission-critical e-commerce applications, for instance, are run at high, guaranteed rates, whereas internal email might get "best effort" status if congestion occurs. There are other vendors with offerings in this space, although many do not have integral SLA reporting tools. Packeteyes from SBE, for example, combines an access router and firewall with software that assigns and controls application bandwidth. There are also software-only products for bandwidth management: The Enterprise Edition software suite from Orchestream, for instance, enforces prioritization of traffic across switches and routers from Cisco, Lucent, and Xedia. On the downside, a lack of standards for policy management has up to now kept products like Orchestream's limited to specific vendors' wares.

Accounting

A key aim of SLM is to keep costs in line. Ironically, products that track the usage of enterprise network services have only recently emerged. These tools, including Netcountant from Apogee Networks, IT Charge Manager from SAS, and Telemate.net from Telemate Software, tap RMON probes and log files in routers and applications in order to tally the amount of bandwidth consumed by a particular application, department, or individual. This data is matched up to a dollar value and placed in a bill. Alternatively, managers can use the data to populate financial reports or forecast the cost of upcoming additions to networking hardware and software.

Because these products are still so new, they haven't reached their full potential yet. It's conceivable, for instance, that by linking these accounting applications to Web load balancers, switches, and bandwidth prioritization gear, IT and network managers could include cost parameters along with network performance in future SLAs. An IT department might, for instance, be able to keep track of how much of a costly leased line or virtual private network a particular group has used in a given month. And if usage threatens to exceed budgeted funds, the department could be notified. Likewise, if more bandwidth is required, a manager can test out various configurations before signing on the dotted line.

Performance

If there is a place of honor among FCAPS functions, performance management can claim it. With few exceptions, most SLM monitoring tools discussed up to this point can be classified as performance management systems because their main purpose is to capture data about how well various portions of the network are performing in terms of uptime, response time, throughput, packet latency, and the like.

Unfortunately, performance management has taken on the "hot topic" status we mentioned at the start of this chapter. Vendors whose products contribute only part of what's required to manage performance—such as event reporting, probes, or protocol analyzers—are "bellying up to the bar" with claims to do the whole job.

In general, products that do performance management share the following characteristics:

- SNMP device management—the capability to gather information from SNMP agents in network devices and systems
- RMON/RMON II or probe links for traffic monitoring—the capability to track the overall performance of network connections
- Response time measurement—the capability to gauge how well applications, databases, and transactions are performing over the intranet
- Real-time event filtering—the capability to generate warnings and alerts when devices break or traffic conditions deteriorate
- Historical trend analysis—storage of performance data over time in order to generate periodic graphical representations of network health and status

A growing number of management systems do provide all the previous features and functions, laying claim to being a new breed of performance management platform. Included are systems like Avesta's Trinity, Loran Kinnetics, Manage.com's Frontline, and NextPoint's S3.

Security

Increased use of the Internet and carrier services in corporate networks has made management of security a full-time job in many networks. Keeping passwords up-to-date, making sure that access is properly assigned, and monitoring software for viruses are just a few of the tasks required to ensure that today's larger, more public networks guard business secrets and avoid resource tampering. A compelling argument for considering security as part of the service level management equation is quite simple. If the security of an environment is compromised, the availability and/or performance of the service can be compromised. Some Service Level Agreements include specific metrics regarding the security of the environment and the data contained therein.

Several vendors of secondary data collectors furnish comprehensive security application suites along with SLM. Unfortunately, many of these products aren't directly integrated with the platform. Exceptions include BullSoft, which offers security management, authentication, monitoring, and documentation as an integral part of its OpenMaster platform.

Reporting Tools

We've spent the lion's share of this chapter describing a framework for selecting products that monitor and capture data for SLM. There's a good reason for this: Without the right input, any SLM project is doomed to failure. Even the best information won't guarantee a successful SLM strategy if the results can't be published effectively. An examination of reporting capabilities is a key part of any SLM product selection.

Unfortunately, when it comes to SLM products, there's a gap between monitoring and reporting—a gap that's not breached by the vendors, who don't like to admit their weaknesses at either end. It's too often assumed that any product that performs SLM monitoring comes with SLM reporting to match. This is definitely not the case. Many primary data collectors like OpenView, for instance, furnish SLM performance data. But they don't ship off the lot with integral SLM report templates. Likewise, some products are designed primarily as reporting tools and rely—at least in part—on imported data from systems like OpenView or BMC Patrol.

In general, it is wisest to keep two things in mind when evaluating SLM reporting tools:

- The information *source*
- The *destination* of reports

Consider the Source

Information sources for SLM refer to the type of data capture already in place, as well as the quality of the data provided. An organization that's invested heavily in a platform like OpenView or Netview, for instance, might want to build on that investment by purchasing the add-on products required for SLM reporting. In contrast, products designed from the ground up for SLM come with their own integral report templates, and if they already hook into other data sources, there's no need to add extra software.

The choice of reporting tool can't be based solely on what's already in place. It's important to consider the type of data that's being captured as well. Management tools in general capture two types of data for SLM: real-time and historical.

Real-time data consists of events reported from the network directly as they occur. Broken routers, congested links, and malfunctioning adapters all generate SNMP alerts that show up as alarms or alerts in fault-management consoles such as OpenView or Netview. This is information that's typically required by network operators in the course of day-to-day troubleshooting and management. In fact, most of the time, management tools with real-time capabilities have the capability to automatically generate a page or dial a phone number to notify operations personnel in the event critical alarms occur. (Operators and other IT personnel can select the particular events ahead of time that will trigger the notification capability.) Still, keep in mind that although real-time data is an important gauge of overall availability and uptime, it can't give the perspective on overall performance required for SLM. Prompt response to an outage can reduce the impact on a particular SLA, or help operations personnel keep to the repair times stipulated in the SLA.

Overall, traditional primary data collectors and fault-management consoles like OpenView don't qualify as SLM tools without some adjustments. Conversely, many early SLM tools, like Infovista's Vistaviews, did not support real-time event handling, although that's now changed as vendors become aware that the ability to pinpoint the number of alarms and outages is a key factor in quantifying network availability.

Historical data comprises metrics of the overall health of specific network segments and connections over time. RMON/RMON II information collected by probes, CSU/DSUs, and packet monitors, for example, can be gathered at specific intervals—daily, weekly, or monthly—and placed in charts or graphs depicting how well service levels were met. The importance of historical data to the overall SLM effort made it easy for performance monitoring vendors like Concord Communications, Desktalk Systems, and Lucent (through their acquisition of International Network Services) to adapt their marketing strategies to fit the SLM trend when it first emerged. That's not to say these vendors didn't proceed to add SLM-specific capabilities to their wares, but getting on the bandwagon was undoubtedly easier for them than for vendors of fault-management applications.

The terms of a specific Service Level Agreement have an impact on the kinds of reports needed. In the case of mission-critical applications, some users will want to know about the occurrence and duration of every device failure. This requires real-time event reporting. In other cases, an SLA might specify that availability of specific devices, such as backbone routers and switches, be reported weekly or even daily, whereas availability for other gear is reported monthly. This makes it vital that an SLM tool be flexible when it comes to the increments of time for which data can be obtained.

Report Destination: Who Will See It?

The other key question to answer about SLM reporting tools is: Who will be viewing the information? Graphs of packet performance over time and host-by-host uptime charts, however useful to a network operator, won't give a technologically challenged executive the needed information about the bottom line. To meet the specific requirements of upper management, SLM vendors generally provide "executive reports" that depict SLM information in more general terms and with a keener eye to the presentation slide. Compuware, Concord, Desktalk, Lucent, Netscout, ProactiveNet, and Quallaby have invested significant effort in creating executive report templates. These vendors also furnish Web access to all reports in an effort to help managers easily distribute SLM data throughout an organization.

A newer trend in SLM reporting is the ability to calculate composite status measurements from a variety of data sources. In this case, data captured from probes, software and hardware agents, and simulation tools is statistically tallied in order to show the overall performance of a specific segment, application, or group. Apptitude, Concord, Desktalk, Lucent, Empirical Software, HP, Netscout, Tavve, and Visual Networks offer composite measurements in their applications.

In some instances, business-level views are also achieved by matching up this performance data with information about the business purpose served. Thus, an executive might be able to see how well the accounting, human resources, and manufacturing divisions were served by information services during the past month. Avesta's Trinity is an example of one system that's geared to furnishing this type of business-level view.

In some instances, managers will need reports that can't be provided by the vendor. For cases like these, many vendors offer APIs and software development kits that allow their wares to be customized. This option might cost extra, however.

Caution

IT managers choosing to use vendor APIs and software development kits (SDKs) sometimes need to spend twice as much as they did to obtain the basic product. Even if APIs or SDKs seem reasonably priced, there might be a need to hire the vendor's professional services team to create customized software that works. In some cases, it might be more practical to simply export data to a third-party reporting package such as Crystal Reports from Seagate rather than going the made-to-order route.

SLM Analysis

It's characteristic of SLM that when it's properly in place in any organization, it starts to exceed its original function. When constituents see the benefits of SLM, they aren't content with a monthly report. Network operators want day-to-day downloads for proactive management. Executives want to see data cut and sifted in various ways to furnish better insight into how the technology they're purchasing is serving the business, and so on.

SLM tools vary widely in their capability to adapt to all these requirements. Some products, such as Desktalk's Trend series, were designed with built-in data analysis flexibility, whereas others, such as the Network Health series from Concord Communications, were advertised from the start as offering off-the-shelf reports that didn't require tweaking. But even if a product furnishes in-depth analytical capability, it might not have the data in hand to do the numbers required. Concord and Desktalk, for instance, have limited real-time data capture capabilities.

Generally speaking, serious data analysis will require the use of sophisticated third-party packages. SAS Institute, the statistical software vendor, now provides a range of data analysis and reporting tools tailored to fit SLM. Among these are the IT Service Vision series, which creates a data warehouse of network, system, and Web performance information. SAS also has added cost accounting, capacity planning, and high-end financial analysis to its suite.

Some organizations will need consulting help to properly analyze SLM data. Cases like these might be best served by reliance on a service from the likes of Lucent, Winterfold Datacomm, or X-Cel Communications. These vendors provide services that can help orchestrate data capture to fuel specially tailored reports and analyses. But as is the case with any kind of customization, extra costs might be involved.

Caution

Vendors usually consider a $2,000-per-day pricetag for consulting help to be a bargain. The value of customized software must be weighed against the outlay beforehand in order to avoid disappointment.

Administration Tools

SLM calls for a new approach to the day-to-day tasks involved in managing and administering network services. After all, it's tough to analyze network costs or ensure ongoing performance if it's not clear what is installed. To make changes as required to improve service levels demands tools that enable network elements to be located and reconfigured quickly and efficiently.

One way to meet these requirements is adoption of better asset-management tools. Products such as N'telligence from Netsuite Development, AssetCenter from Peregrine Systems, and Remedy Asset Management from Remedy can help discover and document network devices, servers, and workstations and keep track of their licenses, service and support records, costs, and configurations. This helps speed up repairs, ultimately boosting service uptime.

Managing software assets is among the biggest challenges in any network. Software distribution tools are offered from vendors like Marimba, which OEMs its Castanet package to a range of framework and console vendors. Specialized packages also are offered to help track servers and desktops throughout multi-site networks and facilitate their upkeep. These include Landesk from Intel, SMS from Microsoft, EDM from Novadigm, Zenworks from Novell, and Netcensus from Tally Systems.

Most of these products deploy SNMP along with proprietary protocols to track and update network software. The Distributed Management Task Force (DMTF) also has created a Common Information Model that can be implemented by vendors to share inventory information across multi-vendor SLM applications. Directories also can help furnish user information to security and accounting applications. The DMTF's Directory Enabled Networks initiative is an effort to standardize the format for directory data, enabling it to be used easily across management applications.

Summary

SLM products span a broad range of functions and formats. What's more, vendors have jumped on the SLM bandwagon in order to promote products that weren't created with service level management in mind. Only by using a framework that keeps the primary purposes and goals of SLM at the forefront can managers hope to make sense of the many offerings crowding the market.

A workable approach is to first look at products according to the SLM functions of monitoring, reporting, analysis, and administration. Then it's important to scope out the monitoring issues—where data is captured and in what format. Careful planning is required to ensure that the right data is gathered in the right spots at the right times to create an adequate basis for service level reporting. When this is accomplished, an organization is ready to choose tools for publishing and analyzing SLM data in ways that meet its particular requirements.

When selecting SLM tools, it is especially important to keep in mind the database format supported by each product. You will need to be able to get data in and out of an SLM system easily. Selecting a system with a proprietary database for back-end functions will limit your ability to customize the software or augment it with third-party products. Many of today's SLM tools are based on open, well-documented databases like SQL Server, so it should not be difficult to select one that meets your requirements.

To be effective, any SLM strategy also needs to be flexible enough to accommodate ongoing information requests. In fact, the test of a successful SLM implementation will be the demands put on the IT department for more information once initial reports are generated. Managers need to be ready to "slice and dice" SLM data in order to meet these demands. Again, in constructing reports, it helps to have an integral database that is familiar to your staff.

Ultimately, SLM monitoring and reporting will lead to a more efficient approach to managing network services; one that calls for improved record-keeping and a tighter centralized control over administrative parameters. The Distributed Management Task Force (DMTF) and other organizations are working to make this happen by creating interoperable schemas for management data in applications, databases, and directories.

PART

III

Recommendations

Chapter

CHAPTER 8

Business Case for Service Level Management

The IT department must ensure that adequate, but not excessive, computing facilities are always available to handle the workloads required by the lines of business with acceptable quality of service. As discussed in previous chapters, this requires proactive service level management during the life cycle of important business applications. Typically, senior management requires a cost/benefit assessment that provides the justification for implementing a service level management strategy.

Cost Justifying Proactive Service Level Management

The cost justification should look across the corporation to determine the benefits of proactive service level management. There are benefits within the IT department, but greater benefits lie in increased productivity within the lines of business, reduced lost opportunity costs, and enhanced customer satisfaction.

Tip

The cost justification for service level management will be much more credible if true business value can be related directly to improved quality of service. This is more powerful than attempting to justify service level management based on cost or staff savings within the IT department.

There might be other, less-tangible benefits such as enhanced brand image and customer loyalty, but it is easier to justify quantifiable benefits that can be objectively measured or calculated.

Key benefits of proactive service level management include the ability to

- Understand the quality of service provided to end users and lines of business
- Optimize the service provided to users of services by automating and centralizing the control of business critical applications and the underlying components such as data, databases, server operating systems, middleware, networks, and server hardware
- Increase business revenue by reducing outages that directly affect business operations
- Increase customer satisfaction and loyalty by ensuring that services used directly by consumers are responsive and available whenever required
- Increase productivity of users within the lines of business through better performance and availability of services
- Proactively plan to meet future business requirements, including workload volumes and required service levels
- Increase the return on investment in IT assets by balancing workloads and obtaining highest levels of component utilization while still meeting service level requirements
- Increase IT staff productivity by implementing proactive planning and management rather than continuously operating in a reactive mode
- Reduce or eliminate penalties associated with contractual commitments to meet specified service levels
- Increase shareholder value by eliminating highly visible outages, which reduce investor confidence

The primary costs associated with implementing service level management are

- IT personnel to plan, implement, monitor, and report against service level agreements
- Software costs for purchasing or developing tools to monitor, diagnose, manage, and report service quality, including problem notification

- Hardware costs for additional servers, workstations, and specialist equipment for supporting the service management software tools
- IT management attention to justify, procure software and hardware, recruit and educate staff, and oversee the operation of a service level management function

During the remainder of this chapter, we will concentrate on methods for identifying and quantifying the benefits because the costs are more easily determined after the service management strategy is determined and appropriate management tools are selected.

Quantifying the Benefits of Service Level Management

A good approach to quantifying service management benefits is to work from the outside inward. That is, look first at the external business impact including the effect on revenue and customer satisfaction, and then examine the impact on productivity within lines of business, and finally, look within the IT department and the effect on IT assets.

Impact on Business Revenue

When critical business applications are unavailable, there is normally an associated loss of business and a reduction in generated revenues. In all cases, this is associated with lost opportunity costs, and in some cases there are flow-on losses due to regulatory penalties and market share losses to competitors.

A recent study of 400 large corporations found that downtime costs an average of $1,400 per minute or approximately $85,000 per hour. The study results are shown in Table 8.1.

Table 8.1 **Costs Associated with System Downtime**

System Availability	Downtime Costs per Year
99%	$7,358,400
99.5%	$3,679,200
99.9%	$736,400
99.99%	$7,000

Note

The cost of downtime varies significantly by industry. Financial trading systems have extremely high costs associated with even minor service disruptions. As more corporations enter the age of e-business, opportunity costs as a result of outages of front office applications will continue to increase.

Business revenue can also be affected by performance degradations that impact the ability to handle the required workload volumes. If the application responsiveness degrades, this can also impact revenues as best illustrated by financial trading systems where additional seconds can lead to significant losses or decrease profits from trades. As e-commerce is used to directly sell goods and services to consumers across the Internet, slow responsiveness can also lead to consumers buying from a competitor.

Quantifying the impact on business revenue requires an understanding of the critical business systems and the associated revenue generated by those systems on an annual basis. This information can be used to calculate an hourly rate, and by assessing the increased service availability due to proactive service management, an associated benefit can be calculated.

Caution

The lines of business should be consulted when calculating revenue impact because they might have manual backup systems that will allow processing to continue in a degraded mode. This produces quantifiable revenues, but at a reduced rate.

Quantifying the impact of slow response times will be more difficult and will require the cooperation of the lines of business. Revenue impact will include any penalties involved in not meeting critical deadlines, as well as the competitive disadvantage associated with reduced effectiveness of internal personnel or lost business due to customers shopping elsewhere.

Customer and Partner Satisfaction and Loyalty

Customer loyalty is becoming more important to most corporations as they attempt to build strong customer relationships, particularly with their best customers. The focus of information technology is shifting from improving the efficiencies within the corporation to improving the effectiveness of the corporation's supply chain as well as its sales channels and marketing efforts. This has led to many front office applications that engage the customer or partner in a dialog and add value to the relationship by providing information or conducting transactions directly with them.

There are a number of methodologies for calculating the value of a deeper relationship with a distributor or customer. One method is to look at the best-penetrated customer of a particular size and in a specified industry. Using that as a guideline, the increased revenue of penetrating all similar customers to the same degree can be calculated. This provides a baseline that must then be scaled to reflect how much of this business potential is affected by improved service quality or would be negatively impacted by failure to meet acceptable service levels for those critical front office applications.

Similarly, the potential of improved relationships with the distribution channels and the effectiveness of supply chain transactions can be used as a basis for calculating the benefit of improved service quality or the negative impact of unacceptable service levels for the critical application services used by these business partners.

End User and Lines of Business Productivity

End user productivity suffers even if other work can be performed when service outages or degradations occur. On average, it takes 20 minutes for an end user to discover an application is restored and get back to the point in the application when the failure occurred. Similarly, if service responsiveness degrades, it takes the service users longer to complete their tasks and business transactions.

Quantifying the benefits of reducing the outages by proactively managing service is a relatively simple matter of calculating the additional time the users will be productive based on increased service availability, and multiplying this by the number of users and the average loaded cost per user per hour.

Tip

When calculating employee costs for productivity calculations, remember to use fully loaded costs, which include salary, bonuses, benefits, equipment costs, real estate, and utilities.

Similar to the benefits of reduced outages, the benefits associated with improved and consistent responsiveness can be calculated by determining how much more work can be performed in a given time period. This can translate into cost avoidance by deferring the hiring of additional employees.

Note

User productivity is also affected by offline activities such as output distribution and information archival and retrieval. When determining the scope of service management in your environment, the service level agreement should extend to cover these offline requirements.

Proactive Business and Capacity Planning

By understanding future business applications and workloads as well as required service levels, it is possible to proactively plan the necessary IT architecture and assets to meet these requirements. This ensures that adequate capacity will be available and it also supports a policy of just-in-time upgrades. Using this approach allows better use of capital, and the net present value of deferring hardware purchases can be calculated along with any associated costs for maintenance charges and upgrading software licenses.

Increased Return on Investment in IT Assets

Proactive management of service levels allows higher utilization levels of IT components because more accurate measurement of service quality is possible and workloads can be better balanced across available resources. This in turn defers the need to upgrade hardware and software.

Similarly, a number of corporations deploy additional resources to provide redundant capacity that can be used in the event of an outage. This might not be a cost-effective approach because redundant systems protect against only one thing: hardware failure, which is the fifth leading cause of downtime. Planned maintenance, application failure, operator error, and operating system failure occur more often. Proactively managing service levels can often meet the requirements of service level agreements without having redundant hardware systems in place because the more frequent causes of outages are reduced or eliminated. This saves the costs of the hardware, software, maintenance, and operating personnel associated with the redundant systems.

Increased IT Personnel Productivity

Industry research firms have found that through the use of a proactive service management methodology and associated tools, IT operational support personnel can increase productivity from 25% to over 300%. By automating tedious and repetitive tasks, human error and subsequent corrective actions are also significantly reduced.

Monitoring and managing a complex, distributed, heterogeneous environment from a service orientation, rather than managing individual components in isolation, significantly increases the quality of services as well as the productivity of network and systems management personnel.

Capturing historical information on the utilization and performance of the IT infrastructure supports proactive analysis of problem areas and enables corrective actions to be taken before problems occur. This results in better utilization of IT staff and reduces reactive fire fighting.

When examining service management tools, it is important to balance the productivity gains with the costs and resources to implement the solution. Chapter 7, "Service Level Management Products," discusses the various management solutions available. Management solutions that focus on specific application services can provide a more rapid implementation that results in cost savings, quicker time to value, and increased IT staff productivity. By utilizing event management tools and setting thresholds on critical items such as application errors, database space availability, CPU utilization, application response time, and other critical components, alerts and warnings can be sent to support personnel to prevent problems before they occur. This increases the effectiveness of IT personnel and allows them to be more proactive.

Tip

When implementing a service level management solution, it is best to start with the most critical or highly visible service provided by the IT department. By focusing on one service at a time, the probability of a successful implementation increases significantly and the initial success leads to continued management support for service level management of additional services.

The decision of whether to develop or acquire service level management tools can also affect IT staff productivity. Acquiring solutions rather than developing and maintaining in-house tools will free up valuable resources for revenue generating applications or other critical applications. In a case in which the application is hosted on unique, old, or specialized hardware, there might be no commercial service level management solutions available. In this case, it is very important to keep development costs associated with building the management tools to a minimum required to provide an acceptable level of monitoring and reporting. Remember to factor in ongoing maintenance when doing the cost/benefit analysis of adding additional functionality.

Quantifying the benefits associated with improved IT staff productivity requires an assessment of the deferred costs associated with being able to do more with the existing or fewer staff. After this assessment is made, calculating savings is easily accomplished using average fully loaded employee costs.

A Sample Cost Justification Worksheet

Table 8.2 is a sample worksheet that was used by one large corporation to calculate the benefits of proactive service level management. Some of the specific formulae used for the calculations follow the worksheet. The following benefit categories are used in the worksheet:

- Employee costs within lines of business—these are the end users of services provided by the IT department
- Average number of personnel using application servers
- IT support personnel costs
- Service downtime—the percentage of time the application service is unavailable during normal business hours
- Lost employee productivity due to service outages that could be prevented by service management
- Lost business due to service outages that could have been prevented by service management
- Cost of customer dissatisfaction due to service outages and degradation that could have been prevented by service management

- Costs associated with failure to meet service level agreements
- Increased IT personnel productivity due to implementing proactive service management and associated tools

---

Note

In the interests of simplicity, this worksheet uses only outages for determining the costs associated with not implementing proactive service management. No costs are calculated for lost revenue and productivity due to degradation in service responsiveness. Nor are the opportunity costs of better utilization of IT assets and deferring upgrades factored into the worksheet.

Table 8.2 **Cost Justification Worksheet**

NUMBERS ARE REPRESENTATIVE OF AN AVERAGE BUSINESS

Employee Costs

Annual salary of personnel using application services	$40,000
Annual salary of IT support personnel	60,000
Percentage of annual salary to add for benefits	30%
Facilities costs per employee per year	5,000
Number of personnel using application services	500
Percentage of their time using the applications	50%
Number of IT operations management personnel	15
Percentage of IT operations time connected to servers	50%

IT Infrastructure – Hardware

Number of application servers	50
Estimated percentage of growth of application servers	10%
Percentage of availability during business hours	99.5%

IT Infrastructure – Software

Number of databases	100
Estimated percentage of growth of databases	10%

Business and Income Numbers

Annual income related to application services	100,000,000
Number of business hours per day	12
Number of business days per week	6
Estimated value of acceptable applications service and related customer satisfaction	500,000
Estimated percentage of business lost due to downtime	3%

SLA Penalties

Penalties per hour outside SLA	2,000
Percentage of application downtime outside SLA agreement	10%

COSTS ASSOCIATED WITH NOT MANAGING SERVICE

Employee Costs

Cost per year of personnel on application servers	57,000
Cost per hour per individual	28.50
Cost per hour total	14,250
Cost per year of IT support personnel	83,000
Cost per hour per individual	41.50
Cost per hour total	1,038

Application Service Downtime

Percentage of application downtime	0.50%
Annual unscheduled downtime in hours for all servers	936
Annual unscheduled downtime during business hours	468

Lost Productivity for Application Downtime

Personnel on application servers	3,334,500
IT support personnel	242,775
Total	3,577,275

Lost Business

Hourly income related to server applications	26,709
Annual lost business due to application downtime	375,000

Customer Satisfaction

Estimated value of customer satisfaction impact	500,000

SLA Penalties Cost

Total SLA cost per year	93,600

Improved IT Staff Productivity

Ratio of servers to IT systems management support personnel	3
Ratio of databases to DBAs	10
Cost avoidance of tools allowing additional IT staff productivity	207,500

SUMMARY

Lost productivity for application downtime	$3,577,275
Lost business	$375,000
Customer satisfaction	$500,000
SLA penalties cost	$93,600
Improved IT productivity	$207,500
Total	$4,753,375

Calculations Used in Worksheet

Most of the items in Table 8.2 are easily calculated. We have included the calculations for representative items in the following sections. These formulae are useful for creating a spreadsheet that can be used to calculate the benefits under various scenarios.

Employee Costs

The costs of the employees should be calculated using fully loaded costs including benefits and facilities costs. These costs will vary based on employee type. In this worksheet, we have only considered two categories of employees: IT personnel and others.

- Cost per year of personnel using application services:

  (annual salary)+(benefits)+(facilities cost per employee)
- Cost per hour per individual:

  (cost per year of personnel using application services)/(2000)
  [40 hours/week×50 weeks/year]
- Cost per hour total:

  (cost per hour per individual)×(number of employees using application services)
- IT operations personnel calculations are similar to the calculations shown here.

Application Downtime

The costs associated with downtime include both unscheduled downtime due to failures as well as planned downtime for maintenance that extends into normal business hours.

- Percentage of application downtime:

  (100)−(percentage of availability during business hours)
- Annual unscheduled downtime in hours for all servers:

  (number of business hours per day)×(number of business days per week)×(52 weeks per year)×(number of servers)×(percentage of downtime during business hours)
- Annual unscheduled downtime during business hours:

  (number of business hours per day)/(24)×(annual unscheduled downtime in hours for all servers)

Lost Productivity for Application Downtime

Application downtime affects the productivity of users within the lines of business as well as support personnel and IT staff.

- Personnel on application servers:

  (cost per hour)×(annual unscheduled downtime during business hours)×(percentage of time using applications)

- IT support personnel:

  (cost per hour)×(annual unscheduled downtime during business hours)×(percentage of time IT & DBAs connected to servers)

Lost Business

When calculating lost income due to unscheduled downtime, we must factor the revenue normally generated by those application services to account for the ability to operate manually in a degraded mode.

- Hourly income related to server applications:

  (annual income related to server applications)/((number of business hours per day)×(number of business days per week))×(52 weeks per year)

- Annual lost business due to application downtime:

  (hourly income related to server applications)×(annual unscheduled downtime during business hours)×(estimated percentage of business lost due to downtime)

- Customer Satisfaction:

  (estimated value of application availability to customers—this is an estimate of future business that will be affected by unacceptable quality of service)

SLA Penalty Cost per Year

Many service level agreements contain penalty clauses for failure to achieve required service levels. This is particularly important if services are provided to external users such as business partners. These penalties should be accounted for in the cost justification.

- Total SLA penalties cost per year:

  (cost per hour)×(annual unscheduled downtime during business hours)×(percentage of application downtime outside of SLA agreement)

Cost Avoidance Due to Improved IT Staff Productivity

Using a proactive service management methodology along with automated management tools can significantly improve the productivity of IT staff, and thus avoid the costs of additional personnel.

- Ratio of servers to IT systems management support personnel:

  (number of application servers)/(number of IT operations management personnel)

- Ratio of databases to DBAs:

  (number of databases)/(number of DBAs)

- The preceding figures are calculated twice—first without tools, and a second time using automated management tools.

- The costs associated with managing the IT environment manually are

  (number of application servers)×(estimated growth of application servers)/(ratio of servers to IT systems management support personnel)×(cost per year of IT support personnel) [plus DBA costs calculated in a similar fashion]

- Cost avoidance of tools allowing additional productivity:

  The difference between the calculation using the ratio of IT personnel to servers without management tools and the calculation using the ratio of IT support personnel to servers using management tools.

Note

Industry analysts have estimated that the practical limit of the number of databases a database administrator can manage manually is from five to ten. Through the use of tools that take proactive actions, this number rises to fifty or more. Similar ratios can be used for system support personnel.

Summary

It is possible to quantify the cost savings associated with implementing proactive service level management strategies and tools. When doing so, it is important to begin with the impact on business revenue, productivity, and customer satisfaction. Additional cost avoidance resulting from improved IT staff productivity, better return on investment in IT assets, and deferring system upgrades can also be used to justify service level management.

Appendix E provides an actual case study of qualitative value and quantitative return on investment for implementing service level management for an SAP application at a service provider.

CHAPTER 9

Implementing Service Level Management

Readers can pause at the start of this chapter. After all, we've covered the fundamental concepts and parameters of SLAs and offered a framework for product selection. Isn't that what implementing service level management is all about?

The answer is a resounding no. In fact, we've only laid the groundwork. Successfully implementing service level management (SLM) calls for more than buying some software and slapping a contract on the desk of the nearest department head. It requires a *strategy*, an organized, flexible plan for introducing SLAs and working with them day to day to achieve maximum efficiency and savings. Without this, projects can fail despite the best efforts to make them work.

Consider the following case: A couple of years back, a network manager working for a large Eastern retailer decided SLM would suit his firm. He hired a consultant to scope out the basics and evaluate products. The CIO signed off. After a large expenditure, software was installed and SLA templates prepared. The first of these was sent to the head of the customer service department, the largest in-house IT user in the company—where it sat on her desk. Time passed. Other divisions were sent SLA forms with similar results. A meeting was called to explain the benefits of the new system, during which the head of customer service asked why she hadn't been given the opportunity to help shape the terms of her SLA. She did not, she pointed out, have time to help IT do its job. The other managers present at the meeting concurred. The next day, the network manager found himself summoned to the boss's office for a long talk about the high cost of his pet project. Two months later, the manager who'd instigated SLM resigned.

This anecdote illustrates that good intentions and products don't constitute an SLM strategy. Instead, what's needed is an in-depth analysis of a company's unique culture and requirements, with a clear sense of information regarding potential pitfalls and opportunities. The network manager wasn't wrong to propose service level management. In fact, he could have been a trendsetter. His products and templates were state of the art. The trouble was, he hadn't bothered to consider how best to introduce SLM to his constituents. He had not focused on soliciting buy-in from all parts of the business, not just IT. He had mistakenly focused on the network layer alone, and he had not followed an *inclusive* strategy that incorporated all services that would be affected by SLM. Inevitably, the vacuum of unanswered questions soon filled with misunderstanding and political rivalry. In the end, our hero fell victim to his own initiative.

Unfortunately, it's a scenario that's repeated all too often in today's business world. But with proper planning, it can be avoided. In this chapter, we'll outline ways to construct an effective SLM strategy, thereby not only avoiding failure, but also planning for best results in real-world situations.

Planning the Rollout

Any business innovation requires some form of planned introduction to succeed. In effect, managers must sell a new technology or procedure to those members of the corporation who'll be charged with making it work. There's a simple reason for this: People resist change. From the shop floor to the boardroom, human nature tends to stick with the status quo, even with its problems and difficulties. Some of this originates in fear: Employees and executives might perceive that adopting a new procedure will threaten their usefulness or position in the company. Some think taking time out to make a change will hinder their ability to meet hectic schedules and deadlines. And of course, political pressures abound.

Any procedure for introducing new technology—including SLM—must be able to meet and overcome most arguments for resistance. Generally, this can be achieved by following specific guidelines:

1. Explain and demonstrate the benefits clearly.
2. Define the goals.

3. Enlist support from significant constituents.

4. Set up resources to assist staff during the transition.

5. Put ongoing controls in place.

An effective SLM strategy will cover all these points. But beware: The procedure isn't as simple as following five steps to success. Read on.

First Things First

A key lesson of the anecdote related previously is that managers can't thrust SLAs on all departments (that is, clients) at once and expect success. Instead, SLM must be introduced on a client-by-client basis. This ensures that the IT manager, acting in the role of service provider to various lines of business, can furnish the maximum attention to each client. It also guards against the confusion—and ultimately, the political upheaval and rebellion—that can erupt when multiple departments clamor at once to grasp new technology. But taking the client-by-client approach means it's vital to choose a starting point that will get the project off on the right foot.

It might come as a surprise that the best place to start an SLM project is not with the first client. Instead, it is within the IT department itself. Make sure that support for SLM is consistent throughout the IT organization—from the CIO on down through the ranks of those operations folk who will be responsible for responding to problem calls and assembling the day-to-day reports the SLA requires.

The necessity for this can be illustrated by another anecdote. Not long ago, the IT manager of a large Midwestern bank decided to start a series of SLAs within her organization. All went well. She was able to enlist the support of top management, purchase the necessary software tools, and set an implementation schedule with her immediate staff. After several meetings, she also obtained the support of two key in-house constituents who seemed eager to start the process. SLAs were assembled, approved, and signed. The process officially began. A few days passed uneventfully. Then late one morning, the executive in charge of one of the constituent departments called the IT manager in a rage. What was the idea of breaking their SLA so soon into the cycle? he thundered. Didn't they have a deal? After some questioning, the IT manager learned that a server had crashed first thing that morning. A call to the IT help desk had failed to produce a fix within the agreed-on time period of three hours. In a panic, the IT manager checked with the help desk, only to learn that her top SLA constituent had been relegated to the bottom of the priority list for that morning, in keeping with usual procedure. Apparently, the help desk hadn't been informed about the existence of a special-case SLA for the department whose server failed.

This story shows clearly what can happen when trouble isn't taken up front to obtain top-down buy-in by all IT personnel, from the CIO down. The concepts of SLM cannot be effective unless all IT personnel are informed of their particular role in making the SLA work.

The First Client

After the IT department itself is fully briefed on its roles and responsibilities, it is time to choose a clientele. Who will be first?

In choosing a first client, it's best to pick according to need and visibility within the corporation. But there are no hard and fast rules, and in the end the best course of action will depend on the company's particular circumstances. The following selection criteria can help:

- **The area most critical to the business**—It's an IT rule of thumb that network applications aren't created equal. A financial services company measures its lifeblood in the uptime of its trading network. An online retailer wants nothing to halt the flow of orders. If SLM implementers succeed in pleasing these tough constituents, it's a safe bet others will fall into line.

- **Where most improvement is needed**—Specific departments might suffer more than others from poor response time and availability. Getting these clients on track first helps demonstrate SLM's capacity for improving network functionality. Also, making substantial improvements lends a sense of drama and achievement to the project.

- **The most disgruntled group**—Every company has departments that routinely require special handling. Perhaps they have the most demanding network requirements (not to be mistaken for the most important or mission-critical ones). Or they might routinely avoid IT, working around standard technologies. Putting the toughest group first might make the rest of the job a breeze.

- **The most politically powerful group**—These are the folks who can make or break any technology initiative. Often, they belong to the area most critical to the business—but there are exceptions. The office of the CEO or CFO, for instance, is often a bellwether for acceptable procedures.

- **Areas of highest/lowest visibility**—Sometimes it's a good plan to start an SLM rollout wherever it will show up the most—or the least. If you're confident of success and want only to make an eye-catching start, choose the shop floor, the trading floor, the customer service center, or another headquarters-based division whose work is widely seen and discussed. The in-house publicity will pave the way forward. Conversely, if you're facing difficulties, choosing an area of low visibility—remote training centers, building maintenance—might help minimize exposure during the start-up phase.

Making Contact

When a starting point for introducing SLM has been chosen, the next step is to initiate contact with the prospective client. This needs to be done from the top. SLM can't succeed without the endorsement of the folks who appear at the head of the client's org chart. Don't make the common mistake of assuming that the boss is too busy or doesn't care about the changes you're trying to make. Also don't assume that those below him in the organization will fall into step on their own.

When you've decided whom to contact, it's time to make your pitch. SLM puts any IT manager in the position of a service provider who must sell the client on a proposal's benefits. Set up a formal meeting with your target executives and give a standard business presentation, complete with graphics (see Table 9.1). This might be your chance to become a corporate hero. Don't reduce your effectiveness with poor preparation.

Table 9.1   **The SLM Presentation: Do's and Don'ts**

DO	DON'T
Contact the top-level personnel in the client department to ask for the meeting.	Assume that the client boss is too busy, orthat underlings will carry the message more effectively.
Call to set an appointment for making your presentation.	Use email alone to contact your target executives.
Create a business-quality presentation for the initial meeting.	Go into the first meeting empty-handed or with handwritten notes.
Prepare a schedule for implementation to share with the client.	Be vague about goals or timelines.
Have a contract template ready for discussion.	Go to the first meeting without a template or thrust a template on the without asking for input client later.
Field all questions calmly and pleasantly.	Get argumentative or defensive when challenged.

After the presentation, be ready for confrontation. Don't expect the benefits of SLM to be immediately evident. Furthermore, the audience (that is, the client) is very apt to be antagonistic to the service provider (regardless of whether it is internal or external). Certainly in a majority of companies today, the IT department is viewed with a mixture of attitudes ranging from mild suspicion to open hostility.

As with any new technology, there will be plenty of questions. Field these pleasantly and with candor. Do not become defensive—if you do become defensive, your client will think you have something to defend. Similarly, any aggressive behavior will work against you.

Going Live with SLM

After SLM has been successfully introduced and a first client chosen, SLM deployment can begin in force. In general, this is a process of the following five steps:

1. Setting up the service management team.
2. Obtaining a performance baseline.
3. Negotiating service levels.
4. Implementing service management tools.
5. Establishing reporting procedures.

We will explore each step in detail.

Setting Up the Team

After the client has committed to participating in the SLM rollout, it's important to select a team as quickly as possible. Ideally, this should start out as a small group comprised equally of top staffers from IT and the client department. Keeping the group small makes it easier to keep the focus, lay the groundwork, and make any adjustments. As time passes, members can be added if need be. Alternatively, folks might opt to drop off the team after things get going.

On the IT side, include representatives of all areas involved. If the service has been properly mapped out from end to end, this will be easy to establish. For example, a customer service department might rely on a LAN and WAN as well as hosted applications. Three different groups within IT might control these elements. Each group needs to be represented on the team, at least initially, to ensure that SLAs are properly defined.

Although the appointment of a single coordinator is practical, in most instances, there is no need to designate an official leader for the SLM start-up team. The reason for this is that in most cases, members of the team need to perceive themselves as partners in the SLM process, not as recipients of another division's policy. Also, both sides represented on the team will play important roles. The client may decide on the time and place for the meeting and kick things off, but IT will be expected to take the lead in presenting choices and making recommendations. Be careful: IT representatives should act as trusted advisers without forcing their will on the group. In the final analysis, both client and IT staffers should play an equal role in decision making.

Obtaining a Baseline

No SLM strategy can begin without a baseline of performance. Baselining, or monitoring the network and systems to determine the present state of performance, is crucial in determining 1) how services need to be changed for more satisfactory performance, and 2) how services will be maintained and guaranteed over time. The operative principle is simple: You must know where you are before you can proceed to a better place.

Taking a baseline doesn't mean racing to the nearest network connector with a portable monitor. Unless all parties agree to a set of fundamental parameters ahead of time—and clearly understand what they're agreeing to—the baseline report will be worthless.

Start by deciding what measurements will be needed to adequately identify existing network and system performance. In most cases, these boil down to *availability*, or uptime of all devices and system, and *performance*, defined in terms of response time, network latency, or job turnaround. As ever, it's important to keep the focus on how the *end user* perceives the service. The end user is the consumer, whereas IT is the service provider. The end-user experience determines how the service is actually meeting key business goals.

Clearly explain all metrics as you suggest them, and make sure that you consult with colleagues in other parts of IT before suggesting anything. Clients are likely to be confused if metrics are explained inadequately or if multiple metrics are presented for the same service. Worse, they might feel IT is attempting to mystify them in order to gain control of the project. Perceptions like these can sound the death knell for SLM.

Next, determine who will be responsible for capturing the metrics, which methodology will be used, and how the data will be captured. If application response time and network availability are determined to be the key baseline elements, two distinct measurements might need to be taken by two IT groups using two distinct types of instruments. The network group, for instance, might gauge uptime via a performance monitor, and the systems group might use a software agent to measure application response time at the server. Choose a time and place for coordinating input from multiple sources.

It's also vital to determine the time values for the baseline. Careful consideration must be given to the time interval over which samples or measurements will be taken, as well as the overall period of time allowed for baseline sampling. These values probably will end up in the SLA itself, so it's important to give this some thought, and perhaps even to run through a few trials before coming to a final decision.

Regarding time intervals for sampling, it's generally best to err on the side of granularity. If you start out with too much data, it can always be reduced to a significant and accurate figure. Too little information, on the other hand, defeats the purpose of baselining. Start by measuring at least on an hourly basis, then tally results into daily and weekly averages.

Let the duration of baseline sampling be determined by the business cycle itself. A payroll application might show the full range of possible variations in response time and availability over the two to six weeks it takes to complete a company payroll. In contrast, a customer service department specializing in seasonal equipment might peak in bandwidth and system requirements for three months of the year, and then show minor fluctuation for the remaining nine months. In that instance, a baseline might have to be taken twice in one year to establish reasonable performance expectations.

Note

SLM team members must agree on the following parameters before baselining can begin:

- WHAT the specific metrics will be

- WHO will measure baseline performance

- HOW the measurements will be taken

- WHERE the baseline will be taken

- WHEN it will be taken (over what time period)

Negotiating Service Levels

After the baseline performance measurement is taken, the SLM team is ready to start finalizing the service levels for the actual SLA. If the baseline has been properly conducted, this step should take care of itself. In many instances, the metrics and sampling intervals chosen for the baseline project can be carried over into the ongoing contract. But lessons learned during baselining should be applied as much as possible. The baseline might reveal, for instance, that response time for a particular application hasn't been up to par. New equipment or network services might need to be procured. When that's done, expectations from IT and the client can be set and an SLA established.

Keep in mind that non-technical clients need help in setting realistic performance expectations. You might need to explain that the nature of technology itself—not a lack of interest on the part of IT—is responsible for making 100% uptime doable only if considerable funds are shelled out for multiple redundancy. Clients might also need counsel in order to avoid shortchanging themselves. One company we worked with recently signed for 99% uptime per month on all WAN links ordered from a particular carrier—but soon found out that metric allowed for several hours of downtime every 30 days. It took some haggling, but adjusting the 99% figure to reflect biweekly rather than monthly performance resulted in significant savings for the company.

Implementing Service Management Tools

It might seem odd to describe SLM tool implementation following a section on baselining. In fact, it's a logical progression. Establishing baseline parameters helps IT managers set goals. That in turn helps them scope out the nature of the work to be done—and assemble the right tools for the task.

In Chapter 7, "Service Level Management Products," we created a framework for product selection, including in-depth coverage of specific product groups and their characteristics. Now it is time to apply that information to your company's specific SLM requirements. At this juncture, it is helpful to list your SLM requirements alongside the tools available to meet them. Table 9.2 illustrates how you might create a worksheet to match your requirements with potential sources of SLM data before going shopping:

Table 9.2   **Charting SLM Tool Implementation**

General Metrics	Specific Metrics	Sources
Availability	Network availability	Network management platforms
		Performance management applications
		Protocol analyzers
		Traffic monitors
		RMON probes
	System uptime	Systems management platforms
		Systems management applications
		System log files
		Some network management systems and performance management applications

continues

Table 9.2 **Continued**

General Metrics	Specific Metrics	Sources
Performance	Network latency	Performance management applications
		Protocol analyzers
		Traffic monitors
		RMON probes
	Network response time (roundtrip from end user workstation; roundtrip from server)	Performance management applications
		Protocol analyzers
		Traffic monitors
		RMON probes
Workload levels	Transaction rates	Log files
		Systems management platforms and applications
	Batch job completions	Log files
Other	Recoverability (mean time to repair)	Asset management systems
	Security	Log files
		Radius servers

Start by taking stock of what you already have. You might have SLM tools that you don't recognize already on hand. Management systems, application log files, and performance management applications all can be used to obtain SLM metrics. By creating a record-keeping database and customized reports, it might be possible to minimize the need to acquire additional products.

Another alternative to acquiring additional products is to upgrade existing tools. For example, most IT organizations use one or more protocol analyzers or network monitors. Nearly all these devices feature upgrades and add-ons for SLM implementation. Not only can these enhancements equip monitors and analyzers with SLA reporting functions, they also can extend their scope of functionality. Vendors like Concord Communications and Netscout now furnish basic application response-time measurement along with traffic monitoring. The same goes for products originally designed only to measure application performance. BMC Patrol, long known for app-management wares, now works with a range of network management platforms and performance monitoring tools. Upgrading existing products can usually be done simply by installing new releases of products to which you are entitled under current maintenance agreements for those products.

Alternatively, although upgrading a product to a new version (as opposed to a new release) will not normally be free, it will usually be much cheaper than acquiring new products.

Many SLM implementers will choose to augment incumbent products with new tools—introducing software from the likes of Quallaby to create databases and reports using output from Openview or BMC Patrol, for instance. When shopping for new tools, however, it's important to build on what's in place. Keep the following checklist in mind during all new-tool evaluations:

- Will it run on the existing network?
- Will it run on existing hardware, or will it require new servers or workstations?
- Will it run under the current operating systems?
- Does it interoperate with or support network or systems management products now in place (for example, HP Openview, BMC Patrol)?
- Does it support databases already installed?

In answering these questions, dig into details. Avoid disappointment and embarrassment by making sure that newly acquired SLM tools match specific releases of operating system, database, and management products in house. Nail down support contracts before officially introducing new tools: Ask all vendors for a commitment to furnish upgrades to ensure that these key parts of your SLM system keep working together.

Establishing Reporting Procedures

When the baseline is taken and tools are selected for ongoing SLM measurement, it is time to think carefully about SLM reporting procedures:

- WHO will generate the reports?
- WHERE will reports be generated?
- WHEN will reports be generated?
- WHO will be on the distribution list?
- HOW will the reports be distributed?

Don't assume that any of this will take care of itself. It is not a given that the same department that takes the SLM metrics will present them to the client. This might in fact be the best approach, but that decision should be reached only after consideration by the SLM team. The chief concern is whether all parties trust the source of SLM reports. If a particular division of IT, for instance, will be taking the metrics, are all team members comfortable enough with that division to ask questions, request adjustments, and make changes as needed? Or will hidden mistrust and rivalries threaten the project? Will the group doing the monitoring have time to deal with all this? Follow your instincts here. Remember, anything shoved under the carpet at this point will surface in one way or another later on. If you sense problems, it might be best to charge one or two team members with reviewing metrics and generating reports.

In many instances, complex SLAs will call for input from multiple departments. If this is the case, create a reporting team to coordinate results. This team also should be accountable for the results—don't enable "buck passing." Pick folks who have the time, the ability, and the diplomacy to get the job done properly.

The next choice is when to issue reports. Much depends on the terms of the SLA itself. If a contract stipulates that IT must live up to a monthly service level, reports should be delivered at a set time each month, preferably in time for the client to obtain credit against next month's bill. In some cases, clients might want more frequent reports, even if the terms of the contract call for once-a-month review. Encourage all parties to compromise in order to reach a frequency that is easy to meet within everyone's schedule, while allowing time for discussion and changes.

Next, establish a report distribution list. This can be tricky. If too many people receive reports, you might be faced with a periodic chorus of opinions and demands (depending, of course, on how well you've managed to field input up front). But too few recipients can lower the project's visibility and value. Each organization will have its own circumstances to consider, but in most instances, itis best to err on the side of having too many rather than too few included in the SLM report loop. If you've done your job ahead of time, report recipients shouldn't have much to complain about or change. And some folks, happy to have been included in the first place, will tend to drop out of active participation over time. An alternative that is growing in popularity is the use of a Web site with authenticated access to make the SLM report information available to clients. However, a study of IT managers by Enterprise Management Associates (see Figure 9.1) found that hard-copy reports are still the most favored method of distributing information about SLM performance.

The capabilities of the SLM tools chosen will help determine how reports are distributed. As noted, many SLM tools today are Web-enabled: Results can be emailed over the Internet or posted to a Web site for general browser access. Where Web distribution isn't possible, the time and trouble it takes to get reports to the right people should influence the size of the distribution list. Alternatively, someone might be designated to supervise the actual publishing and distribution of reports. Using administrative staff or part-time help might be economical ways to get the job done.

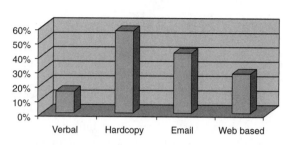

Figure 9.1   *The format of reports to end users.*

Following Through

If you've followed an orderly and well thought out strategy, your SLM rollout should proceed smoothly. But don't rest on your laurels. All SLM projects require continuous care and feeding to stay successful. Part of a winning strategy is a follow-up program of continual improvement. This doesn't mean that you must make changes just to keep up the appearance of flexibility. It does mean that you need to be open to suggestions and willing to make corrections to any aspect of the project as needed.

Sometimes this means parting graciously with pet products and plans. Consider the following case: One IT manager I know implemented SLM in his company using a management system he'd already installed. Working overtime, he prepared SLA templates, a database, and reports tailored to fit the incumbent system. The savings realized from this earned my friend praise and a bonus. Time passed, and the success of the SLM project caused other clients in the company to clamor for their own contracts, based on new parameters. It was clear new tools were needed to meet these requests. One day, one of the man's IT colleagues unexpectedly presented the SLM team with a sweeping proposal for a new suite of tools he'd evaluated. My friend felt slighted and argued publicly against the purchase. Eventually, this caused rivalries to surface, the boss took sides, and my friend felt compelled to take a back seat on the SLM team. By failing to recognize that following new suggestions did not detract from the value of his contribution, my friend stopped reaping the rewards of his success.

This story shows that the right attitude is an important first step in any SLM follow-up plan. But it's just a first step. To ensure continual improvement, you need to get input at the right time and in the right format. A good review process makes this happen. This includes 1) getting input from members of the SLM team in regularly scheduled evaluation meetings, 2) conducting client satisfaction surveys to get input that might not be put forward in a public meeting, and 3) finding ways to keeping ongoing communications open and constructive. We will examine these elements individually:

Meetings—Regular team meetings are key to the ongoing success of any SLM project. Plan to convene at the same time each month. Make sure that all members are present. Keep the focus positive: This is not a gripe session. Instead, use the format of a progress report where suggestions for improvement are welcomed. For instance, don't forget to keep clients informed about technology innovations that might help the cause. The latest traffic monitor or performance management application might offer a way to do the job better. Use your position to inform, not dictate. When changes need to be made, set guidelines for decision-making—use a consensus of opinion or majority vote to establish a plan of action.

Satisfaction surveys—This is a time-tested review method for large organizations. Start by creating a questionnaire. During the monthly team meeting, ask for input and make changes as needed. Then choose a time and place to distribute the survey. If the Web is used for SLM reports, that might be the place to post the questionnaire. Otherwise, you can print it and distribute it in sealed inter-office envelopes. Give participants the option to deliver their responses anonymously. Publish the results in a brief summary for distribution to team members. Then assemble a list of objectives to be met as a result of the survey and set a timetable for meeting those objectives.

Ongoing communications—Don't limit your review process to meetings and satisfaction surveys. Stay proactive and try to anticipate problems. Watch for organizational changes like the regrouping of a department or the departure or arrival onboard of key personnel. When a new person enters the group, take time to stop by and offer to explain procedures or answer questions. Even when SLM procedures run smoothly, don't be lulled into a false sense of security. Maintain regular contact with clients, and when the procedures are in working order, keep up the contact at various levels. Talk to clients who are part of the SLM team, as well as those staffers responsible for using the service in the trenches.

Dealing with Difficulties

In some instances, SLM will meet resistance despite your best efforts. Maybe one department feels snubbed because they haven't been chosen to pilot the new project. Or a new client who is working with an SLA thinks the terms of the contract need changing.

Here, as ever, start at the top. When there is dissatisfaction on the part of a client, it will usually float to the top of the group before it comes across to your department. Often, dissatisfaction in the ranks originates with messages from leading executives. So make sure that you're dealing with senior staff.

When exploring the reason for dissatisfaction, be proactive. If you've heard grum-blings about SLAs, ask for input: "How is the agreement working for you?" "Can we meet to discuss any adjustments that need to be made?" "How can we help make this work better for your group?" Don't wait for the client to become unhappier. Don't think that by hiding in your hole you'll avoid confrontation. If anything, putting off contact will cause disgruntlement to fester and increase the chances of ultimate SLM rejection.

When complaints are voiced, try to defuse them before they get to be insur-mountable obstacles or crises. If a client is unhappy with the time interval being monitored for service level performance, change it. Don't ask for more time or argue against it. Instead, give a simple response such as, "Yes, that sounds like a good idea, let's give it a try." Demonstrating your willingness to act as the client wants will dispel suspicions that you're using your technical expertise to rule the roost.

Sometimes, mistakes will be made. You might fail to be proactive or initiate SLM contact with clients. If this happens, there is a risk that anything you say regarding SLM will be viewed with skepticism. You must accept this. You made a mistake by not being proactive or by responding inadequately to your clients, and you must pay the price. There is no magic fix. Candor and honesty, coupled with open com-munication, stand the best chance of healing the wound over time. So if you find yourself confronted by an unhappy client, be frank. Admit your mistakes, outline your plans to resolve the problems, and move forward. Invite the client to work with you to establish SLAs that will meet their requirements. And keep the lines of communication open. Where problems have occurred, it's important to exceed the minimum level of dialog that the SLA process requires.

Summary

Effective implementation of SLM requires more than good intentions and good products. It calls for a carefully considered strategy that emphasizes cooperation and planning. IT managers can ensure success by first analyzing their company's unique culture; then proceeding with an open mind and a willing attitude to cre-ate a plan that fits it. Putting the plan into action requires assembling a team of professionals who are committed to the rollout. The team must use a thorough, orderly process to create SLAs, track them, and distribute reports in agreed-upon formats. In addition, IT must follow up with ongoing checks on user satisfaction. At every juncture, the time and trouble invested in establishing trust, reliability, and orderly and open communication will determine an organization's success in putting SLM into practice.

CHAPTER 10

Capturing Data for Service Level Agreements (SLAs)

The primary objectives of service level management are to measure, monitor, and improve the quality of services provided to end users. The data collected to support these objectives must measure directly, or provide the ability to derive, the end-to-end service availability and responsiveness experienced by end users.

Metrics for Measuring Service Levels

Rather than measure end-to-end service levels, many IT departments measure the availability and performance of individual resources and components such as the network, servers, or individual devices. This approach does not align the IT department with the lines of business. The lines of business are concerned with end-to-end availability and responsiveness of the critical applications that support their automated business processes. The Service Level Agreements with the lines of business should therefore be based on application services.

Four broad parameters typically used in evaluating service levels are as follows:

- Availability
- Performance
- Reliability
- Recoverability

Availability refers to the percentage of time available for use, preferably of the end-to-end service, but many times of a server, device, or the network. Performance basically indicates the rate (or speed) at which work is performed. The most popular indicator of performance today is response time. However, other indicators are also useful in specific contexts. For example, in a company that performs remote data backups for its clients, an important performance indicator would be the file transfer rate. Reliability refers to how often a service, device, or network goes down or how long it stays down, and recoverability is the time required to restore the service following a failure. These metrics offer high-level views of service quality, whereas response time is a way to directly measure how the end user's productivity and satisfaction are affected by service performance.

Simply providing measurements of availability, performance, reliability, and recoverability is not enough to perform service level monitoring. All aspects of service that affect end-user productivity and satisfaction should be covered by the Service Level Agreements. The characteristic that has the highest visibility among customers is response time. Other aspects to measure and monitor include workload volumes, help desk responsiveness, implementation times for configuration changes and new services, as well as overall customer satisfaction.

Although Service Level Agreements should align with the end-user perception of service quality, IT departments have been reluctant to agree to such SLAs for distributed application services because of the difficulty in measuring actual application availability and performance on an end-to-end basis.

For example, end-to-end response time measurement is an ill-defined concept. Management vendors have differing definitions that vary depending on what their particular product can do. In general, industry analysts agree that end-to-end response time should start and end at the desktop and should measure the time from when a command or transaction request is entered on the keyboard to the time when the resulting actions are completed and the results are displayed on the monitor.

Today's application architectures vary widely and typically use some variation of the client/server model. This results in some processing occurring on the desktop, some on the application server, and in the case of a multitiered architecture, some occurs on back-end database servers. This complicates capturing end-to-end response times because a single business or application transaction will span multiple interactions between the various client/server layers.

With a multitier server structure, end-to-end response time might not provide a detailed enough picture of delays within the underlying components to pinpoint performance problems. Another technique, inter-server response time measurement, focuses on the response time between servers. Providing multitiered response time measurement allows the IT personnel to drill-down and discover the source of performance problems. Undoubtedly the best approach to measuring response time is to implement both end-to-end and inter-server response time measurements.

Today, only a small percentage of IT departments set and measure Service Level Agreements for distributed application availability and performance. Many of these IT departments do so using in-house developed tools and manual processes. These processes are typically based on analyzing end-user service problem calls and correlating the end-user locations with the components that are failing or performing poorly. New technologies are emerging that can assist the IT department to measure distributed application availability and performance in a more automated fashion.

Methods for Capturing Service Metrics

Five emerging methods for proactively measuring application availability and performance are as follows:

- Monitoring all components used by application transactions and aggregating these to derive overall availability and performance measures
- Inspecting network traffic to identify application transactions, which are then tracked to completion and measured for propagation delay
- Using client agents that decode conversations to identify application transactions and measure client-perceived availability and responsiveness
- Instrumenting the application code to define application transactions and collecting information on completed transactions and response times
- Generating synthetic transactions at regular intervals and collecting availability and performance measures based on tracking these transactions

Each of the methods determines application availability by measuring response times of multiple integrated applications used in a business process, a single application, or transaction. Applications with response times recorded above a predefined threshold are considered unavailable. The last three methods provide the most accurate picture of end-to-end response times as perceived by the user community.

Tip

Selecting which method to use depends on a number of factors including access to code for instrumentation purposes, willingness to proliferate and manage agents on desktops, ability to acquire sophisticated network traffic monitors, and the inherent inaccuracies with some of these approaches. In many cases, a combination of approaches deployed pragmatically will provide the best solution.

Use of these techniques does not eliminate the need for measuring the service levels of individual components. In many cases, these techniques will identify service problems based on end-to-end measurements, but this might not be enough to determine where the problem is located or how to correct it. However, by comparing response times by application across various locations, it might be possible to isolate the problem location. For example, if an application is performing poorly across all locations, the server or database is the likely cause. If an application is performing poorly in only one location, it is likely a location-specific problem such as local server, the local area network, or the wide area network connection between that location and the application server.

Caution

These techniques for measuring end-to-end response times aren't able to detect outages of individual desktops. These methods measure availability and performance of application transactions between the user and the business process. This might be an issue for client/server applications in which a significant portion of the application code actually runs on the desktop itself. The IT department should continue to monitor help desk calls and the problem resolution system closely to determine the business impact of individual desktop problems.

We will now examine each of these methods in more detail. As these techniques require data to be collected continuously, we will also discuss some of the common architectures used by data monitoring solutions later in the chapter.

Monitoring Individual Components and Aggregating Results

Infrastructure monitoring involves measuring the availability and performance of individual components such as servers, networks, databases, and clients. To understand the service delivered by a specific application, the availability and performance data across all relevant infrastructure components must be consolidated and aggregated. Figure 10.1 shows the various infrastructure technology layers.

This approach to service level monitoring concentrates on the components in the application dependency stack. Software agents are installed on each technology level to gather information. The information from all the agents is consolidated to provide a single view of the application and its performance. This approach is often referred to as *monitoring by footprint*. It provides a more comprehensive view of the application than simply monitoring one component such as network traffic.

Caution

Monitoring across infrastructure components can use significant system resources to support the data collection agents. It can also be difficult to identify, maintain, and register all the components used by each application, and it can be difficult to consolidate this information and present it in a format that is easy to understand.

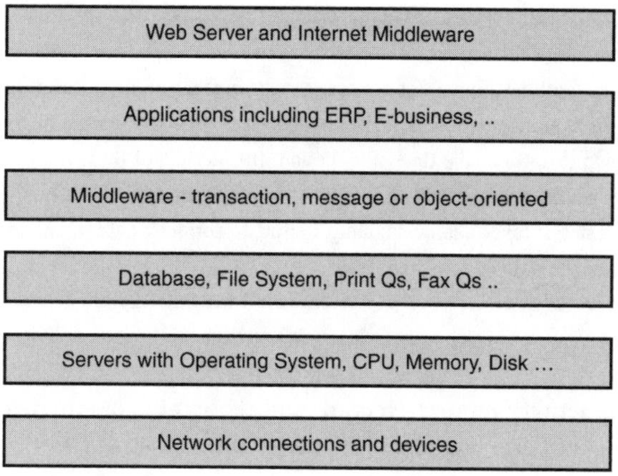

Web Server and Internet Middleware

Applications including ERP, E-business, ..

Middleware - transaction, message or object-oriented

Database, File System, Print Qs, Fax Qs ..

Servers with Operating System, CPU, Memory, Disk ...

Network connections and devices

Figure 10.1 *The infrastructure technology layers.*

A consideration when adopting this approach is the ability to capture management information about the availability and performance of all the relevant components. The primary focus areas for data collection are the servers and the network. The desktops, databases, and middleware also impact availability and performance.

The performance data collected natively for servers varies depending on the operating system platform. OS/390 is a well-instrumented operating system with a significant amount of information available through IBM utilities including System Management Facility (SMF) and Resource Monitoring Facility (RMF), as well as a number of established products from third-party vendors. As these capabilities have been available for a number of years and are well understood, we will concentrate on the distributed systems platforms including UNIX, Microsoft Windows NT, and Windows 2000.

Monitoring UNIX Systems

As mission-critical applications are moved to UNIX servers, the performance and availability of the UNIX server assumes greater importance. However, the UNIX operating system is not constructed to provide complete and accurate performance information. One such important performance metric is the CPU utilization, and the quality of this metric is determined by the capture ratio, which is the proportion of CPU utilization that is accounted for. In most UNIX systems, the capture ratio is not sufficient for sophisticated performance analysis or capacity planning.

Note

UNIX systems come with a variety of performance measurement utilities. Unfortunately, these utilities were designed as standalone tools, and each addresses the particular problem the utility designer was trying to solve at the time of its design. The outputs of these utilities vary between UNIX variants. In addition, the procedure for underlying measurement is not well documented and supported. As a result, it takes a large amount of effort to correctly collect, understand, and interpret UNIX performance data in consistent ways.

The utilities generally available with the UNIX operating system include

- *Sar*, system activity reporter, records and reports on system-wide resource utilization and performance information, including total CPU utilization. CPU utilization is measured using the tick-based sampling method. A system counter accumulates the number of CPU ticks during which non-idle process was running. This counter is sampled at specified intervals to compute the average CPU utilization between samples. This method leads to the problem of relatively low capture ratio.

- The *accounting* utility records the resources used by a process upon the process's termination. The principal drawback of this method is that no information is available for the process until it terminates. Accounting reports summarize these statistics by the command or process name and username.

- The *ps* utility provides a snapshot of the processes running on the system as an ASCII report. It reports the amount of CPU used by the process since its inception. When reporting information on all the processes, overhead is quite high.

As seen from this quick overview, these tools primarily provide resource utilization information and don't measure the end-user response times or application transaction throughput. The output of these utilities differs among the assorted UNIX variants and doesn't provide historical or trend information.

A number of performance monitoring products are available from independent software vendors. Most of these collect data through a standard UNIX interface called the /dev/kmem kernel device driver. The advantages of the third-party products include the ability to normalize and compare the data across different UNIX variants as well as greater productivity through enhanced user interfaces and reports, including trend analysis reports.

Monitoring Windows NT and Windows 2000

Microsoft ships performance management tools with Windows NT and Windows 2000. These include

- *Perfmon* monitors performance and server resource usage (including CPU, memory and disk I/O). It uses counters from the Windows registry, and the data can be logged and viewed online or charted in reports.

- *Taskmanager* provides information on all the processes and services running and the amount of memory and CPU they are using.

- *Process Explode* monitors processes, threads, and the committed mapped memory. This is primarily of use to developers.

- *Quick Slice* is a basic tool for viewing the per active process CPU usage.

Similar to the standard UNIX utilities, these Windows facilities focus on resource utilization and don't directly measure or monitor the service levels experienced by users. The event logs can also provide a significant amount of information about activity on an NT system. The NT Resource Kit Utilities allow these logs to be dumped and imported into a database for easier manipulation and analysis.

Monitoring the Network

The Simple Network Management Protocol (SNMP), and associated Management Information Bases (MIBs), is used by most network device vendors to provide configuration, fault, and performance information about the network components. This information is useful for diagnosing failures and service degradation. The Remote Monitoring (RMON) MIB provides additional information that can be useful for determining traffic patterns and for understanding bandwidth utilization by protocol and traffic type.

Later in this chapter, we discuss in more detail how analyzing network traffic provides additional information about the quality of service delivered to end users.

Monitoring the Database

The SNMP protocol can be used for high-level database monitoring as most database vendors support the RDBMS MIB. However, for more detailed monitoring and database management, additional tools are required either from the database vendor or third-party software vendors.

Aggregating the Component Information

To build the composite picture of availability and performance, the standard utilities will generally need to be augmented by third-party performance monitoring tools. Additionally, a management database and a mechanism for loading captured data from servers and the network provides a central repository for answering queries and producing reports. Similarly, performance information should be captured from other components such as middleware, databases, and Web servers and loaded into the same repository.

When the information has been placed in the repository, analysis tools that support a specific application service are required to correlate and aggregate information across all components. It is typically easier to use this method to determine end-to-end availability than it is to determine end-to-end response times.

Inspecting Network Traffic for Application Transactions

Two mechanisms for inspecting the network traffic are as follows:

- Decoding network packets
- Intercepting socket traffic

In both cases, the network traffic is examined to identify the end-points in the connection, including which application is participating in the conversation. This allows transaction times to be calculated by linking the transaction pairs in a dialogue and determining elapsed times between requests and responses.

Decoding Network Packets

This approach known as *wire sniffing* or *network packet decoding* involves using a technology that intercepts and analyzes every network packet. Typical technologies are pure software approaches that do not require a hardware card. This technology manipulates the Network Interface Card (NIC) by placing it in promiscuous mode, which sends the packets through the software components that analyze the packet data.

The analysis of these packets is by no means a trivial task. Simple network packet data is relatively easy to gather. For example, mapping of packets to sockets and port numbers can be useful in analyzing bandwidth usage by application. However, decoding the packets to find the application-level transaction start and finish points is more difficult. ASCII protocols such as DNS, telnet, and HTTP are not hard to decode. However, proprietary protocols such as SQL*Net from Oracle or those of ERP applications such as SAP R/3 are more difficult to decode. This difficulty is the main reason why such approaches are not amenable to in-house development and available only from management solution vendors.

One advantage that arises from current LAN technology is that the network packet collector need not sit on the server or client machine. It can run on any machine within the network segment, thus allowing flexibility to perform analysis on the server or on a dedicated workstation.

Intercepting Socket Traffic

Another technology with similar promise as network packet decoding involves intercepting network traffic directly from the kernel stack. Network traffic on a system (server, workstation, or desktop) passes through a software layer before continuing into or out of the system. Typically, this collection method involves replacing some low-level network libraries or intercepting traffic from existing low-level operating system features.

This technology sees all incoming and outgoing network traffic. Analysis can be simplistic such as byte counts or complex protocol decodes. The same comments about decoding traffic packets and protocols apply here as they do for network packet decodes from wire sniffers. ASCII protocols such as DNS and HTTP are easier than proprietary vendor protocols.

The main advantage of this technology is the opportunity for actual optimization and compression, rather than just measurement. This idea can be implemented on either the client or server machines, or on both sides.

Caution

The primary drawbacks of analyzing network traffic are the inability to define transactions in user terms and the difficulty of matching all traffic. Additionally, these techniques do not capture response time stemming from desktop application components.

End-to-End Service Level Measurement

The problem of measuring end-to-end service levels including availability and response times is gaining significant interest from IT departments and the vendor community. There are multiple methods for addressing this issue and new technology is rapidly emerging. Three basic approaches to this problem are as follows:

- Capturing information from the end-user's desktop to understand the application transactions as they occur
- Instrumenting the application to identify transactions with markers that can be monitored in real time
- Generating sample transactions that simulate the activities of the user community and that can be monitored

Using Client Agents to Decode Conversations

This approach involves loading every client machine with a small agent that non-intrusively watches events such as keystrokes or network events. The client agent then attempts to detect the start and end of a transaction, and measure the time between these events. Typically, the client agent then sends back measured data to a central place where broader analysis occurs.

These client agents capture response time from the client perspective without having to instrument the application itself. For example, some capture information on Web browser interactions such as the response time for page retrievals or downloads. Similarly, some can decode client transactions for popular ERP applications. The primary benefits of this method are the granularity of collection, for example at an individual screen level, lack of application instrumentation, and the ability to analyze user interaction from the detail data.

Tip

The primary drawback of this approach is the large volume of data captured. To mitigate this issue, place agents on representative desktops rather than on every desktop in the organization. Using a sampling mechanism can also reduce the volume of data while still providing reasonable availability and response time metrics.

These client capture agents might also be appropriate for user workflow analysis in addition to capturing the service quality from the end-user perspective.

Instrumenting Applications

The next approach involves building application programming interfaces (APIs) that provide monitoring directly into the application. These API calls allow a monitoring tool to query the application for end-to-end response times, as well as run application management actions on the application, for example backup and recovery routines. This approach is still developing, as an industry accepted standard for these API calls has not emerged yet.

Even after a standard becomes widely accepted, many popular applications will likely go through several releases before they fully support the standard. This embedded API approach offers the best accuracy for measuring application response time. The Application Response Measurement API (ARM), discussed in Chapter 5, "Standards Efforts," is a good example of an API used to measure response time.

The instrumentation APIs define the start and end of business transactions and capture the total end-to-end response times as users process their transactions. This technology is invasive to the application itself. The strength of this approach is that transactions are defined in terms of business processes. The primary drawback is application invasiveness, which is an expense that most enterprises are willing to incur for only their most critical applications. Further, instrumentation adds overhead that could impact the runtime performance of the application.

Caution

The main issue with this approach is the high costs of modifying legacy application code and the lack of coordination between most IT operations staff and applications development departments. The need for application modification makes this approach inapplicable to older, noninstrumented versions of an application. Hence, this intrusive instrumentation approach is best used in a situation in which a full revision and upgrade of the application is already required or under way.

Generating Synthetic Transactions

Generating synthetic transactions can be accomplished using scripts and intelligent agents or by using tools that capture transactions and then later play them back against an application service. These mechanisms allow a simulated response time to be measured, and can be very effective provided sufficient thought is given to ensuring the transactions are truly representative of typical user behavior and that all locations are also represented.

The implementation can be as simple as writing a small script that launches the application's client, command-line interface (CLI), or application programming interface (API) to perform a simple read or other controlled sample transaction. The length of time taken can be subject to alerting, notification, and further actions for deeper diagnosis or perhaps corrective attempts. The script can be scheduled to run at regular intervals using an intelligent agent or task scheduler.

Capture/playback tools have traditionally been used for applications testing. These are now evolving to also report availability and performance metrics. A number of capture/playback products are available from testing tool vendors that can be retrofitted or customized to provide availability and performance metrics. Capture/playback tools record user keystrokes and can play them back at regular intervals while measuring response time. By using distributed server resources or placing dedicated workstations at desired locations to submit transactions for critical applications, a continuous sampling of response times by location is captured and reported. The strength of this method is in its ability to provide the end-user experience using samples rather than having to collect large volumes of data across all transactions from all end users.

There are two important considerations when implementing the synthetic transaction approach. The first is to use a broad enough sample base to capture the service quality across all critical applications and end-user locations, while ensuring that the number of transactions generated does not place too much overhead on the application environment. The second issue is that as the applications change, or measurement criteria change, modification will be required to the scripts or the transactions will have to be re-captured for future playback.

Commands like *ping* and *traceroute* are special cases of simulated transactions. They measure only the response time of the network round trip, and do not include any information about the application server or database. These approaches can be useful in detecting network congestion, diagnosing if a problem is network or server related, and separating measured transaction times into network and non-network times. As an example of the latter, transaction-level synthetic transactions correlated with network-level pings can provide a reasonable division of response time into network and server times.

Tip

Synthetic transaction generation, together with built-in sampling capabilities, offers the best approach to measuring availability and response time metrics for the widest variety of business transactions. This approach is not intrusive into the application, and it requires less technical skill to implement.

Common Architectures and Technologies for Data Capture Solutions

The most common approach to monitoring applications uses intelligent autonomous agents to gather information on the application as well as the underlying infrastructure components. These agents use a variety of measurement techniques to collect the data that is then used for event management and problem diagnosis and stored for trend analysis and reporting. In most cases, a management console is used to display the information for administrative purposes.

When deploying management agents for data collection, the captured information must be consistent and accurate. One issue to consider is the potential problem of managing the widespread proliferation of agents. This can be achieved by ensuring both efficient management agent architecture as well as an efficient data collection mechanism.

Management Agent Characteristics

Management agents perform a number of functions including scheduling the collection of data, determining event conditions, forwarding this event information to consoles, executing recovery actions, and storing metric and event information for historical purposes. Simple agents are normally slaves to a master console. They collect data and perform some event detection based on simple threshold analysis. They then pass the collected data and events to a management console that has built-in intelligence to know how to react to the event. As outlined in Chapter 7, "Service Level Management Products," there are a number of vendors that provide network, operating system, database, middleware, and application agents as part of their management solution. All these agents perform similar tasks, but the functionality differs based on certain agent characteristics.

True intelligent agents have the following characteristics:

- Autonomous—Operates independently of the management console including the ability to start, collect data, and take actions.
- Social—Communicates with other agents, management consoles, and directly with users.
- Reactive—Detects events and initiates actions based on the event.
- Dynamic—Operates differently depending on time and the context of other activities that might be happening.

There are also a number of technical aspects of an intelligent agent including

- Asynchronous—Does not need a permanent link to the initiating event or console.
- Event-driven—Reacts to events and runs when only certain events occur.
- No active user interaction—Does not require constant user intervention to run.
- Self-executing—Has the ability to run itself.
- Self-contained—Has all required knowledge to perform its task.

To avoid excessive overhead on the servers, the number of agents should be limited. This might be best achieved by acquiring agents from as few different vendors as possible. When selecting agent vendors, agent-to-agent integration capabilities, agent intelligence, and agent security are important considerations.

Tip

Before deploying agents, implement a pilot to measure CPU, memory, and bandwidth consumption of agents and consoles under a variety of operating conditions. By estimating the number of events and the overhead required to manage that number of events, the agent impact on the system can be accurately planned.

Procedures to control, rationalize, and optimize the scope of agent execution in both function and execution time should be developed. For example, ensuring that only a fault detection agent is run continuously will limit the impact on overall system performance. Some data collection agents can be run at regular intervals, for example as a response to a detected condition that requires additional data for diagnosis. Historical data should be held for trend analysis so that the root causes of problems can be identified.

Tip

Multiple agents that duplicate agent functionality on a server should be avoided wherever possible. This can be achieved by careful coordination across management disciplines such as network management, database administration, and systems management. Each management discipline should be responsible for controlling agent deployment within its functional area. Policies and procedures should be developed for deploying and managing distributed agents.

Measurement Techniques

Before using a specific performance metric, it is important to have a clear and unambiguous understanding of its semantics. This is particularly important when using multiple metrics in conjunction to derive end-to-end service quality or to solve a problem of service degradation. Almost all operating systems and management solutions have had some metrics with ambiguous meaning at some point in time. Measurement techniques for collecting performance data can be divided into two general categories, which are event-driven and sampling-based.

Event-Driven Measurement

Event-driven measurement means that the times at which certain events happen are recorded and then desired statistics are computed by analyzing the data.

For example, when measuring CPU utilization, the events of interest are the scheduling of a process to run on a processor and the suspension of its execution. The elapsed time between the scheduling of a process to run and suspension of its processing is added to the CPU's busy counter and the process's CPU use counter, which can be sampled and written periodically to a log file or repository. With this method, both the total CPU utilization and the CPU utilization for each process are measured.

The same method can be used for collecting other information including end-to-end response times based on instrumentation APIs or synthetically generated transactions.

Sampling-Based Measurement

The sampling method of data collection involves taking a scheduled periodic look at certain counters or information access points. For example, when measuring CPU utilization by sampling, the measurement method periodically takes a sample to see if any process is running on the CPU, and if so, it increments the system busy counter as well as the CPU usage counter for the process. The data collector will typically sample these counters and record values in a log file.

The sampling method is generally more efficient because it places less overhead on the system under measurement.

Comparative Analysis

The event-driven collection method is generally the most accurate, but it does have some limitations. Its accuracy depends on the level to which the events are traced. There can also be discrepancies depending on the nature of the event interrupt and when the actual measurements are taken. Depending on the frequency of events, the overhead of the event-driven measurement can be significantly larger than that of sampling-based measurement, and it can potentially distort the measurements significantly.

On the other hand, the sampling-based method is subject to errors when multiple activities occur or processes run between two samples. The activity occurring at the time of the sample will be allocated the entire length of the sample interval. Other activities or processes are not allocated any time during that sample. Similarly, if an activity takes place totally within a sample or if a process is created and terminated between two samples, it is not allocated any time at all.

Note

The amount of error in the sampling depends primarily on the sampling frequency. Longer time between the samples will result in larger potential errors. The trade-off is that more frequent sampling will increase the overhead of this technique.

Summary

There are multiple data collection techniques and agent architectures that are used to collect data that is useful for measuring and monitoring service levels. Careful consideration should be given to the nature of the technology used and the deployment of collection agents. The goal is to ensure that sufficient data is collected to accurately measure service quality, while not placing excessive overhead on the computing environment.

It is also very important to ensure that service levels are measured from an end-to-end basis so that the end-user experience is captured. A number of techniques can be used to measure end-to-end availability and response times. When selecting a method to use, considerations include access to code for instrumentation, agent proliferation, and the level of expertise in house for implementing and supporting the management solution. In many cases, adopting a pragmatic approach utilizing synthetically generated transactions that are measured using sampling techniques will provide sufficient scope and accuracy of information.

Very critical and time-sensitive applications might require more sophisticated techniques such as intrusive application instrumentation or client agents to provide more comprehensive, accurate information.

CHAPTER 11

Service Level Management as Service Enabler

The benefits of service level management can be clearly delineated for any organization that takes the time to make it work. But SLM can be especially advantageous for those companies seeking to sell their IT services to outside users. In fact, the growing ranks of Internet service providers (ISPs), application service providers (ASPs), and outsourcers testify to the value of SLM.

By defining the parameters of acceptable service and setting clear goals and expectations for providers and users, SLM provides a framework in which providers can offer more and better services, while maximizing the potential of existing ones.

SLM also is the key to helping users ensure that they get the most value from their growing investment in outside services. In most organizations, increased demands on IT are accompanied by staff shortages and budget constraints. IT managers are turning to external providers for help. SLM gives them a way to quantify and get the level of performance and capacity they require.

In this chapter, we'll take a closer look at how SLM is playing a role in the emerging world of online services. In doing so, we will attempt to focus on SLM issues from two perspectives—the service provider's and the end user's.

The Ascendance of IP

First, we will take a look at the types of services that are most often used by corporate customers to extend their internal networks. These services vary, but there is a preponderance of demand for IP-based services. The reasons are clear: Internet access is inexpensive compared with the costs of dedicated, private networks. The Internet is a fast and easy way to extend the corporate network without adding new facilities. An Internet presence gives companies with limited geographic scope a way to market their wares to 55 million computers in 222 countries.

Improved security and performance on the Internet also make it a unique environment for .com businesses such as Amazon.com that exist solely in cyberspace. The market for firms like Amazon.com that conduct business-to-consumer electronic commerce over the Internet is expected to exceed $100 billion over the next three to four years. And business-to-business electronic commerce, in which companies use the Internet to support transactions with partners and suppliers, is even bigger. Estimated revenue for companies in this space is expected to top $1 trillion within the same timeframe.

Market opportunities like these are forcing SLM into the spotlight, as providers and their customers seek ways to establish and maintain ever-higher levels of network performance and availability in an increasingly service-oriented environment.

Note

The Advantages of Internet-based Services are as follows:

For end users: A quick, inexpensive way to extend in-house networks and interact with customers and suppliers

For service providers: Fast deployment of services at low cost; worldwide reach; and unique environment for services like electronic commerce

A Spectrum of Providers

As demand rises for Internet-based services, the market is becoming increasingly segmented. Internet service providers (ISPs) tout a range of offerings IT professionals can use to increase their companies' online capabilities, including standard Web access and hosting, email, virtual private networks, electronic commerce networking services, remote access, and voice-over IP services. According to investment banker Credit Suisse First Boston (New York), projected worldwide revenue for ISPs will exceed $45 billion by 2002.

Meanwhile, an emerging segment of application service providers (ASPs) offers remote access to specific applications, such as enterprise resource planning (ERP) applications, corporate databases, and complex vertical applications, over the Web. Market researchers such as Forrester Research (Cambridge, MA) and International

Data Corp. (IDC, Framingham, MA) estimate this market will grow at rates over 90% annually, reaching $2 billion to $6 billion by the end of 2001.

Companies also are turning to outsourcers for assistance. Consultants and systems integrators often take over all or part of the duties of the data center, including supervision of local and wide area network services, maintenance and management of assets, network monitoring, and security. According to IDC, worldwide revenue for outsourcing services now exceeds $100 billion and is expected to reach $151 billion by 2003.

What's an ASP?

The demands of e-business are driving companies to sign on with service providers who offer them online access to mission-critical applications. This approach reduces the initial investment organizations must make, and it saves development and implementation time. It also eliminates the need to hire extra IT talent to run new systems.

But, like all technology "buzz phrases"—such as service level management—the term ASP seems to take on new meanings every month. And as this profitable services segment grows, the term is likely to become even more inclusive—at least to marketing experts. Outsourcers, integrators, and even consultants are jumping on the revenue bandwagon and are labeling themselves as ASPs.

On a more down-to-earth level, the question of who really qualifies as an ASP is more limiting. According to the ASP Consortium (Wakefield, MA), "An application service provider manages and delivers application capabilities to multiple entities from data centers across a wide area network." Market research firm International Data Corp. (Framingham, MA) gives this definition: "Application service providers (ASPs) provide a contractual service offering to deploy, host, manage, and rent access to an application from a centrally managed facility. ASPs are responsible for either directly or indirectly providing all the specific activities and expertise aimed at managing a software application or set of applications."

These definitions leave room for two kinds of providers—those who offer applications from their own facilities, and those who rely on the cooperation of other carriers or Web hosting companies to furnish the necessary network services. In either case, the ASP is charged with the direct management of its own servers and holds ultimate responsibility to the customer for maintaining agreed-on levels of service.

The generally accepted definition of ASP does not include those companies that provide applications over a customer's own network, such as systems integrators. And in most instances—although there is some disagreement about this—it does not include network outsourcers. In some cases, however, these providers might host customer applications from their own servers, using the Web as the transport medium.

The ASP market has many helpers, as evidenced by the list of ASP Consortium members, which includes hardware vendors like Compaq and Cisco, which furnish the servers and network infrastructure gear for ASPs, as well as software suppliers like Citrix, Great Plains Software, and IBM. Still, these companies do not qualify as ASPs by themselves.

The Importance of SLAs in the Service Environment

Emerging e-commerce and e-business services rely on network availability. In the volatile environment of the Internet, where traffic levels vary dynamically and an error in one location can snarl traffic worldwide, it isn't as easy to guarantee performance levels as it is in the world of dedicated links. Thus, Service Level Agreements (SLAs) are playing a key role in the spread of today's IP-based services. Users demand them, and service providers are finding them to be a necessary differentiator as competition increases.

This is not to say that today's SLAs for IP-based services are without problems. On the user side, there is much to be desired. Users say most SLAs for standard Internet services from ISPs are too simplistic to be truly effective. What's more, if something goes wrong, many IT professionals report difficulties in getting reimbursement from their providers (see Figure 11.1).

For their part, service providers embrace SLAs as much as their customers. But many service providers believe that they can standardize their SLAs in order to simplify life for themselves. They cite the difficulties involved in negotiating individual SLAs for many customers. "We'd never get services out if we spent all that time creating SLAs," said one provider. "If we do our job correctly, we can keep customers satisfied and keep SLAs uniform."

There are exceptions: Large, powerful customers that enlist multiple services from one provider usually can negotiate their SLA terms as part of an overall service contract. Getting the best results, however, requires the input of a strong negotiator. It also calls for the customer to establish a reliable means of monitoring ongoing service performance (see Sidebar).

Get It In Writing

Don't try to sell corporate networkers on the merits of the honor system. What works well at West Point shows flaws outside the walls of the academy, especially when it comes to SLAs: Can customers really trust that carriers will meet the pledges they make, and make restitution when they come up short?

Ask David Giambruno, the global transition program manager for medical equipment manufacturer Datex-Ohmeda, a subsidiary of Instrumentarium Corp. (Helsinki, Finland). He suffered days of downtime on AT&T's international frame relay network last October, and while he was fixing the problem, he discovered AT&T had charged him for five years of service he never knew about.

"'We had PVCs (permanent virtual circuits) in Canada that weren't even hooked up to routers,' he says. To top it off, AT&T (Basking Ridge, NJ) refused to make compensation—pointing out the SLA (Service Level Agreement) didn't cover either problem. AT&T declined to comment, but Giambruno is blunt: 'I've learned that unless you can actually see what's going on in your network, it's going to cost you.'"

From the article, "SLA Monitoring Tools, Heavyweight Help," *Data Communications* magazine, February 7, 1999.

Do you have SLAs (Service Level Agreements) with WAN service providers?	
Yes	54%
No	46%

How do you measure SLA performance?	
Commercially available product	32%
Part of the service	52%
Product or solution developed in-house	28%

Are you satisfied with the terms of your SLAs?	
Yes	72%
No	28%

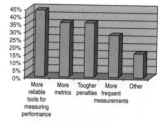

How could your SLAs be improved?	
More reliable tools for measuring performance	44%
More metrics	36%
Tougher penalties	36%
More frequent measurements	28%
Other	16%

If you do not have SLAs in place, why not?	
Provider does not honor them	43%
Provider unwilling to negotiate	33%
Provider responds to performance problems case by case	33%
Confident in provider performance without them	29%
Other	5%

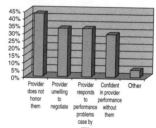

Figure 11.1 *The role of SLAs in WAN services.*

Different Strokes

The burgeoning growth in IP services—and the variety of services now on offer—presents a challenge when it comes to SLM. New services such as e-commerce and ASP services will not always fit a single SLM mold because an extension or modification of existing SLM parameters is required. And in some cases, it might be necessary to set new parameters.

When it comes to e-commerce, for instance, availability, performance, and other SLM parameters will be affected not only by the customer's own network but also by those of the business partners and suppliers who support the customer's online presence. Callers who place an online order with an e-commerce retailer, for example, might experience a response time delay if the supplier on whom the retailer depends suffers a network failure. Although the retailer is not technically responsible for the delay, it will affect his ability to deliver service to his customers. He is liable to compensate those customers if response times fall below promised service levels. The retailer is legally the provider of service, regardless of the components that service contains. Any SLAs set up with e-commerce providers—and/or SLAs made between providers—need to reflect these new facts of life in the world of online services.

Emerging ASP services also present special challenges. ASP services are still so new that users and providers have not determined the precise elements that will constitute service-level criteria. New types of services are changing the rules. Do ASPs, for instance, offer their customers SLAs based on user response time, server response time, overall network uptime, or a combination of all these? Questions like these are still in debate as the market for services develops.

There are other SLM challenges presented by emerging services: In many instances, a service might include interdependencies between Web hosting providers and carriers offering the underlying network facilities. SLAs will need to be established between the multiple providers as well as between providers and customers.

Smart Implementation

Regardless of the complexities of particular SLA criteria, all the suggestions and templates for creating and maintaining SLAs covered so far in this book can be successfully applied to the service environment. From the perspective of the user of services as well as the provider, it is important to set up a task force, define SLA parameters, and agree on continual methods of monitoring and follow-up.

The service environment also presents unique SLM implementation challenges, both from the user and service provider perspectives. It is important to be aware of these from the beginning in order to ensure success.

Fundamentally, these distinctions center on the fact that the service provider holds the advantage in relation to its customers. By offering the vital services on which the customer's business is run, the provider is virtually in control of the customer's business itself.

Advice for Users

The unequal nature of the user/provider relationship makes it vital for users to be thorough in establishing SLAs right from the start. Remember that any loopholes left will be sure to surface to the users' disadvantage later on. Ask lots of questions: As noted, most service providers have prefabricated SLAs they use as standard. They will not offer to extend these SLAs unless they are asked to do so.

Note

Remember: Like it or not, corporate customers are the underdogs in the service relationship. Controlling the business infrastructure gives the provider control over the customer's business. It is therefore vital to clarify all terms of the SLA and its implementation right from the start.

IT professionals can give themselves a better chance for success by keeping several things in mind when setting up a SLM relationship with service providers:

- Know what you're talking about—Enter negotiations armed with baseline measurements. Know what constitutes adequate performance and capacity for all business functions that the provider will be expected to support. Also know exactly how long you are willing to wait to have something fixed if it breaks.

- Establish a common frame of reference—Make certain up front that the terms used in the SLA match those the service provider uses. Also, agree with the provider on what methods and products you'll be using to monitor conformance with parameters. Some providers might not support your products, and vice versa, making it tough to make a case for compensation if something goes wrong.

- Document everything—Make sure that you ask your provider to endorse all SLA parameters, including reimbursement in the event of outage or failure. If your requests are not documented, the provider will be under no obligation to follow them. And the fact that the provider has so many customers will make it resistant to extending special unasked-for privileges.

- Be ready to pay for extras—Providers will often prove flexible when asked to extend the terms of their one-size-fits-all SLAs. But most will ask for additional payment beyond a certain point. This situation is normal; expect to pay for the terms you need.

- Get your act together—Make sure that your in-house SLM team is well prepared and unified. Recordkeeping is a key part of the SLA and needs full support on your end. If something does go wrong with the service you are contracting, it will be vital for team members to work as a well-informed team in order to get repairs and compensation.

- Keep an open mind—Our advice so far is based on the fact that users need to take extra precautions in setting up SLM with their providers. But don't maintain a defensive attitude: Remember that most service providers intend to do the best possible job for their customers in order to keep themselves in business. Encouraging an atmosphere of cooperation will serve you better than harboring an adversarial attitude.

Advice for Service Providers

SLM can work as well—or better—for service providers as it can for their customers. But there are unique considerations from the service provider perspective. Providers might start from a position of power relative to their customers, but this does not mean that they themselves are not vulnerable. In many ways, today's service providers are just as vulnerable as their customers. After all, their business is to offer reliable service. If they fail to do that, they cannot stay in business.

SLM does more for service providers than merely offer protection from liability. It helps them create a frame of reference for new and existing services. Knowing the level of performance they can guarantee allows them to pass along SLAs to their customers that differentiates them from other providers.

SLM also helps in the creation of *differentiated services,* in which different groups of users are offered disparate guarantees of service, based on their payment plan. "Gold" customers, for instance, might be offered continuous availability at an agreed-upon level of response time; "silver" customers would get response times within a certain range of measurement; and "bronze" customers would receive "best effort" service. SLM provides the input that enables the service provider to offer differentiated services; and it also gives them the ongoing framework for implementing them with customers. Table 11.1 illustrates a typical model used by providers of differentiated services.

Table 11.1   **A Typical Model of Differentiated Services**

Service	Rate	Response time	Availability
Gold	10Mbps	<1 second	99.9%
Silver	5 to 10Mbps	<3 seconds	Over 90%
Bronze	2 to 5Mbps	<5 seconds	Over 80%
Standard	Best effort	Best effort	Best effort

In general, service providers have the same problems their customers do, often on a grander scale. Also, service providers face a range of challenges that their customers do not. Specifically, they must ensure that other providers and suppliers on whom they depend can furnish a level of performance, availability, and capacity that enable them to pass along a single, consistent level of service to their customers. In effect, many of today's online services, such as e-commerce services, depend on a group of suppliers maintaining a chain of performance. A break in the chain will affect the ability of all participants to meet service-level expectations.

In some cases, service providers will need to take the initiative in establishing SLA parameters ahead of industry trends. Many ASPs, for instance, are breaking new ground when it comes to service models. They find themselves creating SLAs in a vacuum, where no precedents exist to guide them. That said, there are rules providers can follow to help them navigate the uncharted waters of today's service offerings:

- Make infrastructure serve your SLAs—Service providers can make the most of service level management by building it into their infrastructure through the use of technologies like Quality of Service (QOS), which uses intelligence built into routers and switches to control the flow of network traffic. It is worth the investment of time and effort to find and take advantage of these new resources for guaranteeing performance.

- Stay in tune with customers—Most providers are focused more on determining the *kinds* of services customers want than on ways to present new SLAs. Still, it pays to keep in touch with demands for SLA improvements, particularly as the quality and content of SLAs will increasingly differentiate services from multiple providers in emerging segments.

- Take the lead with other participants and suppliers—Many types of services today call for cooperation among multiple providers. E-commerce is one example. Leave nothing to chance if you have these kinds of interdependent relationships. Remember, your business depends on all the links in the chain performing consistently.

- Keep an open mind—Stay flexible with your customers and business suppliers. Rigidity will not serve you well in a market in which new competitors are ready to take business from you at a moment's notice.

Summary

The burgeoning services market is a proving ground for SLM. Users need to be firm and clear in negotiations with providers. Providers need to stay in touch with customer demand and remain flexible and open to new methods, while ensuring a consistent level of performance and availability in multiprovider situations. Over time, the demands of the service environment will no doubt help service level management develop beyond its present scope.

CHAPTER

Moving Forward

We have covered a large amount of information on the state of service level management in the industry today. However, the story has only just begun. We anticipate many advances during the coming months and years. The continuing maturity of the understanding and best practices of service level management will happen more rapidly if IT managers share information, monitor the evolution of standards, and push vendors to provide more capable solutions.

This chapter recaps some of the more salient aspects of the current state of service level management and also suggests a mechanism for commencing and continuing a dialog to assist in the maturation process for service level management.

Establishing the Need for Service Level Management

As corporations and organizations move forward with using information technology for business effectiveness, the quality of services delivered by the IT department becomes more critical for business success. Most corporations are rapidly moving to greater use of technology, particularly Web and Internet technologies, to communicate more effectively with employees, business partners, and consumers.

In general, the business goals for the IT department in the new millennium can be characterized as

- Improving internal business efficiency through intranets, knowledge management, data mining, and information sharing
- Improving the cost effectiveness of the supply chain by integrating enterprise applications, connecting to business partners via extranets, and outsourcing non-mission-critical elements
- Enhancing customer and distribution channel relationships and loyalty through one-to-one marketing, sales force automation, personalized Internet Web sites, and data mining

These goals cannot be fully realized unless the quality of the services delivered by the IT department is adequate. If internal systems are not available or responsive enough, employee and business productivity degrades. If supply chain applications are not delivering the right level of service, business partner linkages will not be as effective; in many cases, costs will rise, rework might be required, and upstream processes might be negatively impacted. If the problems are severe enough, the business partnership might be placed in jeopardy.

Similarly, many corporations are moving to a direct self-service model for interacting with their customers using the Web as the communication mechanism. Hundreds of millions of dollars are being spent to attract customers to those Web sites. If the site is not available, the Internet application is not responsive, or the customer feels vulnerable from a security or privacy perspective, he will not have a good experience. Not only will he be reluctant to buy something or conduct a business transaction on the initial visit, it is unlikely that they will return to the site, or it will take significant marketing dollars to attract them again.

Chapter 8, "Business Case for Service Level Management," provides a business case for service level management along with a sample cost justification worksheet. Hopefully, these won't be needed in order to convince senior management of the need to carefully manage service quality in the same way as they would monitor and manage other valuable business assets.

Defining the Services to Be Managed

The initial step in any service level management initiative is to clearly define and prioritize the services delivered by the IT department. This must be done in conjunction with the lines of business so that the true business value and importance of each service is clearly understood.

Each service should have identifiable business owners as well as responsible IT management personnel assigned to them. The locations where each service is delivered together with the user community served should be identified and documented. This will help to assess the business impact in the event of a service outage or degradation. It also allows the IT department to identify who needs to be involved in negotiations for the Service Level Agreements.

Communicating with the Business

One of the most crucial aspects of successfully implementing a service level management strategy is the ongoing communication between the IT department and the lines of business. Service Level Agreements, if constructed appropriately, provide the IT department the ability to discuss goals, responsibilities, and issues with the lines of business in terms they will easily understand. Service management aligns the IT department with the business and will raise the credibility and value of the IT department in the eyes of the business managers.

Tip

If the IT department is seen as overhead and treated as a cost center, implementing a proactive service management strategy is an excellent initial step in changing that perception. As increased competition forces the lines of business to look for competitive and market advantages, the IT department can take an increasingly stronger leadership role in delivering capabilities to improve business and market effectiveness. However, when the IT department takes on this challenge, it will be even more important to ensure consistent, high-quality service delivery.

The dialog with the lines of business is important when defining services and negotiating Service Level Agreements. Reporting on service quality when problems occur, as well as when excellent service is delivered, is another important aspect of building trust and credibility. It will also be important to jointly conduct, with the lines of business, regular satisfaction surveys and reviews of the Service Level Agreements. This helps the IT department to stay in touch with changing business requirements and user perceptions of service quality.

Negotiating Service Level Agreements

Service Level Agreements can never be set by the IT department alone. They must be developed in conjunction with the lines of business and, where necessary, negotiated as with any other contract. There is an inherent balance between the service levels that can be achieved, the workload that can be supported, and the cost of delivering the service. When that is understood by all parties to the negotiation, there will typically be ample opportunity to formulate an agreement acceptable to the IT department as well as the lines of business.

All the agreements used by the IT department should follow a similar format, but the actual terms and conditions can vary from one agreement to another. The detail required within each agreement could also vary, particularly when the business importance and time criticality of the services vary. The Service Level Agreements should include the conditions under which the agreement should be re-negotiated to remove any contention in the future.

Managing to the Service Level Agreement

When the Service Level Agreements are in place, the difficult task begins of ensuring that the required service levels specified in the agreements are met. Service level management is not simply reacting to problems and reporting the achieved service levels. Properly implemented, service level management includes proactively developing the right procedures, policies, organization structure, and personnel skills to improve service quality and to ensure that users and the business are not impacted by any service difficulties.

The starting point is to first capture the end-user experience of service quality, particularly the end-to-end availability and response times. There are a number of viable approaches to capturing and collecting metrics that provide this information. When the end-to-end service quality is being continuously monitored, service degradation or trends that indicate Service Level Agreements are in jeopardy can be detected. Upon this type of event detection, procedures should be followed to isolate and correct the problem, along with proactive notification to end users, alerting them to the issue together with an estimate of when normal service will be resumed. This proactive approach to service management increases the credibility of the IT department and also increases the willingness of lines of business to work with the IT department.

Skilled technicians are required to diagnose and correct problems when service degradation or potential degradation occurs. Wherever possible, these diagnostic and recovery routines should be automated so that if the same condition occurs again, it can be recovered in machine speed rather than having to wait for operator intervention.

Proactive service level management is a combination of structuring the right organization, ensuring that the staff have appropriate skills, defining and implementing the right methodology and procedures, and using an appropriate management solution to monitor and improve service quality.

Tip

The organization structure should align front-line operational teams with each service rather than the traditional approach of aligning operations personnel by technology layers; for example, separate teams of network managers, database administrators, and system managers. This provides a much better interface to the lines of business, and the service teams become the advocates for the lines of business within the IT department.

It might also be beneficial to align some component of compensation for IT personnel with the service quality and meeting Service Level Agreements. In some corporations, incentives have also changed to encourage more proactive automated approaches to ensuring that service level objectives are met, rather than providing incentives for reactive fire-fighting problem correction practices.

Using Commercial Management Solutions

Initially collecting information and monitoring service levels might be performed using standard utilities and manual techniques. This might be sufficient to establish some baselines of service quality, but it will very quickly be inadequate for proactive service level management. Although it might be tempting for the IT department to develop scripts and other automated mechanisms for capturing service level information, it is generally more efficient to use commercial solutions for service level management. Chapter 7, "Service Level Management Products," provides information on a variety of solutions that are generally available. It is unlikely that a single product or solution from a single vendor will meet all your service level management requirements.

Even having to integrate solutions from multiple vendors will generally be an easier proposition for most IT departments than attempting to develop solutions completely in-house. Applications change, as do the underlying database, middleware, operating system, and network hardware and software. Maintaining currency with the individual new versions as well as the various combinations of components can be an onerous task for a single IT department, whereas independent software vendors can distribute the development costs across a number of customers.

Continuously Improving Service Quality

One aspect of service level management that must be recognized is that user expectation and business requirements will continue to increase over time. This is why adopting a very proactive approach to service level management is very important; because operating in a reactive mode will not support continuous improvement.

There is a natural maturation process associated with service level management that involves

- Monitoring the service quality by monitoring individual components and evolving to monitoring from the end-user perspective.
- Managing the service to reduce the impact of service degradations.
- Controlling the service in an automated fashion to proactively detect and correct problems. This also ensures consistency of management actions and removes the potential of human error.

- Delivering service continuity by predicting future business requirements and the associated resources that will be necessary to support the business with appropriate levels of service.

- Moving to a virtual environment where many of the supporting services provided by the IT department use online interfaces and capabilities to provide better service to the end users while reducing the overhead on the IT department. This allows the IT department to use freed staff resources for more proactive activities such as planning future capacity requirements.

Tip

Building on the experience of others is a very effective way of enhancing your service level management practices. Attending trade shows and conferences and using the opportunity to network with other attendees is one mechanism for achieving this. Later in this chapter, we suggest another mechanism using a Web site.

Keeping track of advancements in standards efforts and solution technology will assist your understanding of the state of the art in the industry. This knowledge will help you continue to enhance service level management procedures and practices within your IT department.

Evolution of Service Level Management Standards

Today there are no real industry-accepted standards for service level management, Service Level Agreements, or metric definitions for capturing data to monitor service levels. We can expect standard definitions to evolve during the early years of the new millennium.

These standards initiatives are most likely to evolve from the Distributed Management Task Force (DMTF), IT Service Management Forum (ITSMF), and the Internet Engineering Task Force (IETF). Chapter 5, "Standards Efforts," provides the Web site addresses of these organizations, which contain status information that makes tracking their progress very easy.

Although we can expect standards to evolve, the criticality of implementing proactive service management means that most IT departments should adopt pragmatic service management approaches prior to standards becoming available.

Evolution of Management Solution Capabilities

The capabilities of commercial management solutions will also continue to evolve. Most management vendors started with network management offerings and augmented these with system management capabilities. Additional capabilities for managing other components such as databases and middleware are available and are maturing rapidly.

A new breed of solution has evolved over the last few years. Typically referred to as application management, these solutions seek to manage from an application perspective and drill into the underlying technology layers where necessary to resolve problems. This provides a much better alignment between the IT department and the lines of business and is more attuned to supporting a service level management initiative. These solutions are being augmented to capture the end-user experience, which provides the basis for understanding and improving service quality.

Several vendors are also providing more sophisticated service reporting capabilities based on the ability to either capture directly or derive the end-to-end availability and responsiveness of critical application services.

The future direction of management solutions will include advances in the following two important areas:

- Enhanced intelligence built into the solution as it is delivered from the vendor

- Broader solution scope to provide service management of the entire business processes

Enhanced Management Solution Intelligence

Today's management solutions typically require significant customization before they are able to effectively monitor and manage service quality. Some vendors provide off-the-shelf knowledge for various components in the environment. However, relating the components to the supported service and to the end users using the service is difficult and generally requires customization. We can expect advances in this capability through the use of directories, repositories, and advances with standards such as the common information model (CIM).

The ability to capture the relationships between the various components also provides the basis for more sophisticated event aggregation and correlation, as well as root cause analysis. This capability will increase the level of automated problem diagnosis, allowing the IT department to concentrate on solving the specific problem causing the service degradation. Reducing the time required to diagnose problems will also allow the IT staff to spend more time on automating recovery actions, proactively planning future requirements, and working with the lines of businesses on supporting strategic business initiatives.

Reading relevant articles in trade publications as well as research reports from industry analyst firms is one way of keeping abreast of technology and solutions advances.

Service Management of Business Processes

The most sophisticated management solutions today manage a single application at a time. This provides service level management for users and business processes that use a single application. However, as businesses seek greater effectiveness, enterprise application integration is becoming more important as supply chains are connected with manufacturing systems, and back-office applications are connected with front-office systems. This means that managing service quality from a business process perspective requires management solutions with a greater scope and the ability to span multiple applications.

A number of vendors offer enterprise consoles that have the capability to provide multiple views onto the business environment, and these are rapidly evolving to deliver business process views.

Caution

As with any new initiative within the industry, vendor hype around business process management will confuse the marketplace. When evaluating these claims, it is a good idea to go back to the basics. A business process spanning multiple applications can't be effectively managed unless the solution has visibility into, and can manage, the individual applications. Similarly, a single application can't be effectively managed unless the solution has visibility into, and can manage, all the supporting infrastructure layers.

Establishing and Continuing the Dialogue

The intent of this book has been to examine the state of service level management today and to provide some practical help in implementing a service level management initiative. We anticipate that the topic of service level management will continue to be of major interest to most IT professionals. As stated previously, we also expect that the capabilities and general understanding of service level management methodologies and technology will continue to evolve.

We would like to participate in that evolution and extend an invitation to you, the reader, to also be involved in the progress of service level management. To this end, we have set up a Web site at www.nextslm.org. On this site, you will find some of the templates provided in the appendix to this book, as well as other material we felt would be beneficial to share. There are chat capabilities as well as instructions on how to post material to the site.

We hope the Web site will promote sharing of best practices and a continuing dialog between like-minded professionals seeking to advance service level management. We thank you for your interest in this book, and in advance, for sharing in the forthcoming dialog.

PART IV

Appendixes

Appendix

Appendix A

Internal Service Level Agreement Template

About the SLA

This section provides a general description of the intent of the service level agreement (SLA) as well as the owners, approval and review process, and a definition of the terms used in the document.

Statement of Intent

This service level agreement (SLA) documents the characteristics of an IS service that is required by a business function as they are mutually understood and agreed to by representatives of the owner groups. The purpose of the SLA is to ensure that the proper elements and commitment are in place to provide optimal data processing services for the business function. The owner groups use this SLA to facilitate their planning process. This agreement is not meant to override current procedures, but to complement them. Service levels specified within this agreement are communicated on a monthly basis to the owner group representatives.

Approvals

Table A.1 shows which business groups and IS groups share ownership of the service, and which of their representatives have reviewed and approved this SLA.

Table A.1   **Organization Representation**

Ownership Type	Organizational Group	Representative
Business Function	*Name of business unit supported by this service*	*Business unit representative*
IS Service	*Name of service*	*Service manager*
Computing Services	*Support team for service*	*Team leader*

Review Dates

Last Review: *Date of last SLA review*

Next Review: *Scheduled date for next SLA review*

Time and Percent Conventions

This SLA uses the following conventions to refer to times and percents:

Times expressed in the format "hours:minutes" reflect a 24-hour clock in the central standard time zone.

Times expressed as a number of "business hours" include those from the hours from 8:30 to 17:30.

Times expressed as a number of "business days" include business hours, Monday through Friday, excluding designated holidays.

The symbol "---" indicates that no time applies in a category (for example, no outages are scheduled for a day).

About the Service

This section provides a description of the service and the user community, including their physical location.

Description

The *service management* group provides the following service:

- Ensures that the *specify name* application is available for users to log on and to *specify business purpose of the service*
- Responds to and resolves user questions about, problems with, and requests for enhancements to the application

User Environment

The business function is conducted in the following data processing environment as shown in Table A.2.

Table A.2 **Service User Community Characteristics**

Number of Users	Approximately *number of service users*
Geographic Location	*Specify physical locations of users*
Computer Platform	*Specify actual systems and desktops used to support the service; include any prerequisites in terms of operating system, database, and so on*

About Service Availability

This section provides information about the normal schedule of times when the service is available. It also describes the process for enhancing or changing the service.

Normal Service Availability Schedule

Table A.3 shows the times the service is available for customer use.

Table A.3 **Service Availability**

Times	Sunday	Monday	Tuesday	Wednesday	Thursday	Friday	Saturday
Start	0:00	0:00	0:00	0:00	0:00	0:00	0:00★★
Stop	24:00	24:00	24:00	24:00	24:00	24:00	24:00

★★Adjusted when necessary for scheduled outages and nonemergency enhancements

Scheduled Events that Impact Service Availability

Regularly scheduled events can cause a service outage or have an impact on performance (such as slow response time). Table A.4 shows when these are scheduled to occur.

Table A.4   **Scheduled Outages for the Weekly Server Reboot**

Times	Sunday	Monday	Tuesday	Wednesday	Thursday	Friday	Saturday
Start	3:00	---	---	---	---	---	---
Stop	4:00	---	---	---	---	---	---

Nonemergency Enhancements

All changes that take more than four hours to implement or that impact user workflow are reviewed by the *service name* Advisory Board for approval and prioritization.

Enhancements and changes that do not require a service outage and that do not impact user workflow are implemented upon completion.

Enhancements and changes that require a service outage are scheduled on Saturday mornings. Users are notified at least two business days in advance when a nonemergency service outage is required to implement an enhancement or change.

To request an enhancement, submit a problem by *specify problem submittal process.*

Change Process

Changes to any hardware or software affecting the application should be requested by *specify change request process.*

Requests for New Users

To add a new user to an existing team requires notifying the *specify appropriate representative*, or submitting a completed User Request form, and specifying the team name and the user job role (or a pattern user). Requests are usually satisfied within two business days.

To set up a new team requires notifying the *specify appropriate representative.* These requests are treated as enhancement requests and are prioritized by the *service name* Advisory Board.

About Service Measures

The *specify service management team* monitors and reports the service quality. Table A.5 shows the service measures that are reported along with the performance targets.

Table A.5 **Service Quality Measurement**

Measurement	Definition	Performance Target
Service Availability Percent	The percent of time that the application is available during the normal schedule minus the impact time from any events (scheduled or unexpected) other than loss of network or system availability	*Insert target percentage*
User Response Time	The time taken for the application service to complete a user request and user request and user request and return a response	*Insert targets— normally specified as X% of transactions of type Y to be completed with Z seconds*
Problem Response Time	The time required for a user to receive a response after reporting a problem to the Help Desk	1–High Priority— *insert target time* 2–Medium Priority— *insert target time* 3–Low Priority— *insert target time*
Problem Circumvention or Resolution Time	The time required for a user to receive a circumvention or a solution after reporting a problem to the Help Desk	1–High Priority— *insert target Time* 2–Medium Priority— *insert target time* 3–Low Priority— *insert target time*

The Help Desk prioritizes requests for support according to the following priority-level guidelines:

1–High Priority

Service name is not operational for multiple users.

A major function of *service name* is not operational for multiple users.

2-Medium Priority

> *Service name* is not operational for a single user.
>
> A major function of *service name* is not operational for a single user.
>
> A user needs to access a locked record.

3-Low Priority

> A minor function of *service name* is not operational for one or more users (who can continue to use other application functions).
>
> A user has questions about *service name* functionality.
>
> A user needs administrative assistance.
>
> Enhancement requests are logged as Priority 3-Low Priority, but are reviewed and scheduled by the *service name* Advisory Board.

Appendix B

Simple Internal Service Level Agreement Template

The *insert service name* is used by *insert description of user community* to *insert description of the service capability.* The IT department guarantees that

1. The *service name* will be available *insert percentage* of the time from *insert normal hours of operation including hours and days of the week.* Any individual outage in excess of *insert time period or sum of outages* exceeding *insert time period per month* will constitute a violation.
2. *Insert percentage* of *service name* transactions will exhibit *insert value* seconds or less response time, defined as the interval from the time the user sends a transaction to the time a visual confirmation of transaction completion is received. Missing the metric for business transactions measured over any business week will constitute a violation.
3. The IT department will respond to service incidents that affect multiple users within *insert time period*, resolve the problem within *insert time period*,

and update status every *insert time period*. Missing any of these metrics on an incident will constitute a violation.

4. The IT department will respond to service incidents that affect individual users within *insert time period*, resolve the problem within *insert time period*, and update status every *insert time period*. Missing any of these metrics on an incident will constitute a violation.

5. The IT department will respond to noncritical inquiries within *insert time period*, deliver an answer within *insert time period*, and update status within *insert time period*. Missing any of these metrics on an incident will constitute a violation.

Appendix

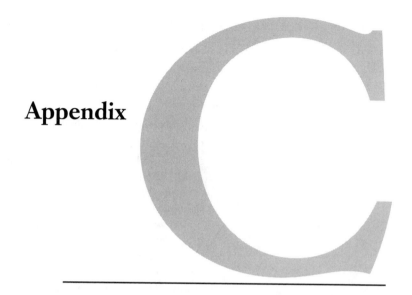

Sample Customer Satisfaction Survey

Thank you for taking the time to provide feedback regarding the services provided by the IT department. There are three areas that you may evaluate:

- Customer Service Orientation
- Results Orientation
- Expertise of Staff

There is also an area for general comments and future IT requirements.

Rating Service Quality

The quality ratings to be used are

- Poor: Service was significantly below expectations
- Fair: Service was below expectations
- Good: Service met expectations
- Very Good: Service exceeded expectations
- Excellent: Service significantly exceeded expectations

If you enter a Fair or Poor rating, we ask that you provide additional comments.

Table C.1 shows the qualities and skills descriptions that should be used when making evaluations.

Table C.1   **Quality and Skill Descriptions**

Area	Qualities and Skills Evaluated
Customer Service Orientation	Courteous, congenial, responds in a timely manner, gets along with customers, cost-efficient, professional, enthusiastic
Results Orientation	Maintains focus, persistent, strong commitment, organized, 'can-do' attitude, takes initiative, takes pride in work, achieves goals, takes responsibility, dependable
Expertise of Staff	Technical knowledge, effective oral and written skills, good listener, perceptive, objective, thorough, analytical, decisive, insightful, intuitive

Please complete Table C.2 by rating each of the services against the three attributes.

Table C.2   **Service Ratings**

Service	Customer Service Orientation	Results Orientation	Expertise of Staff
	BUSINESS APPLICATIONS		
Financial Application			
H/R Application			
Email			
Web Access			
	DESKTOP SUPPORT		
PC Hardware/Software			
UNIX, X-terms			
	NETWORK SUPPORT		
Local Network			
Remote Network			
Phones/Voice mail			
	TECHNICAL SUPPORT		
Mainframe			
UNIX Servers			
NT Servers			

General Comments

Please make general comments in the following areas:

Customer Service Orientation:

Results Orientation:

Expertise of Staff:

What things do you feel the IT department does well and what things could we do better? What works and what does not? Please be specific.

Current Usage

This section helps the IT department gain a better understanding of the service usage and support patterns of our customers. Please answer the following question.

How would you describe your reliance on information technology to perform your job?

- Extremely Heavy
- Heavy
- Moderate
- Light
- Very Light

Please indicate in Table C.3 the most frequent contact you have with the IT department in each of the designated areas.

Table C.3 **IT Department Contacts**

Contact Type Annually	Daily	Weekly	Monthly	Quarterly
Reporting a service problem				
Requesting a new application project				
Requesting an application enhancement				
Adding a new user				
Requesting new network access				
Requesting service access				

Future Requirements

In your opinion, what specific areas should the IT department focus on during the next year? Please be specific.

Optional Information

Please provide the following information so that we can follow up with you:

Name: _____

Department: _____

Location: _____

Appendix

Sample Reporting Schedule

The following outline recommends report content and frequencies. The reports are additive. At the end of a quarter, the monthly, weekly, and daily reports would be produced in addition to the quarterly report.

Daily Report

The daily report is a tactical report showing sufficient detail to allow the IT department and IT management to have a good understanding of the service quality of the previous day. These reports are typically kept online for two weeks. The contents include

- Outage report by application by location
- Response time report by application by location summarized at 15-minute intervals for the prime shift, and at 30-minute intervals for the off-shift
- Problem reports by priority, including a brief description of the problem for critical and severe problems

- Average problem response time by priority
- Problems closed and outstanding by priority
- Security violations and attempted intrusions

Weekly Report

The weekly reports are used by both the IT department and the lines of business to review the service quality delivered by the IT department. These reports are kept online for eight weeks. The contents include

- Workload volumes by application summarized by shift by day
- Outage summary by application by shift by day
- Recovery analysis for all outages of significant duration
- Cumulative outage duration for the month by application
- Response time percentiles by application
- Security violations and attempted intrusions

Monthly Report

The monthly report is a management report that focuses on how well the IT department is servicing the lines of business. The monthly reports are kept online for six months. The contents include

- Report card summary
- Workload volumes by application
- Service level achievement summary by application service
- Highlighted problem areas and analysis

Quarterly Report

The quarterly report is a business report focused on identifying trends in service quality as well as overall satisfaction. It also provides information on future initiatives. The quarterly reports are kept online for four to six quarters. The contents include

- Workload trend report by application and user community
- Customer satisfaction survey results
- Service level achievement trends
- Cost allocation summary
- New IT initiatives

Appendix

Sample Value Statement & Return on Investment (ROI) Analysis for a Service Provider Delivering an SAP Application

This appendix contains a case study of the justification for implementing service level management at an application service provider. The name of the company has been suppressed. In addition to a qualitative discussion of the value from implementing service level management at this company, there is a quantitative analysis of rates of return on investment.

The value proposition is explained by looking at two different categories of value: benefits and ROI. A *benefit* refers to the soft value that is typically harder to quantify in direct dollar revenue generation or cost savings. People, productivity, and perception frequently fall into this category. *Return on Investment*, or *ROI*, refers to hard real-dollar savings or direct revenue generation or direct dollar cost savings.

Summary of Value

The nature of the service provider business is providing application availability. Inherent in this is a guarantee of a certain level of availability and performance. The Service Level Agreement (SLA) evidences this with our customers. We provide for a penalty when this level of availability is not met. The major service level management value comes from providing the exact methodology and tools needed to manage at the required level.

The ROI value areas are

- Avoid paying a financial penalty by meeting service level objectives for a customer
- Slower growth (hiring) of the support and operations staff
- Reduce the number of help desk calls
- Eventual possible elimination of the help desk operations
- Software licensing savings

The benefit value areas are

- Lost customer credibility with excessive downtime or poor response time
- Time savings of the operations staff
- Time savings of the shared group
- Greater credibility of the SLA numbers
- Sales competitive advantage
- Reduced time and manual effort for the billing staff

Return on Investment (ROI) Value Areas

These are the hard-dollar savings or increased revenue that can be generated as a result of implementing proactive service level management.

Avoid Paying a Financial Penalty by Meeting Service Level Objectives for a Customer

Service Level Agreements provide for giving our customers performance credits when a service level is not met in some defined area.

How Service Level Management Contributes Value

Proactive service level management monitors and manages the very thing that is in the Service Level Agreement with your customers. There is no stronger statement of value that service level management can make than this.

Metrics Needed to Quantify

- Past frequency of missing service levels
- Cost of a performance credit and the formula for determining when real money is lost due to performance credits given

Expected Service Level Management Benefit

A reduction in number of times of missing a service level and the resulting lowering of performance credits given. This will result in fewer dollars lost due to performance credits.

Slower Growth (Hiring) of the Support and Operations Staff

Automation of certain routine tasks and recovery processes means that the support and operations staff has more time to spend on other nonroutine tasks and projects. That means as the workload increases, new staff will not have to be hired as fast as the growth of new customers.

How Service Level Management Contributes Value

Proactive service management provides the automation, notification, email, and paging capabilities to make this possible. Also, because the service level management methodology helps to better determine which roles are responsible for what service areas, problem detection and determination time are reduced as well.

Metrics Needed to Quantify

- Projected new customer and user frequency
- Projected support and operations staff increases

Expected Service Level Management Benefit

A slower than projected growth rate of support and operations staff.

Reduce the Number of Help Desk Calls

Quicker recovery of certain routine tasks along with real-time Web posting of application statuses will reduce the number of calls to the help desk. There is a direct cost associated with the resources needed to staff and operate a help desk.

How Service Level Management Contributes Value

Proactive service level management includes the Web posting and communication facilities to customers and end users so that they will not have to call the help desk as often to report a problem or find out information. In other companies, this process has resulted in calls to the help desk being reduced by as much as 85%. Using certain assumptions based on cost of resources and time to complete a call, other companies have estimated the cost of a single help desk call to be in the $20–$25 range. Multiplying this cost multiplied by the expected reduction in number of calls demonstrates that this process can result in substantial savings.

Metrics Needed to Quantify

- Cost per hour of help desk and support resources
- Average time spent on a single help desk call

Expected Service Level Management Benefit

Substantial reduction in the number of help desk calls and a corresponding decrease in cost.

Eventual Potential Elimination of the Help Desk Operations

Elimination of the help desk function that involves actually answering the phone to take all problem and request calls can be accomplished over time through the implementation of proactive service management and can result in significant savings.

How Service Level Management Contributes Value

The service management center, through its Web posting and virtual help desk enabling capabilities, can help the IT staff to align systems statuses and problem reporting alike so that users and customers are presented with the same levels of drill down. This alignment also means that problems are directed to the proper support resource in the same way that the IT department alerts staff automatically of internal problems. This has been an observed and demonstrated benefit at other companies. Several companies have no help desk staff. All problems are logged through the internal Web page, system and application statuses are posted to the internal Web site, and a backup telephone number using automated voice recognition (AVR) technology directs callers automatically using the same prompts as on the internal Web site.

Metrics Needed to Quantify

- Annual cost of help desk staff
- Current help desk staffing levels and projected growth rates
- Cost of AVR technology

Expected Service Level Management Benefit

Eventual elimination of the help desk staff.

Software License Savings

By using information on active and inactive users of a software package in an environment where license purchase is based on concurrent usage, the number of licenses needed can be managed to be much less than the observed maximum number of concurrent users.

How Service Level Management Contributes Value

Proactive service management provides the capability to understand which users of an application are active and inactive, and how long inactive users have been in that state. Through a baselining process, you can determine how many concurrent licenses you need if you automatically logged off users who have been inactive longer than a certain period of time. Then the service management center performs the automatic logoff to keep you in license compliance. This has been an observed and demonstrated benefit at other companies. Hundreds of thousands of dollars have been saved in just a few years by using this information.

Metrics Needed to Quantify

- Type of licensing arrangements
- Cost of a license for specific application packages
- Expected growth rate of users
- Current license usage levels

Expected Service Level Management Benefit

Dollar savings in fewer concurrent licenses needed and growth containment in new licenses needed.

Benefit Areas

Benefits include soft dollar areas such as people productivity, customer confidence, and brand perception that are harder to quantify and use as a justification for service level management, but are nonetheless important.

Lost Customer Credibility with Excessive Downtime or Poor Response Time

A service provider will quickly lose credibility with customers who frequently experience what they perceive to be excessive down time or poor response time. Even though the service provider will pay a penalty for not meeting service level objectives with customers, the intangible loss of credibility can ultimately cost the service provider new and existing customers in the long run.

How Service Level Management Contributes Value

Proactive service management manages both availability and performance to customer needs. These are two of the items that can significantly contribute to loss of credibility.

Time Savings of the Operations Staff

Automation of certain routine tasks and recovery processes means that the existing support and operations staff has more time to spend on other nonroutine tasks and projects. Having more time to spend on projects means performance improvements across the board. This also helps improve morale of the staff because they would prefer to work on the more challenging and less routine aspects of their jobs.

How Service Level Management Contributes Value

Proactive service management provides automation, emailing, and paging capabilities, which free up time for the staff to perform nonroutine tasks and projects.

Time Savings of the Reporting Group

The reporting group has the responsibility of collecting the data and analyzing this information to prepare and publish SLA data. This is a manual effort today, which is time-consuming. As the company grows in size of number of customers, this effort will take even more time. Automation of the collection and publishing of this information can save substantial amounts of time, as well as result in greater accuracy.

How Service Level Management Contributes Value

Proactive service management is based on collecting the information needed to produce SLA reports. This will eliminate the manual effort of the reporting group for collecting the information, comparing it to defined SLAs, and reporting it.

Greater Credibility of the SLA Numbers

Most IT environments that report service levels for availability and performance collect numbers based on assumptions and memory recall, and few facts that can be validated. Proactive service management reports on numbers that are based only on true, measured availability, and response times from an application, as well as an end-user perspective.

How Service Level Management Contributes Value

Proactive service management collects availability information from all technology components involved in an application service and records exact uptimes and downtimes. There is no guesswork involved and everything is automated. When the entire application service is covered through electronic means, the numbers have credibility.

Sales Competitive Advantage

Besides access to applications, high availability and good performance of business transactions are the biggest benefits a service provider offers to potential customers. Having the infrastructure tools, processes, and resources aligned in the same way can be a selling point with potential customers.

How Service Level Management Contributes Value

Service level management contributes value in this area by providing the means to manage and improve availability and performance.

Reduced Time and Manual Effort for the Billing Staff

The billing staff must collect accurate information on availability by application and customer in order to calculate the bills and credits properly each month. This effort can be reduced with proactive service level management that automatically collects these numbers, thus saving time and money of the billing staff.

How Service Level Management Contributes Value

Service level management contributes value in this area by providing accurate availability numbers electronically in whatever format is desirable. This comes from a service monitoring database where these numbers are consolidated from all technology components involved in the process.

Return on Investment Analysis

Along with the qualitative analysis, a quantitative analysis has been produced show-ing three-year rates of return on the investment required to implement proactive service level management. These results are shown in Figure E.1.

Sample Service Provider
Project ROI Analysis

3 Year Utilization

Benefits/Costs	Year 0	Year 1	Year 2	Year 3
Slower Rate of Hiring - Systems Support	$0	$140,000	$210,000	$280,000
Reduce Help Desk Hiring Rate / Eliminate HD	$0	$140,000	$210,000	$280,000
	$0	$336,000	$840,000	$1,344,000
	$0	$616,000	$1,260,000	$1,904,000
Professional Services - SAP SLM	$0	$450,000	$0	$0
Product Cost - SAP	$0	$480,000	$1,080,000	$960,000
	$0	$930,000	$1,080,000	$960,000
Annual Net Cash Flow	$0	($314,000)	$180,000	$944,000

Internal Rate of Return	104.4%
$ Above Hurdle Rate	$341,358

Figure E.1   *An ROI analysis for service level management of an SAP application at a service provider.*

Summary

The implementation of proactive service level management at this sample service provider shows an excellent rate of return on the level of investment required for the implementation.

Appendix

Selected Vendors of Service Level Management Products

$\mathbf{A}$s this book went to print, the ever-expanding market for service level management included over 800 vendors, each with a claim to provide at least one SLM solution. In reality, many products cover just one aspect of SLM, such as event monitoring or historical reporting. But this limitation does not stop vendors from selling their wares as comprehensive SLM solutions. Given these claims, it is difficult, if not impossible, to assemble a complete list of SLM products that does full justice to the market—and the prospective buyer. The information that follows is intended as a sampling of representative offerings that readers can use to start the evaluation process.

ServicePoint Series

The ServicePoint Service Delivery Unit (SDU) is a WAN access device that combines termination, monitoring, and control. It maps specific types of services, such as ATM, frame relay, or IP WAN service, to business applications, according to user-specified parameters. ServicePoint Explorer is a real-time software package that centrally collects data from multiple ServicePoint devices, displaying performance parameters such as utilization, congestion, and delay and monitoring WAN use within organizations. ServicePoint Reporter is a non-intrusive data collection tool for monitoring frame relay service levels and overall network performance. It works with ServicePoint SDUs and with ADC Telecommunications' DataSMART Frame Monitoring DSU/CSUs. Reporter monitors frame relay performance and graphically displays key statistics on circuit availability, delay, and data delivery rates. It also exhibits individual and aggregate circuit performance on a day-to-day basis and over time, giving IT staff a basis for circuit troubleshooting and WAN bandwidth planning.

ADC Telecommunications Incorporated

Access Products Division

14375 NW Science Park Drive

Portland, OR 97209

+1-503-643-1681

800-733-5511

http://www.adc.com/access

IQ Series

The Adtran IQ series of intelligent performance monitoring devices provides detailed statistics on the overall health and performance of frame relay networks at rates from 56Kbps to 2.048Kbps. It is specifically targeted at Service Level Agreement verification for frame relay subscribers. In-depth diagnostics for circuit management and troubleshooting also are furnished. The IQ family features IQ View, an SNMP management program that runs under Windows NT. This software manages IQ devices while providing a database and trend analysis of the frame relay statistics gathered.

Adtran Incorporated

901 Explorer Boulevard

Huntsville, AL 35814-4000

+1-256-963-8000

800-923-8726

http://www.adtran.com

EnView

EnView software monitors service levels for distributed applications and alerts IT managers when objectives are not being met, so problems can be resolved proactively. The software runs under Windows NT and is designed to continuously provide response-time information from the end-user perspective. The software identifies trends in response time over long periods of time to spot potential problems before they interfere with business and to identify growth patterns for capacity planning. To facilitate this, detailed service-level data generated by EnView can be stored in a central reporting repository. Thus, availability and end-user response time might be tracked historically by application and location, enabling service-level trending for IS management and the end-user community.

Amdahl Corporation

1250 East Arques Avenue

Sunnyvale, CA 94088

+1-408-746-7830

http://www.amdahl.com

Appvisor Application Management

Appvisor is a software package designed to work with Microsoft Exchange and Lotus Notes. It provides service level monitoring, performance reporting, help desk services, and ongoing usage analysis. Appvisor users can associate resource use with specific departments or individuals in order to manage user behavior, correct inefficiencies, and illustrate how resources are being consumed. Appvisor also supports real-time monitoring of application transactions and monitors the impact of application workloads on server performance and user response time. The product also creates illustrations of baseline performance.

Appliant Incorporated

3513 NE 45th Street

Seattle, WA 98105-5640

+1-206-523-9566

877-227-7542

http://www.appliant.com

Spectrum Service Level Management Solutions

Aprisma, formerly the Spectrum division of Cabletron, offers a range of service level management products, both independently and through partnership with selected third-party vendors. Products that have been integrated with the vendor's Spectrum management platform include Concord Network Health, Gecko Saman, ICS Continuity, Micromuse Netcool/Omnibus, Opticom EIS, and Optimal Application Expert. In addition, Spectrum itself offers a range of products that support SLM, including the SpectroWatch real-time alarm notification package for applications, hosts, and network devices; Spectrum Alarm Notification; and SpectroRx inferencing solution. Spectrum also offers a range of applications designed to report performance and manage availability for specific types of networks. These include Spectrum ATM Services Manager, Remote Access Services Manager, and VLAN Services Manager. A series of functional applications for Spectrum enhance IT's ability to furnish comprehensive SLM measurements and reports. These include Spectrum Data Warehouse, Spectrum Data Mining, Spectrum Capacity Planning, and Spectrum Accounting and Billing. Spectrum software runs under a range of operating systems, including most versions of UNIX.

Aprisma Management Technology

121 Technology Drive

Durham, NH 03824

+1-603-337-7000

http://www.aprisma.com

Attention!

Attention! provides immediate notification of system, network, and environmental events via pagers, telephones, audio announcements, message boards, and custom notification techniques. The software filters events and activates alerts in support of user-specified escalation procedures. It also furnishes statistical reports detailing how well performance meets specified thresholds. The product runs in mainframe, UNIX, and Windows NT environments and supports most RS-232 devices.

Attention Software Incorporated

2175 N. Academy Circle, Suite 100

Colorado Springs, CO 80909

+1-719-591-9110

http://www.attentionsoftware.com

Trinity and eWatcher

Avesta Technologies, acquired in February 2000 by Visual Networks Inc., offers two SLM products. The first of these, Trinity, helps enterprises, service providers, and electronic commerce organizations to apply priorities and workflow policies to IT problems and report real-time and historical service levels to their customers. Trinity's Enterprise Service Model performs real-time root cause and impact analysis for diagnosing problems, allowing IT managers to resolve critical problems before service is disrupted and increasing availability. Trinity runs under UNIX and Windows NT.

Avesta Technologies' eWatcher is a Web management software solution that provides continuous monitoring of Internet-based applications and services. The package automatically discovers existing Web environments and tests service performance against established thresholds. eWatcher also locates bad links and scripts proactively. In the event of changes to home page content, eWatcher will alert IT personnel. It also delivers real-time availability and performance information. The product runs under UNIX and Windows NT.

Avesta Technologies Incorporated

2 Rector Street, 15th Floor

New York, NY 10006

+1-212-285-1500

800-822-9773

http://www.avesta.com

PILOT

PILOT is a performance tuning and capacity planning tool for mainframes. It features reporting, tracking, forecasting, and modeling. PILOT tracks response times, identifies peak periods, builds simulations of current and future systems for capacity planning and justification, and produces reports that facilitate timely problem diagnosis and resolution. Versions of PILOT are offered for MVS, CICS, and SMF environments.

Axios Products Incorporated

1373-10 Veterans Highway

Hauppauge, NY 11788

+1-631-979-0100

800-877-0990

http://www.axios.com

Patrol, Best/1, Command/Post, MainView, MAXM

BMC Software solutions are designed to ensure that businesses meet specified goals of availability, performance, recovery of business-critical applications, and service level management agreements. The solutions run on a range of operating platforms, including OS/390, most versions of UNIX, and Windows NT. Specific BMC Software solutions are available in four key areas: Application Service Management ensures that applications meet accepted service levels. Products in this area include Patrol, Command/Post, Best1, and MainView. In the area of data management, products ensure enterprise data availability and integrity. Solutions in this area include MAXM.

BMC offers Incontrol software for IT process automation and Resolve for rapid recovery and storage management. In addition to these products, BMC offers service level management in customized Service Assurance Center solutions. These combine a management methodology with products and professional services for a variety of platforms and applications.

BMC Software Incorporated

2101 CityWest Boulevard

Houston, TX 77042

+1-713-918-8800

800-841-2031

http://www.bmc.com

Keystone VPNview and Keystone CNM

Keystone VPNview software allows customers to proactively monitor SLAs and manage performance of carrier services such as frame relay. It reports real-time and historical data on bandwidth utilization and availability of individual circuits and routed segments. IT professionals can partition data so that in-house customers view only the data specific to their portion of the network. The software supports SNMP and runs under UNIX and Windows NT. Keystone CNM (Customer Network Management) gives service providers the ability to furnish end users with access to their network information via the Web. An integral real-time repository ensures security and enables individual customers to further partition their data views by subsidiary, geography, division, or department. The software monitors performance on ATM, frame relay, IP, and Sonet networks based on switches from Ascend, Cisco, Lucent, and Newbridge. A topology application provides graphical representation of specific nodes and circuits.

Bridgeway Corporation

PO Box 229

Redmond, WA 98073-0229

+1-425-881-4270

http://www.bridgeway.com

OpenMaster

BullSoft, the worldwide software division of Groupe Bull SA (Paris), offers OpenMaster to manage multi-vendor IT networks, systems, and applications. OpenMaster, based on UNIX, incorporates an object-based repository and management services to allow IT staff to easily deploy software, manage assets and configurations, manage availability and performance of IT, and secure IT components. OpenMaster also furnishes service-level reporting on all IT elements across geographical, functional, or business process boundaries. Reports are provided on network devices, desktops, servers, and applications. Information is delivered on configuration, significant events, and security parameters. A range of report formats are offered for a variety of media, including the Web via graphical Java interfaces. In addition, multi-dimensional analysis tools are available for more complex tasks, such as return on investment evaluations or analyses of the overall performance of critical components over long periods of time.

BullSoft

300 Concord Road

Billerica, MA 01821

+1-978-294-6000

800-285-5727

http://www.bullsoft.com

eBA*ServiceMonitor and ServiceNetwork, ETEWatch, RTN, PMN

eBA(e-Business Assurance)*ServiceMonitor is a Windows NT- and UNIX-compatible software package that measures Web site performance from the end-user perspective, enabling IT and Web managers to set Service Level Agreements and ensure customer service thresholds. eBA*ServiceNetwork is a business information service that studies Web service levels, historical trends, and usage over time and automatically issues reports.

ETEWatch is software that runs under Windows NT and measures end-to-end application performance management. Versions are offered to support Citrix MetaFrame, Lotus Notes, R/3 monitors, PeopleSoft, and custom applications.

Candle's Response Time Network (RTN) is a service that monitors applications from the end user's point of view. RTN is based on Candle's ETEWatch and lets users see how applications are performing for any site, time, user, server, or time period right at the desktop. An advanced online application process engine structures the data into information that can be customized. Candle's Performance Monitoring Network (PMN) automates the transformation of performance data into intelligent business analysis. The service provides daily, weekly, monthly, or quarterly information on service levels, capacity, and application monitoring.

Candle Corporation

201 N. Douglas Street

Los Angeles, CA 90245

+1-310-535-3600

http://www.candle.com

CiscoWorks 2000 with Service Level Management Suite

Cisco offers a service level management suite with XML-based interfaces for use on networks that deploy its routing and switching equipment. The suite relies on specially developed Service Assurance Agents (SA Agents) within routers and switches. These agents extend the integral capabilities of Cisco devices to measure Web, voice, and data services. The results obtained by SA Agents are used to monitor network Service Level Agreements. The Cisco Service Level Management Suite also furnishes business-oriented reporting for IT managers on services deployed from outside providers. By using XML, the agents can be extended across multiple partners' networks using the Internet delivery model.

The service level management suite runs under Windows NT and is also part of Cisco's Management Connection Service Management Program, which enables enterprise customers to choose their applications and to construct a service management solution consisting of multiple horizontally integrated partners. Vendors in the program have committed to deploying solutions based on Cisco's service management technology and open XML-based interfaces. The initial vendors in the program include: Compuware, Concord Communications, Desktalk Systems, FirstSense Software, Ganymede Software, Hewlett-Packard, InfoVista Corporation, Inverse Network Technology, Manage.Com, NetScout Systems, Network Associates, NextPoint Networks, ProactiveNET, Response Networks, TAVVE Software, Valencia Systems, Visionael, and Visual Networks.

Cisco Systems Incorporated

170 West Tasman Drive

San Jose, CA 95134

+1-408-526-4000

800-553-6387

http://www.cisco.com

Unicenter TNG Advanced Help Desk and ServiceIT Enterprise Edition

CA's Unicenter TNG products offer service level management according to user-definable rules that can be associated with business policies as well as network or system elements. Users can define service thresholds according to a specific condition or set of conditions. Actions can be set to be performed when service thresholds are exceeded, or when a condition is not present. Alerts, evaluations, or specific automated routines can be set for activation after an elapsed time interval. All actions can be associated with assigned service priority levels. The software runs under UNIX and a range of other computing platforms.

Computer Associates International Incorporated

One Computer Associates Plaza

Islandia, NY 11788-7000

+1-516-342-5224

800-225-5224

http://www.cai.com

EcoSCOPE and EcoTOOLS

EcoSCOPE uses a software probe technology to monitor the network nonintrusively. It automatically discovers applications, tracks application flows through the LAN/WAN infrastructure, and collects detailed performance metrics. EcoSCOPE correlates this information into a user interface with a scorecard format that automatically identifies poorly performing applications, the servers and users impacted, and the magnitude of the performance problem. Users can drill down to understand the root cause in order to solve problems quickly. EcoSCOPE also can be used to determine which applications are contending for network resources, who is using them and for how long, and whether there are any predictable patterns in application usage. EcoTOOLS enables an IT administrator to manage availability and service levels across e-commerce, messaging, and ERP applications running under Windows NT, UNIX, and Novell NetWare. EcoTOOLS uses a single, consistent Windows NT interface to furnish at-a-glance scorecard reports for management and the general user population in addition to the in-depth operational reports required for the daily management of applications and servers. Customizable reports also are available.

Compuware Corporation

31440 Northwestern Highway

Farmington Hills, MI 48334-2564

+1-248-737-7300

800-521-9353

http://www.compuware.com

Network Health—Service Level Reports

Concord's Network Health—Service Level Reports allows service providers to optimize service quality and document Service Level Agreement compliance. It also enables them to add value to transport services by offering customized reports tailored to individual organizations. These reports can be a valuable bargaining tool in service contract negotiation, the vendor says. Network Health—Service Level Reports runs under UNIX and Windows NT. Concord says its approach leverages the vendor's ability to gather performance information from multiple enterprise resources and present it in a concise, single-page report that's easy to understand. The reports include the Executive report, a high-level summary of quality of service across the enterprise and by business unit; the IT Manager Report, which offers a more detailed picture of enterprise trends and service performance by region and individual devices; and Service Customer Reports, which document the quality of service delivered by providers to their customers.

Concord Communications Incorporated

600 Nickerson Road

Marlboro, MA 01752

+1-508-460-4646

http://www.concord.com

CrossKeys Resolve

CrossKeys Resolve is a software suite designed to help service providers define, set, and meaasure service level goals. The product also includes performance reporting software. The Solaris-based package enables service provider to deliver sets of network and service performance reports to their customers and internal users via the

Web. The application correlates network information with links to customer information and Quality of Service (QoS) objectives—to provide an end-to-end service view for service provider customers.

CrossKeys Systems Incorporated

1593 Spring Hill Road, Suite 200

Vienna, VA 22182

+1-703-734-3706

http://www.crosskeys.com

TREND

DeskTalk's TREND product automates the collection and analysis of performance data and delivers business-critical reports out of the box. TREND collects performance data from industry-standard sources such as SNMP MIBs, as well as from application monitoring partners such as FirstSense Software and Ganymede Software. Utilizing these heterogeneous data sources, TREND reports deliver a cohesive view of network, system, and application performance, providing IT organizations with an end-to-end service level picture of the entire business process. TREND is built on a distributed architecture with a Web interface for report creation and viewing. TREND users can add new data sources, update polling polices, fine tune threshold definitions, and create customized performance reports. A predictive analysis feature warns network managers in advance of impending slowdowns so they can prevent problems and quickly identify the root cause of any delay. TREND operates on and between AIX, HP-UX, Solaris, Windows 95, and Windows NT platforms.

DeskTalk Systems Incorporated

19191 South Vermont Avenue, Suite 900

Torrance, CA 90502

+1-310-630-1000

http://www.desktalk.com

RPM 3000 with WANwatcher

Eastern Research's Router/Performance Monitor (RPM) 3000 is a multifunctional branch office frame relay router with integral DSU/CSUs that includes trend analysis monitoring capabilities. Using interface cards, it can be upgraded to support a range of data rates up to T1. The RPM 3000 measures throughput, bandwidth utilization, and network delays on up to 32 frame relay PVCs (permanent virtual circuits) and assures that a carrier is delivering the promised SLA bandwidth. WANwatcher takes the data gathered by the RPM 3000 and provides IT with statistical trending information on the utilization, link status, and interface detail as well as other parameters vital to the frame relay network. WANwatcher collects the network statistics in real time or on an hourly, daily, or weekly basis or at preset intervals. It can handle data on up to 1,280 channels in the network. Statistics can be viewed in a range of report formats.

Eastern Research Incorporated

225 Executive Drive

Moorestown, NJ 08057

+1-856-273-6622

http://www.erinc.com

Empirical Suite

Empirical's flagship product, the Empirical Suite, covers the planning, measurement, and prediction functions associated with improving enterprise service levels. The suite is comprised of three products: Empirical Planner, Empirical Director, and Empirical Controller. The applications are sold either individually or as a bundled solution. Empirical Planner helps IT managers set baselines, define corporate service levels, and implement requirements. Empirical Director runs under Windows NT, UNIX, or VMS and tracks actual application service, sending alerts when performance falls below an optimum level, and diagnosing the source of a problem. IT managers can also use the application to perform trend analysis for capacity planning and long-term troubleshooting purposes. Empirical Controller performs corrective actions to fix service level issues. The application makes promises to help administrators automate the tuning of application SQL and the database's physical structure.

Empirical Software Incorporated

1151 Williams Drive

Aiken, SC 29803

+1-803-648-5931

877-289-8100

http://www.empirical.com

Envive Service Level Suite

Envive's Service Level Suite (SLS) provides SAP service level and performance management based on real-time monitoring and analysis of end-user response time performance by business unit, department, or geography. SLS develops a baseline analysis to determine normal system performance. It then applies a series of knowledge-based rules against the baseline to identify abnormal behavior that can lead to performance problems. Engineers can drill down and learn more about the abnormal behavior and perform what/if analyses to see how changes in loading can improve system performance. Basis engineers can also enhance Envive's health check by adding additional knowledge rules using their own SAP knowledge. SLS runs on a separate architecture from the database system itself, enabling it to perform analyses even when R/3 is down.

Envive Corporation

1975 El Camino Real, Suite 303

Mountain View, CA 94040

+1-650-934-4100

888-236-8483

http://www.envive.com

FirstSense Enterprise

FirstSense, which was acquired by Concord Communications on January 2, 2000, offers FirstSense Enterprise, software that continuously monitors application performance and availability from the end-user perspective. FirstSense says this approach provides IT organizations the information necessary to measure true application quality of service. FirstSense Enterprise uses patented lightweight intelligent autonomous agents on end-user client systems to continuously monitor and collect information on business transactions that affect the end user. The agents track end-to-end response times (in real-time) comparing actual availability and performance against service-level thresholds. When a transaction exceeds defined service-level thresholds, FirstSense Enterprise captures diagnostic information at the moment the exception occurs and at every tier involved with that specific application transaction. FirstSense sends notification of an alarm, and compares values at exception time to normally observed behavior. These "normalcy profiles" provide a baseline of application behavior so that IT can determine what is typical for a particular environment. The baseline data and exception diagnostics provide IT with the context for resolving problems, whether on the client, network, or server.

FirstSense Software Incorporated

21 B Street

Burlington, MA 01803

+1-781-685-1000

http://www.firstsense.com

Pegasus

Ganymede Software's Pegasus monitoring solution is designed to minimize the time and effort required to detect, diagnose, and trend network performance problems. The Pegasus Application Monitor component gives a user's view of application performance. It passively monitors the performance of end-user transactions, so IT professionals can identify, prioritize, isolate, and diagnose application performance problems. It tells staffers if an application on a particular desktop is being constrained by the client, the network, or the server so that they can deal with these problems before end-users are aware of them. If the network is causing an application to slow down, Pegasus identifies which network segment is causing the performance degradation by using active application flows of known transactions to determine where performance is being constrained. In addition, key system statistics can be monitored to see how they are affecting application performance.

This information can be used to establish trends, set SLAs, and monitor conformance to agreed-on criteria.

Ganymede Software Incorporated

1100 Perimeter Park Drive, Suite 104

Morrisville, NC 27560-9119

919-469-0997

http://www.ganymede.com

Gecko Service Level Agreement Manager (SAMAN)

Gecko SAMAN provides service level management and reporting for mission-critical networks. It is designed to allow net managers to define, monitor, and report on the achievement of service level commitments, either by in-house organizations or external service providers. The product models Service Level Agreements and furnishes executive-quality business reports based on information from a wide variety of different sources including Spectrum, HP OpenView, and Tivoli NetView. Using this information, customers can build Service Level Agreements that include availability (uptime, mean time between failure, mean time to repair), network performance (bandwidth and latency), and people-related performance from workflow management systems.

Gecko Software Limited

P.O. Box 5

PINNER, HA5 1US

Middlesex, UK

+44 700-004-3256 (UK)

or

19925 Stevens Creek Boulevard

Cupertino, CA 95014-2358

+1-408-725-7105 (US)

http://www.geckoware.com

HP OpenView ITSM Service Level Manager

ITSM Service Level Manager uses a configuration management database to identify the components that reside in the IT infrastructure and the corresponding IT services the components provide. IT professionals can then use this information to create a service catalog to formalize operational performance agreements between IT groups and their customers. The HP application tracks actual service versus service level objectives. This makes it possible for organizations to set progress monitors and escalation rules to manage the incidents and ensure that Service Level Agreements will not be violated.

Hewlett-Packard Company

3000 Hanover Street

Palo Alto, CA 94304-1185

+1-650-857-1501

http://www.hp.com

Continuity

Continuity software is designed to help IT organizations manage service requirements in complex distributed environments. It gathers baseline information on normal network performance and then tracks information on availability, performance, response time, throughput, service levels, and operational risks—in terms that both IT operations managers and business managers can understand. Continuity provides real-time, correlated diagnostics to maximize availability and performance by helping managers to correct and prevent service disruption quickly. By monitoring business transactions as users experience them, the product aims to address problems before users are aware they exist.

Intelligent Communication Software GmbH

Kistlerhof Str. 111, 81379

Munich, Germany

+49-89-748598-35

http://www.ics.de

InfoVista and Infovista Web Access Server, VistaViews

InfoVista offers a suite of tools specially designed for SLM. Features include wizard-driven report creation, drill-down between reports, complex data structure handling, full-database query capabilities, and complete developer kit (with C, Perl, and Visual Basic support) for customization.

The InfoVista Web Access Server is a Web application (Java-based and HTML compliant) for report browsing. Web Access Server, like the InfoVista core product, is fully customizable. Key features include exporting reports by specifying filters, exporting reports by specifying instances, batch or on-demand report distribution, and intelligent online updating of performance information. VistaViews are ready-to-use report templates for use with the InfoVista Report Builder. These include comprehensive reports covering networks, systems and applications, ATM and frame relay WANs, Ethernet switches, routers, and LAN segments, among other elements. The Vista Plug-in for NetFlow is an integrated package for InfoVista that provides an efficient means of managing high-volume NetFlow data from Cisco devices. All InfoVista products run on Windows or UNIX platforms.

InfoVista Corporation

12, avenue des Tropiques

91955 Courtaboeuf cedex

France

+33.1.46.21.87.87 (Europe)

or

5950 Symphony Woods Rd

Columbia, MD 21044

+1-410-997-4470 (United States)

`http://www.infovista.com`

Service Management Architecture

Jyra measures the quality of service and response times delivered to Web commerce customers, desktop users, and branch locations. Jyra's products are built around its Service Management Architecture (SMA) that continually monitors services to identify weaknesses in network configuration, hardware failures, congestion, or other issues that are having a negative impact on e-commerce performance.

Jyra's SMA uses a mid-level manager to collect and aggregate response time data from Service Level Monitor (SLMs), agents distributed throughout the networked environment. SLMs notify the mid-level manager of when response times exceed a defined level. The mid-level manager can, in turn, forward that data to upstream management stations. SLMs can also be used for local reporting.

Jyra Research Incorporated

2880 Zanker Road, Suite 203

San Jose, CA 95134

+1-408-432-7235

http://www.jyra.com

NETClarity Suite

The NETClarity Suite of network performance management and diagnostic tools allows the network manager to monitor, measure, test, and diagnose performance across the entire network. The suite's six network performance tools are Network Checker+, Remote Analyzer Probe, Load Balancer, Service Level Manager, Capacity Planner, and NETClarity Complete. All the tools are based on technology and methodologies taken from LANquest's independent LAN/WAN testing services.

LANQuest

47800 Westinghouse Drive

Fremont, CA 94539

+1-510-354-0940

800-487-7779

http://www.lanquest.com

PerformanceWorks for E-Business and PerformanceWorks WebWatcher

PerformanceWorks for E-Business software monitors the performance of end-user workstations, back-end servers, databases, and other system-level components of enterprise services. PerformanceWorks WebWatcher monitors the performance of Web servers and end users in e-commerce sites.

PerformanceWorks software runs under a range of platforms, including UNIX and Windows NT, as well as mainframes. Optional packages are offered for adding predefined alarms and reports, specialized agents for specific servers and databases, capacity planning, and application performance management.

Landmark Systems Corporation

12700 Sunrise Valley Drive

Reston, VA 20191

+1-703-464-1300

800-488-1111

http://www.landmark.com

VitalSuite

NetCare Professional Services offers a full suite of enterprise performance management solutions under its VitalSuite trademark software brand.

The suite includes VitalNet (formerly, EnterprisePRO), a network performance reporting and SLA compliance management system—VitalAnalysis, a performance reporting system for mission critical applications; VitalHelp, a proactive, real-time fault detection and troubleshooting solution; and the Business Transaction Management System—which manages network, application, and user activity. In addition, NetCare Professional Services provides comprehensive consulting services to assist clients—both enterprise and service provider—in designing, deploying, and administering effective, business-oriented SLAs.

Lucent Technologies NetCare Professional Services (formerly INS)

1213 Innsbruck Drive

Sunnyvale, CA 94089

+1-650-318-1000

1-888-4-NETCARE

http://www.lucent.com/netcare

ServiceDesk for SAP R/3, Service Level Analyzer for SAP R/3

Luminate's ServiceDesk for SAP R/3 generates end-to-end performance profiles according to user-defined parameters, including SAP R/3 SID, user ID, transaction code, and date/time. The Luminate software analyzes performance from several perspectives, from identifying general end-to-end problems to diagnosing very specific transaction code issues. The application breaks down response time into network response time, system queue time, application response time, and database response time. Luminate's Service Level Analyzer adds a business user perspective to its analysis of service levels issues, associating the impact technical performance has on corporate divisions, geographic sites, and individual users.

Luminate Software Corporation

2750 El Camino Real

Redwood City, CA 94061

+1-650-298-7000

http://www.luminate.com

Netcool

Micromuse's Netcool suite is designed to help telecommunications and Internet service providers ensure the uptime of network-based customer services and applications. The Netcool ObjectServer is the central component in the suite. The ObjectServer is an in-memory database optimized for collecting events, associating events with business services, and creating real-time reports that show the availability of services. The ObjectServer performs all formatting and filtering of this data, allowing operators to create customized EventLists and views of business services. The suite also contains ObjectiveView, an object-based topographical front-end toolset that allows operators to build clickable maps, icons, and other graphical interfaces to ObjectServer data and EventLists. ObjectiveViews are used by managers in the network operations center because they supply a concise, global summary of event severities and service availability throughout the entire network.

Micromuse Incorporated

139 Townsend Street

San Francisco, CA 94107

+1-415-538-9090

http://www.micromuse.com

Do It Yourself (DIY) and Custom Network Analysis

NetOps offers products and services in the areas of network fault analysis and event correlation. The company's solutions focus on uncovering the root of a problem that might be diminishing network service levels. DIY (Do It Yourself), the company's Internet-based software, identifies network problems and offers IT managers possible solutions. DIY uses proprietary mid-level managers called Distributed Status Monitors (DSMs) that model what networked system behavior should be and then collect actual performance information and report problems. The DSMs speak SNMP. An SNMP polling hierarchy of monitors is configured for centralized aggregation of all threshold-crossing events in real-time. Non-critical events that might be signs of future problems are collected for fault avoidance analysis. NetOps also provides a service called Custom Network Analysis in which the company integrates the DSMs into the network and interprets the information from the agents. NetOps then offers suggestions to correct network deficiencies.

NetOps Corporation

501 Washington Avenue

2nd Floor

Pleasantville, NY 10570

+1-914-747-7600

http://www.operations.com

NetPredict

NetPredict software monitors the end-to-end performance of specific applications on user-selected paths through a network. To perform this function, the software collects key data obtained from SNMP and distributed RMON sources. That information is then stored in a relational database for long-term trending and historical review. By comparing this data against measured traffic on the network, NetPredictor is able to perform accurate predictions of the effects of changes in the network or the application. With this capability, IT personnel can accurately gauge their capacity requirements to improve the performance of both their applications and networks. NetPredict supplies a tool for creating and tracking Service Level Agreements. IT managers can use it to estimate what their actual requirements are and then use the technology to measure the application performance end user's experience on a day-to-day basis.

NetPredict Incorporated

1010 El Camino Real, Suite 300

Menlo Park, CA 94025

+1-650-853-8301

http://www.netpredict.com

Wise IP/Accelerator

The Wise IP/Accelerator enables carriers and ISPs to offer SLAs for IP-based virtual private networks (VPNs). The IP SLAs supported by Wise/IP Accelerator furnish point-to-point bandwidth availability guarantees for virtual private networks (similar to the committed information rate or CIR of a frame relay network). By utilizing Wise/IP Accelerator to offer SLAs for IP VPNs, carriers and ISPs can generate additional subscribers among companies looking for an inexpensive alternative to dedicated network services.

Netreality

2350 Mission College Boulevard, Suite 900

Santa Clara, CA 95054

+1-408-988-8100

http://www.nreality.com

NetScout Manager Plus, NetScout Server, NetScout Webcast

NetScout Systems monitors the performance of enterprise applications for the purpose of tracking SLA compliance. NetScout Manager Plus integrates data from distributed RMON probes and embedded agents throughout the network. The software then analyzes that information to produce service level baseline and historical trend reports. Another component, NetScout Server, makes enterprise-scale network monitoring possible by logging RMON data from probes and switches, allowing more frequent polling while minimizing management traffic. NetScout Server shares data with NetScout Manager Plus to create enterprisewide reports. The server generates reports on demand or on a daily, weekly, or monthly basis.

NetScout WebCast works with NetScout Manager Plus and NetScout Server to give IT managers access to reports and alarms at any time via the World Wide Web.

NetScout Systems Incorporated

4 Technology Park Drive

Westford, MA 01886

+1-978-614-4000

http://www.netscout.com

NetSolve Services

NetSolve offers a range of remote network management and security services that allow companies to selectively outsource specific management tasks to increase the reliability and the performance of their enterprise networks. The company essentially acts as an extension of its client's internal IT staff.

Besides supplying network implementation services, NetSolve provides security services and turnkey management services for both LANs and WANs. The company's WAN and LAN management services encompass network design verification, installation, 24X7 fault management, configuration management, performance management, and ongoing documentation.

NetSolve's performance management practice collects service level information from the customer's site and uploads that data to NetSolve's Network management center. A NetSolve engineer analyzes that data and produces a summary of those statistics. If changes are necessary, the report will include recommendations.

NetSolve Incorporated

12331 Riata Trace Parkway

Austin, TX 78727

+1-512-340-3000

http://www.netsolve.com

Netuitive Service Level Monitor

Netuitive SLM uses Netuitive's patented Adaptive Correlation Engine (ACE) to identify network performance thresholds automatically, and then predict problems before they occur. ACE technology analyzes the performance data about critical online business systems from a range of data streams in real-time. These data streams can be gathered by the software itself or through its access to the databases of products like DeskTalk TREND and Visual Network IPInsight. Netuitive uses this input to correlate performance variables, identify the correct baseline for normal network performance, and then predict abnormal performance up to four days in advance. Deviations between the SLM-predicted performance for each data stream and the baseline are reported to network managers as an alert. The sensitivity to these alert conditions is configurable globally across all inputs that are being predicted, or for groups of inputs.

Netuitive Incorporated

3460 Preston Ridge Rd., Suite 125

Alpharetta, GA 30005

+1-678-256-6100

http://www.netuitive.com

Bluebird

N★Manage supplies Service Level Agreement monitoring software for systems and networks. Bluebird, N★Manage's SLA tracking software, collects service and availability data for IP, email, FTP, HTTP, NFS, and other applications. Bluebird uses a distributed architecture and a Java client to present network health information. Bluebird issues real-time alerts when network performance exceeds acceptable thresholds or availability falls below an acceptable level.

N*Manage Company

Raleigh, NC 27606

+1-919-362-8866

http://www.nmanage.com

Optivity SLM and Preside Performance Reporting

Nortel produces service level management products for both the enterprise and the service provider. Optivity SLM, the centerpiece of its enterprise management offerings, gathers and aggregates application performance and availability data directly from the network to provide information on both a user and application basis. Optivity SLM is designed to quickly isolate and respond to network faults that impact business-critical applications. It also features remote access support, allowing end users dialing in remotely to run a six-step diagnostics check before calling their help desk. Optional application modules enhance transaction visibility for Oracle database applications and IMAP email applications.

Preside Performance Reporting provides trending and historical reporting capabilities for networks based on a range of vendors' devices, including those from Cisco and Nortel Networks. The software comes with a range of graphical reports. The software was added to Nortel's product line after its acquisition of X-Cel Communications in 1999.

Nortel Networks Corporation

8200 Dixie Road, Suite 100

Brampton, Ontario L6T 5P6

+1-905-863-0000

http://www.nortel.com

Executive Information System or iView

Opticom's Executive Information system consolidates reporting on all aspects of the service management process within the infrastructure—assets, services, availability, capacity, and performance. The product includes software modules that track specific metrics of applications, carrier services, and systems from the perspective of the end user. The EIS integrates into the existing management infrastructure. A component called ServiceView compares metrics based on the business impact of an outage. It also offers multifaceted service views. Users have the ability to define services of all types, ranging from network transport services to complex business processes.

Opticom Incorporated

One Riverside Drive

Andover, MA 01810

+1-978-946-6200

http://www.opticominc.com

Energizer PME

OptiSystems designs and sells products to manage the performance of SAP R/3 systems. The company also offers management products for R/2 applications. Energizer PME (Performance Management Environment) for R/3 dynamically analyzes system usage and reacts to events as they happen in order to improve system performance.

The data collection engine for the Energizer PME for R/3 products runs as an R/3 task and captures real-time interval data, as well as summary data, for all system components using SAP's own data collection routines. As a result, Energizer's overhead is negligible (less than 1%, according to the vendor) and R/3's own data collection is not needlessly duplicated. In addition, the data collected by the Energizer data collection engine is used as the basis of the Energizer PME for R/3 product modules. After one of the modules is installed, any one of the other modules can make use of the same data.

OptiSystems Incorporated

1100 Fifth Avenue South, Suite 404

Naples, FL 34102

+1-941-263-3885

http://www.optisystems.com

PacketShaper

Packeteer supplies products to both enterprise customers and service providers for managing network bandwidth. PacketShaper detects and classifies network traffic, analyzes traffic behavior, offers policy-based bandwidth allocation for specific applications, and provides network reports. PacketShaper automatically detects over 150 types of traffic. It can categorize traffic by application, service, protocol, port number, URL or wildcard (for Web traffic), hostname, precedence bits, and IP or MAC address.

PacketShaper tracks average and peak traffic levels, calculates the percentage of band-width that's wasted on retransmissions, highlights top users and applications, and measures performance. PacketShaper's high-level network summaries record network trends. The product also has the capability to measure response times and then compare those numbers to what is deemed acceptable response time performance.

Packeteer

10495 N. De Anza Boulevard

Cupertino, CA 95014

+1-408-873-4400

http://www.packeteer.com

OpenLane

Paradyne's OpenLane network management application features support for diagnostics, real-time performance, SNMP-managed narrowband, and broadband networks through its access device product lines. OpenLane collects and reports performance against the terms of an SLA. Support is provided for Paradyne's FrameSaver Frame Relay Access Units as well as Paradyne's Hotwire xDSL and MVL products. OpenLane also supports Paradyne's 31xx, 7xxx, and NextEDGE 9xxx T1 and subrate access products.

Paradyne Corporation

8545 126th Avenue North

Largo, FL 33773

+1-727-530-2000

http://www.paradyne.com

Foglight

Foglight software ensures the reliability and performance of electronic commerce sites, enterprise resource planning (ERP) systems, and information technology infrastructures.

Foglight monitors business applications for their availability and performance; alerting system managers to actual or potential application problems, and allowing them to effectively identify and correct potential problems before end users are impacted. Foglight keeps critical applications up and running properly, monitors and reports on application service levels, and provides a solution to scale e-business systems growth through accurate capacity planning.

Quest Software, Incorporated

8001 Irvine Center Drive

Irvine, CA 92618

+1-949-754-8000

http://www.quest.com

Solo DSU/CSUs with WANview

The WANview Network Management System is a complete SNMP-based system for managing wide area networks that includes Service Level Agreement (SLA) monitoring and reporting for the vendor's Digital Link Solo Select family of intelligent DSUs. Using industry-standard measurements based on the Frame Relay Forums' FRF.13 specification, IT managers can ensure the levels of service they have contracted for. As a complement to its SLA features, WANview incorporates a customer database, accessible via a Web browser, making it easier for service providers to partition data on a per-customer basis and enabling them to generate new services such as SLA verification and selectable quality-of-service levels (QoS) for their customers. WANview is a UNIX-based application that runs under HP Openview. The Digital Link Solo series includes intelligent monitoring DSU/CSUs for use on frame relay networks at 56Kbps, T1, or fractional T1 rates and leased lines at up to T1 rates.

Quick Eagle Networks

217 Humboldt Court

Sunnyvale, CA 94089-1300

+1-408-745-6200

http://www.digitallink.com

ResponseCenter

ResponseCenter is an active testing solution that provides comprehensive, end-to-end transaction performance and problem diagnosis for e-business and e-commerce sites. ResponseCenter diagnoses the response time of a complete e-transaction across networks, servers, databases, middleware objects, and application components, breaking down the individual components of total end-to-end performance. The product is designed to help e-businesses get an early warning of potential application brownouts or outages before e-commerce service is interrupted.

Response Networks Incorporated

2034 Eisenhower Avenue, Suite 290

Alexandria, VA 22314-4650

+1-703-739-7770

http://www.responsenetworks.com

Statscout

Statscout is a network performance monitoring package based on SNMP. It runs under FreeBSD-3.X UNIX, a little-known flavor of UNIX comparable to Linux. Statscout boasts that its software can monitor thousands of devices and ports simultaneously while requiring minimal disk space. The software measures network health statistics, including average response time (calculated by measuring ping response times), utilization, and errors. Statscout also produces SLA summary reports that include information on SLA non-conformance, as well as detailed network management statistics.

Statscout

One World Trade Center, Suite 7967

New York, NY 10048

+1-212-321-9282

http://www.statscout.com

SOLVE Series

Sterling's SOLVE products monitor network performance and diagnose any problems that could have a negative impact on enterprise service levels. The software supplies IT managers with utilization information so that they can adequately allocate network resources and control spending. Sterling claims their SOLVE product line can instantly determine the location of a problem and accelerate resolution. Sterling offers SOLVE products for a variety of platforms and environments. Included among those are software solutions for SNA, TCP/IP, CICS, and MVS.

Sterling Software

300 Crescent Court, Suite 1200

Dallas, Texas 75201

+1-214-981-1000

http://www.sterlingsoftware.com

Frame Relay Access Probe and Sync Performance Manager

The Frame Relay Access Probe (FRAP) line of circuit management solutions from WAN access hardware vendor Sync Research is designed to deliver proactive service level management and troubleshooting capabilities to both enterprise and service provider users. These FRAPs, placed in strategic areas of the network, collect statistics and act as troubleshooting devices. An accompanying product called the Sync Performance Manager is designed to help companies establish and maintain SLAs, plan for future growth, and manage network change by compiling statistics over time and analyzing that data for trend information. Sync also offers an SNMP-managed CSU/DSU.

Sync Research Incorporated

12 Morgan

Irvine, CA 92719

+1-949-588-2070

http://www.sync.com

Tivoli Service Desk

Tivoli Service Desk software works with the vendor's Tivoli Enterprise management framework to give customers comprehensive, centralized control over IT service levels. The product contains Asset Management, Problem Management, and Change Management modules, as well as a Service Level Agreement Module that allows organizations to identify, define, configure, administer, and measure all aspects of IT service delivery. All components of Tivoli Service Desk are integrated with the Tivoli framework. The vendor says this approach enables IT managers to not only monitor SLAs, but also to proactively maintain network and system performance as well as to automatically fix problems as they occur. Tivoli Service Desk provides bi-directional integration with both Tivoli NetView and the Tivoli Enterprise Console.

Tivoli Systems Incorporated

9442 Capital of Texas Highway North

Arboretum Plaza One

Austin, TX 78759

+1-512-436-8000

http://www.tivoli.com

Vantive Help Desk

The Vantive Corporation offers internal help desk software that promises a number of functions to help improve and then sustain enterprise service levels. The company's help desk solution includes asset management, enterprise tracking capabilities, and technical support functionality that can be customized to fit the needs of an individual enterprise.

Vantive says its Help Desk is designed for fast access to diagnostic information, streamlined problem resolution, robust change management, and inventory tracking. The company says its approach cuts support costs and improves employee productivity by reducing downtime. The software integrates with a number of network and system management consoles including HP OpenView and Intel LANdesk management packages.

The Vantive Corporation

2525 Augustine Drive

Santa Clara, CA 95054

+1-408-982-5700

http://www.vantive.com

WANsuite and NetVoyant

Verilink Corporation WANsuite series of intelligent, software-based integrated access devices (IADs) is designed to combine voice, data, and network traffic over a single transmission facility, and targets public and private line services at DDS, T1, E1, and HDSL2 delivery. An accompanying Windows NT-based element management system, NetVoyant, tracks performance data for use in WAN SLM. NetVoyant includes an ODBC compliant database, CORBA IDL (Interface Definition Language) for customization and flexibility, real-time diagnostics, and extensive reporting and trending application support. NetVoyant gathers statistics from any SNMP-based networking device.

Verilink Corporation

127 Jetplex Circle

Madison, AL 35758

+1-256-772-3770

800-926-0085

http://www.verilink.com

Visual Uptime and Visual IPInsight

Visual UpTime integrates expert monitoring capabilities with access equipment to fully automate the collection, interpretation, and presentation of service level data across fast-packet IP, frame relay, and ATM networks. The product includes Analysis Service Elements (ASEs) that embed the functionality of a protocol analyzer and transmission monitor into a CSU/DSU or a passive-monitoring device. ASEs are available for DS3, T1/FT1, 56K DDS, V.35, EIA-530, RS-232, RS-449, and X.21 circuits. For transmitting network data back to the centralized management console, either an Ethernet or a Token Ring LAN interface is available, as well as a backup SLIP interface via a standard serial port.

Visual UpTime comes with a series of SLA monitoring and reporting tools that track performance of frame relay and ATM network services on a daily, monthly, or multimonth basis. A Visual UpTime Burst Advisor continuously measures one-second usage over each port and PVC. From this information, the system automatically makes recommendations on correct bandwidth allocations. A series of executive reports puts this data into a format suitable for presentation to CEOs and top-level executives.

Visual IP InSight leverages technology that the company picked up as part of its acquisition of Inverse Network Technology to give service providers and enterprises the tools required to manage IP connectivity and applications such as dedicated and remote access and Web sites from the perspective of the end user.

Visual IP InSight comprises three application suites that let IP services managers provide and track service level agreements, offer new levels of end-user customer care, and monitor end-to-end network performance. The service level management suite includes Service Level Performance Reports: a series of programs that gather actual end-user performance information via the network operator's deployment of the Visual IP InSight client. Single Visual IP InSight installations can take feeds from as few as 500 clients, scaling to the millions, the vendor says.

Visual IP InSight service level management reports can be used with other suite applications in order to manage a user's end-to-end experience. The reports can be used, for instance, with Visual IP InSight Dial Care to furnish information about access functionality at end-user desktops, or with Visual IP InSight Dial Operations to proactively manage network access, be it in-house or outsourced. The suite also can be used to track and manage the performance of application services, such as virtual private networks, Web, email, and news.

Visual Networks Incorporated

2092 Gaither Road

Rockville, MD 20850

+1-301-296-2300

http://www.visualnetworks.com

Glossary

Like other specialized areas of information technology, service level management (SLM) has acquired a language of its own. For the most part, the terms used in SLM are derived from the fields of networking, general IT, enterprise management, and software development. Here is an alphabetical list of key terms you'll encounter in most SLM activities and interactions:

Access control: The process of defining and controlling which users have access to which resources or services, and determining the nature of the authorized access.

Agent: Software designed to collect data about the status and functionality of a device, system, or application for reporting purposes. See the definition of Manager later on.

Application service provider (ASP): A company that provides applications remotely to user companies over external facilities, typically including the Internet.

ARM: Application Response Measurement. An industry-wide effort launched by Hewlett-Packard and other vendors to create a set of APIs (application programming interfaces) designed to be written into applications in order to measure business transactions from an end-user perspective.

Availability: The percentage of time that a service is available for use.

Baseline: The present state of performance, as monitored by an analyzer or other measuring tool. Baselines are obtained in order to determine how services need to be changed to obtain more satisfactory performance, and how services will be maintained and guaranteed over time. The operative principle is simple: You must know where you are before you can proceed to a better place.

Batch job concurrency: A measure of the number of background jobs that can be run on a computer system concurrently. The optimal number of jobs varies with operating system and the characteristics of the jobs themselves.

Capacity planning: The process of calculating the amount of system resources and network bandwidth that will be required to support a service in the future.

Capture ratio: The proportion of CPU utilization that is actually used, compared with what is allocated for processing. In most UNIX systems, the capture ratio is not sufficient for sophisticated performance analysis or capacity planning.

Common Information Model (CIM): An object-oriented information model created by the DMTF to manage systems, software, users, and networks. The DMTF also provides a conceptual management framework that establishes object definitions and classes for use with CIM.

CPU utilization: The amount of time an application requires to process information in a computer's central processing unit (CPU). CPU usage governs the response time a computer can deliver.

Critical deadlines: The specified times at which certain jobs or tasks must be completed in order to satisfy external vendors or regulations.

Data currency: An indication that data is timely and up-to-date. Some measure of data currency is particularly important to have when data is distributed across multiple data stores such as replicated databases, data warehouses, and data marts.

Data integrity: The accuracy and consistency of data and database structures.

Decode: The process of using special technology to intercept and analyze data packets as they traverse a network. Used to troubleshoot and determine overall quality of data transmission.

Differentiated services: The assignment of specific levels of service to different groups of users, based on cost or other criteria. *Gold* customers, for instance, might be offered continuous availability at an agreed-upon level of response time; *silver* customers would get response times within a certain range of measurement; and *bronze* customers would receive "best effort" service.

DMTF: Distributed Management Task Force, which is a consortium of users and vendors dedicated to leading the development of management standards for desktop, network, and system environments.

DMTF Service Level Agreement (SLA) Working Group: A task force of DMTF members who are focused on extending the DMTF's Common Information Model (CIM) to allow the definition and association of policies, rules, and expressions that enable common industry communications with respect to service management.

Downtime: The amount of time during which a system or network element or a service itself is not available because of technical failure.

End-to-end service: A view of IT service that includes each of the end users of a service and their locations, together with the path they take to access the business application providing the core part of the service.

End-user's perspective: The performance of a service as it is experienced by the user at the desktop. This perspective is the ultimate measure of service quality.

Expectation creep: The basic characteristic in human nature to always want more and better—regardless of the subject. In service level management, expectation creep describes how users will pressure IT to exceed service levels. With SLAs in place, IT is assured that performance and capacity increases will be acknowledged and perhaps paid for by the client, instead of being taken for granted.

External SLA: A Service Level Agreement between a service provider and a client in another organization.

FCAPS: The initials of the five basic categories of tasks included in any comprehensive network management scheme: specifically, *F*ault management, *C*onfiguration, *A*ccounting, *P*erformance management, and *S*ecurity management.

Historical data: Measurements over time of the overall health of specific service elements. Examples include RMON/RMON 2 information collected by probes, CSU/DSUs, and packet monitors at specific intervals—daily, weekly, or monthly. This data is placed in charts or graphs depicting how well service levels were met.

IETF Application Management MIB: The Internet Engineering Task Force's Request for Proposal 2564: Application Management Information Base. This spec defines units of work in a system or application and specifies ways of measuring response time, monitoring resource usage by application (such as via I/O statistics and application layer network resource usage), and controlling applications (by stopping, suspending, resuming, and reconfiguring them as needed). While not focused on service level management, RFC 2564 can assist in measuring and managing service quality.

In-House SLA: A Service Level Agreement between a service provider and a client within the same organization.

Interactive responsiveness: The time taken to complete a request on behalf of a user. The quicker the requests are completed, the more responsive the service.

Internal SLA: A Service Level Agreement used by the service provider to measure the performance of groups within the service provider's organization. An example might be the SLA between a network services group within IT and the overall organization, or perhaps the CIO.

Intrusion detection: The process of monitoring the IT environment to detect unauthorized access or attempts to access resources illegally.

ISP: An Internet Service Provider, or a carrier who offers dedicated or dial-up access to the Internet for consumers and business customers.

IT Infastructure Library: A documented methodology for managing IT services created by the UK Government's Central Computing and Telecommunications Agency (CCTA).

Kernel: The inner portion of a UNIX operating system that interacts directly with the hardware of a computer system in order to govern the order in which resources (files, data, and so on) are handled. The kernel is the source of multitasking capabilities in UNIX environments.

Latency: The amount of time during a service transaction that is consumed by the processing of network devices such as routers.

Layered monitoring: An approach to SLM in which data from agents installed on each network device, system, or application is consolidated in order to obtain a comprehensive view of performance.

Lines of business: Those parts of an organization that function as separate business entities when viewed from the highest level.

Manager: Software designed to gather, consolidate, and display management data about network devices, systems, and applications. See the definition of Agent earlier in this glossary.

Mean time to recover: The average amount of time taken to cease processing, restore a stable environment, recover corrupted data, and recreate lost transactions.

Performance: The responsiveness of an application or a network to interactive users. Performance is expressed in response time of a service to end users, in the time required for a server to deliver a response to a user command, or the time required for a request to be fulfilled or a batch job to be processed on the mainframe.

Physical layer performance: The uptime of cable links and device interfaces on a network.

Primary data collector: A management tool that captures data directly from the network elements underlying the service (bridges, routers, switches, hubs, and so forth). Some primary data collectors also gather input from software programs that affect overall service availability (applications, databases, middleware, and the like). Although not dedicated to service level management, these tools are often key to facilitating it.

Privilege class: A group of staffers or operations personnel who are awarded a particular type of access based on job function, job level, organization structure, physical location, or some combination of these.

Probes: Standalone hardware devices containing RMON and RMON 2 agents along with packet parsing and filtering engines similar to those used in protocol analyzers.

Real-time data: Events reported from the network directly as they occur. Examples include broken routers, congested links, and malfunctioning adapters.

Recoverability: The ability to resume processing after unplanned outages as rapidly as possible.

Registry: A database, directory, or file that is used to hold and maintain security information about users and resources. The use of a registry can simplify the administration of user groups and the assigning of access privileges to resources.

Replicated data: Data that is copied from one location to another in the course of completing specific business processes or transactions.

Resources: The services, data, applications, systems, and network elements involved in delivering a particular service to users.

Response time: The time required for a user to get a reaction from a server, mainframe, or other system entity after pressing a command on the keyboard.

RMON and RMON 2: Remote network monitoring management information base; an SNMP MIB designed to track packet-level activity on network links and connections, as opposed to monitoring the status of specific devices, systems, or applications. RMON 2 is a later version of the MIB that identifies traffic on particular subnets.

Scheduled maintenance: The performance of IT functions such as backup during scheduled downtimes.

Secondary data collector: A management tool that does not communicate directly with the managed environment (although some secondary data collectors are able to do so, if necessary). Secondary data collectors extract data from other products that are primary data collectors.

Security: The actions involved in defining who can access a service, the nature of the access, and the mechanisms used to detect, prevent, and report unauthorized access.

Service Level Agreement (SLA): A contract between IT and its clients that specifies the parameters of system capacity, network performance, and overall response time required to meet business objectives. The instrument for enforcing SLM.

Service level management (SLM): The continuous process of measuring, reporting, and improving the quality of service provided by the IT organization. Includes a proactive, disciplined methodology for establishing acceptable levels of service in keeping with business processes and costs.

Service subscription: An SLM model in which users agree to a level of service that adds up to a specified amount of IT resources during a given time period.

Simulated transactions: Software routines that mimic the activity of specific business tasks on a corporate or service provider network; often used to obtain consistent readings on response time and availability.

SLM domains: Those components of a network service that must be monitored and measured as part of a service level management strategy. SLM domains typically include network devices and connections, servers and desktops, applications, databases, and transactions.

SNMP: The Simple Network Management Protocol (SNMP), created by the Internet Engineering Task Force (IETF), is a coding scheme that uses Management Information Bases (MIBs) to retrieve configuration, fault, and performance information about network components.

Socket: A programming call that links various portions of an application to one another in a networked environment; for example, a client portion of an application to the server portion.

Transaction: The performance of a business task by one or more users of a computer system that results in a change to the state of a business application or the data associated with it.

Turnaround time: The time required for completion of processing that does not require direct interaction with either the user or system operator. Turnaround time refers to actions that take place in batch mode or as background tasks.

WBEM: The DMTF's Web Based Enterprise Management (WBEM) specifications, which include CIM data descriptions, XML transport encoding, and http access.

Workload level: The volume of processing performed by a particular service, typically measured in the number of transactions, client/server interactions, or batch jobs performed.

Index

Other Related Titles

Implementing SAP R/3: The Guide for Business and Technology Managers
0-672-31776-1
Vivek Kale
$39.99 USA / $59.95 CAN

Sams Teach Yourself SAP R/3 in 24 Hours
0-672-31624-2
Danielle Larocca
$24.99 USA / $37.95 CAN

Sams Teach Yourself SAP R/3 in 10 Minutes
0-672-31495-9
Simon Sharpe
$12.99 USA / $18.95 CAN

SMS Administrator's Survival Guide
0-672-30984-X
James Farhatt, et al.
$59.99 USA / $84.95 CAN

Maximum Linux Security
0-672-31670-6
Anonymous
$39.99 USA / $59.95 CAN

Microsoft SQL Server 7.0 DBA Survival Guide
0-672-31226-3
Mark Spenik, et al.
$49.99 USA / $71.95 CAN

Peter Norton's Maximizing Windows 98 Administration
0-672-31218-2
Peter Norton
$29.99 USA / $42.95 CAN

Maximum Security: A Hacker's Guide to Protecting Your Internet Site and Network, Second Edition
0-672-31341-3
Anonymous
$49.99 USA / $70.95 CAN

SAMS
www.samspublishing.com

All prices are subject to change.